WORDSWORTH
A RE-INTERPRETATION

WORDSWORTH
A RE-INTERPRETATION

F. W. BATESON

LONGMANS, GREEN AND CO
LONDON · NEW YORK · TORONTO

LONGMANS, GREEN AND CO LTD
6 & 7 CLIFFORD STREET LONDON W 1
ALSO AT MELBOURNE AND CAPE TOWN

LONGMANS, GREEN AND CO INC
55 FIFTH AVENUE NEW YORK 3

LONGMANS, GREEN AND CO
215 VICTORIA STREET TORONTO 1

ORIENT LONGMANS LTD
BOMBAY CALCUTTA MADRAS

First published 1954

PRINTED IN GREAT BRITAIN BY
SPOTTISWOODE, BALLANTYNE AND CO. LTD.
LONDON AND COLCHESTER

PREFACE

IT IS ONLY within the last few years that a comprehensive critical discussion of Wordsworth has become possible. Until Miss Helen Darbishire completed with her exemplary edition of *The Excursion* (1949) the definitive edition of Wordsworth's Poetical Works 'from the manuscripts' of which Ernest de Selincourt's memorable *Prelude* (1926) was the first instalment, the standard edition of the poems was still that of William Knight (1882–6; partly revised 1896). Knight had had access to the manuscripts, but he used them perfunctorily and uncritically—and of the crucial early poems that Wordsworth never printed himself, or else revised so drastically that they are barely recognisable, Knight's editions give hardly a hint. It is the same with the letters and Dorothy Wordsworth's Journals. Until de Selincourt published his six-volume edition of the letters of Wordsworth and his sister (1935–1939), the critic who wished to use Wordsworth's life to illustrate the poems had to rely on Knight's incomplete and inaccurate *Letters of the Wordsworth Family* (1907), and such supplementary facts as he could pick up in Christopher Wordsworth's dreary *Memoirs* (1851) of his uncle and Knight's woolly and muddled *Life* (1889). The Annette Vallon episode, if the most dramatic, was only one of the skeletons that were kept carefully locked in the family cupboard. It is true Knight did publish the Journals, but his expurgations from them removed much that is of the greatest biographical and psychological interest, and the notes are slipshod and unreliable. His edition has now been superseded by de Selincourt's *Journals of Dorothy Wordsworth* (1941), to which de Selincourt's attractive and scholarly *Life of Dorothy Wordsworth* (1933) may be regarded as a pendant.

In addition, and in some ways this is the most important event of all, all the manuscripts that had remained in the possession of the Wordsworth family are now available to the *bona fide* student at Dove Cottage and the new Wordsworth Museum, Grasmere. As almost all the other surviving manuscripts, except for a few letters, are either already in print or easily accessible in public libraries, this means that it is now possible to read Wordsworth on the same sort of terms as Spenser or Milton or Keats. If there is a difference it is that we know a good deal more about Wordsworth than we do about Spenser and Milton, or even Keats. Such is the wealth of manuscript material at Grasmere—almost all of it catalogued by the indefatigable Miss Darbishire, the present Chairman of the Trustees of Dove Cottage, who are the legal owners of the manuscripts—that it is probably true to say that more is known, or at least is now knowable, about the evolution of Wordsworth's poems than about those of any other English poet down to our own time. Biographically, too, there is a similar accumulation of material, which I have been at some pains to excavate, in Victorian memoirs and in the more casual reminiscences contributed to such journals as _Notes and Queries_, the _Athenæum_ and the _Academy_. And new facts are continually turning up even today.

This book may be regarded, in intention at any rate, as an introductory critical report on Wordsworth as a poet and a man —the two are indissoluble, as I soon discovered—in the light of the information that is now available. It makes no claim, however, to say the last word about any aspect of the Wordsworthian problem, either critical, biographical or historical. The point of view and the tone of voice are perhaps the distinctive features. Wordsworth has been the subject of too much bardolatry and too little criticism. It is true that the form of critical worship has changed since Arnold launched his famous attack on the Wordsworthians. Ironically, indeed, Arnold's own essay has led to the growth of a new Wordsworth sect—we may call them the Arnoldians. Books like the late Lascelles Abercrombie's _The Art of Wordsworth_ (1952) and Miss Darbishire's _The Poet Wordsworth_ (1950), though useful and expert in their own ways, essentially say over again, with only the minutest variations of emphasis, either what Arnold himself said in 1879 or what such Arnoldians as Walter Raleigh, A. C. Bradley or H. W. Garrod have said after him. The New Criticism, on the other hand, by which I mean not only the American critics, but the whole critical movement that derives from T. S. Eliot, has contributed curiously little to our understanding of Wordsworth. With the exception of Sir Herbert Read's *Wordsworth* (1930) there has been nothing in book-form, as far as I know, that can be said to have been written from a specifically twentieth-century point of view,[1] and most of the shorter essays by such critics as Eliot himself, F. R. Leavis, G. Wilson Knight, Cleanth Brooks, Lionel Trilling and William Empson, have been disappointingly perfunctory or marginal. Read's book was, of course, a useful corrective when it was first published, but it is most inaccurate and the habit of finding Annette lurking behind every rock, stone and tree becomes monotonous and irritating. Its permanent value derives from its recognition of the essentially subjective nature of Wordsworth's poetry. The conclusion I have myself been finally driven to is that Wordsworth, far from being the central figure in the English Romantic Movement, is in truth the extreme instance of Romanticism—a more subjective poet not only than Coleridge or Keats but also than Blake or Shelley. His greatness lies, in my opinion, in the heroic and agonised efforts that he made to break out of his own subjectivity. I am aware that a re-interpretation of Wordsworth on these lines is not likely to convince all the readers of this book. I can only hope that it will make a very great poet more real and more sympathetic to some of them—a man speaking to men, as I see him, instead of the egocentric rhapsodist of the text-books.

I wish to record my special gratitude to the Trustees of Dove Cottage for allowing me access to the manuscripts and for their permission to quote from some of the unpublished material. I have had the privilege of discussing a number of problems with Mrs. Mary Moorman who is now at work on what is likely to be the definitive biography of Wordsworth. Without her generous

---

[1] *The Egotistical Sublime* (1954), by my colleague Mr. John Jones, of Merton College, appeared too late for me to benefit by his close and sensitive reading of Wordsworth's text.

co-operation Appendix I, my time-table of Wordsworth's comings and goings down to 1800, would be much less detailed and comprehensive. I am also grateful to Lady Pinney, of Racedown Lodge, Dorset, who has allowed me to consult and quote from various Racedown documents, including letters written to or about Wordsworth by members of the Pinney family.

January, 1954.   F. W. BATESON.

CONTENTS

Chapter One

THE TWO VOICES

There are two Voices: one is of the deep;
It learns the storm-cloud's thundrous melody,
Now roars, now murmurs with the changing sea,
Now bird-like pipes, now closes soft in sleep.
And one is of an old half-witted sheep
Which bleats articulate monotony,
And indicates that two and one are three,
That grass is green, lakes damp, and mountains steep.
And, Wordsworth, both are thine . . .

J. K. STEPHEN[1]

I

WORDSWORTH has been parodied more often and more successfully than any other English poet. This disconcerting fact typifies the peculiar challenge that his poetry presents to the modern reader. Something in it, some contradiction between its intentions and its achievements, seems almost to invite parody. In a sense, indeed, any fool can parody Wordsworth. The temptation to rush in, as we emerge from a reading of these extraordinary poems, with their calculated oddities and their unpredictable sublimities, is almost irresistible. The interesting thing, however, is that Wordsworth's best parodists have also been some of his most discriminating and enthusiastic readers. This was true even in his own life-time. Horace and James Smith—whose "Baby's Debut" in *Rejected Addresses* (1812) was the earliest, as it is certainly one of the most amusing, of the nineteenth-century parodies—are known to have been fervid admirers of some of Wordsworth's

---

[1] Originally contributed to *Granta*, June 1891 (as "A Sonnet"). Reprinted in *Lapsus Calami and Other Verses* (1896).

poems.[1] So was Shelley—in spite of that masterpiece of critical parody *Peter Bell the Third*. So too was Hartley Coleridge—in spite of his unkind perversion of the Lucy poem:

> He lived amidst th' untrodden ways
>   To Rydal Lake that lead;
> A bard whom there were none to praise,
>   And very few to read.
>
> Behind a cloud his mystic sense,
>   Deep-hidden, who can spy?
> Bright as the night when not a star
>   Is shining in the sky.
>
> Unread his works—his 'Milk-white Doe'
>   With dust is dark and dim;
> It's still in Longman's shop, and oh!
>   The difference to him! [2]

---

[1] See the preface added by the Smiths to the 18th edition of *Rejected Addresses* (1833), p. xii. *The Simpliciad* (1808), which has some claim to be the earliest parody of Wordsworth, is something between a parody and a satire. Although dedicated 'To Messrs. W–ll–m W–rdsw–rth, R–b–rt S–th–y, and S. T. C–l–r–dg–' most of the fun is at Wordsworth's expense. Lines 94–101 are a fairly favourable specimen of the author's wit:

> Poets, who fix their visionary sight
> On Sparrow's eggs in prospect of delight,
> With fervent welcome greet the glow-worm's flame,
> Put it to bed and bless it by its name;
> Hunt waterfalls, that gallop down the hills:
> And dance with dancing laughing daffodills;
> Or measure muddy ponds from side to side,
> And find them three feet long and two feet wide.

There are also not unamusing notes identifying the passages ridiculed. Wordsworth took *The Simpliciad*'s criticisms much too seriously and re-wrote many of the lines it had made fun of (see the de Selincourt-Darbishire edition of *The Poetical Works, passim*). He seems to have thought the anonymous author was Richard Mant, later Bishop of Down—see his letter to Quillinan, 10 Sept. 1830— but Mant's acknowledged *Poems* (Oxford, 1806) are very different from and greatly inferior to *The Simpliciad*.

[2] Hartley Coleridge's parody was originally sent to *Notes and Queries*, 19 June 1869, by a correspondent with the initials G. E., who wanted to know who it was by. It was identified in the next issue by another correspondent who had heard Hartley recite it 'and have an impression that G. E. does not quote it with perfect accuracy'. A better text has not, however, turned up.

Why is this? Why does a proper appreciation of Wordsworth seem to demand the ability to ridicule him? Perhaps one reason may be that all parodies are necessarily, to some extent, the product of exasperation tempered by affection. If the parodies of Wordsworth's poems are better than those on other poets, that may be because of the intensity both of exasperation and affection that his poetry arouses. Since he *can* write so well, why *must* he insist so often on writing so badly?

The co-existence of the Two Voices has been the Wordsworth problem *par excellence*. Matthew Arnold's prescription, as is well known, was selection. If only Wordsworth could be relieved of a great deal of the poetical baggage which encumbers his collected works, his supreme greatness—'after Shakespeare, Molière, Milton, Goethe, indeed, but before all the rest' since Dante—would immediately be apparent to the world.[1] The suggestion must have seemed an obvious one, and it is probable that Arnold's elegant little volume of selections (1879) in the Golden Treasury Series did in fact do a good deal to revive an interest in Wordsworth's poetry that had rather flagged after his death.[2]

But Arnold's diagnosis did not reach the root of the problem. The odd thing about Wordsworth's poetry is that the more selective one is, the more one pares away the allegedly dead wood in his works, the smaller he emerges in poetic stature. The point was first made by Arthur Hugh Clough in a brilliant though little-known "Lecture on the Poetry of Wordsworth". 'Had Wordsworth been more capable of discerning his bad from his good,' Clough wrote, 'there would, it is likely enough, have been far less of the bad; but the good, perhaps, would have been very far less good.'[3] In some peculiar way, that is, the 'bad' poems —except perhaps the *senilia* (Wordsworth's 'dotages' are a separate problem)—are somehow an essential part of Words-

---

[1] *Poems of Wordsworth chosen and edited by Matthew Arnold* (1879), p. xi.

[2] According to Thomas Hutchinson (*Academy*, 21 Oct. 1893), Arnold's selection caused a Wordsworth boom 'not unlike in kind, though inferior in degree of intensity, to the earlier boom which lasted throughout the third decade of the century'.

[3] *The Poems and Prose Remains of Arthur Hugh Clough. Edited by his Wife* (1869), I, 318–19.

worth's poetic greatness. There are long, enormously boring stretches even in *The Prelude*, which are a pain and a grief to the sensitive reader. But they cannot, alas, be skipped. *The Prelude* without them, if in some ways a more attractive poem, would be a much smaller poem, in terms of quality as well as mere length.

Here, in fact, is the essential crux. There *are* Two Voices, and up to a point they are necessarily contradictory. The bleat of the half-witted sheep *is* an anticlimax to the roar of the mountain torrent. But the contradiction is not total. There ought to be an inherent logical incompatibility between the poetically sublime and the poetically ridiculous, but in Wordsworth's case curiously enough there isn't. In his most characteristic poems, like "Resolution and Independence"—which A. C. Bradley rightly called 'the most Wordsworthian of Wordsworth's poems, and the best test of ability to understand him'[1]—the Two Voices turn out to be complementary instead of being contradictory. The bathetic elements, or what at first seem such, serve to guarantee the authentic humanity of the more lofty passages, which in return lend a poetic suggestiveness to the prosaic details that precede or succeed them. The possibility must, I think, be faced that what is true of "Resolution and Independence" is true of more of Wordsworth's poems than his critics have been prepared to admit. Clough, for example, seems to have thought that Wordsworth only wrote four really good sonnets, and that not more than 'a few lines' are worth preserving from some books of *The Prelude*.[2] A certain amount at any rate of the poetical baggage may prove to reflect a limitation on the part of his critics rather than on Wordsworth's own part. After all the eighteenth century detected Two Voices in Shakespeare's tragedies—a dualism that nineteenth-century criticism found no difficulty in reconciling. A similar process of reconciliation is perhaps in progress among the more recent critics of Wordsworth. It is certainly suggestive to compare A. C. Bradley's comment on "Resolution and Independence" with Coleridge's in *Biographia Literaria*. Coleridge also thought it a poem 'especially charac-

---

[1] *Oxford Lectures on Poetry* (1909), p. 130.
[2] *Poems and Prose Remains*, I, 319.

teristic' of Wordsworth—'There is scarce a defect or excellence in his writings of which it would not present a specimen.'[1] To Coleridge, however, there was no connection whatever between the defects and the excellences. Fortunately Wordsworth's defects were not only entirely deplorable, they were also easily removable. One of the Two Voices could be silenced! And in poem after poem Coleridge did manage to persuade Wordsworth to delete or tone down the disconcerting undignified details. The effect of the changes, on Coleridge's hypothesis, should have been to improve the poems immensely as poetry. But were they improved? Did the substitution of the turtle-shell for the washing-tub make "The Blind Highland Boy" a better poem? Curiously enough even Coleridge's own family soon began to have their doubts. It is interesting to consult Sara Coleridge's notes in her elaborate edition of the *Biographia Literaria* (1847). Time and time again, as when discussing the textual changes not only in "The Blind Highland Boy" but also in "Resolution and Independence", "There was a Boy" and "Intimations of Immortality", she modestly admits a preference for Wordsworth's earlier readings before her father had intervened to emasculate them. 'Such are the whims', she says, 'of certain crazy lovers of the Wordsworthian Muse, who are so loyal to her former self that they sometimes forget the deference due to her at present.'[2] What Sara Coleridge's whims amount to, though she would never have put it in so many words, was an obstinate conviction of an inherent underlying harmony in the Two Voices. And there can be little doubt, I think, that she was right.

II

But what were the Two Voices? It is time to define the Wordsworthian Sublime and the Wordsworthian Ridiculous rather more precisely.

---

[1] Ch. xxii.

[2] II, 136. Sara Coleridge was one of the most perceptive of the early devotees. She has an admirable note on the structure of "Song at the Feast of Brougham Castle" (II, 152) and a particularly intelligent defence of *The Waggoner* (II, 183-4). The edition of *Biographia Literaria* was begun by her husband (and cousin) H. N. Coleridge and completed by her after his death.

J. K. Stephen's second Voice, that of the half-witted sheep, is presumably to be identified with the naïve realism of *Peter Bell* and most of the *Lyrical Ballads*, as well as with such later poems as "Alice Fell", "Beggars", "The Sailor's Mother" and *The Waggoner*. The discovery that 'two and one are three' seems to be a gibe at the notorious third stanza of "The Thorn" in its original mensurational form:

> Not five yards from the mountain-path,
> The thorn you on your left espy;
> And to the left, three yards beyond,
> You see a little muddy pond
> Of water, never dry;
> I've measured it from side to side:
> 'Tis three feet long, and two feet wide.

Five yards, three yards, three feet, two feet.

In contradiction to the colloquial realism of Wordsworth's second Voice, the first Voice, in J. K. Stephen's account, is an impressive and elevating one, reverberating with all the magnificence of a force of nature. This is the voice of "Lines written a Few Miles above Tintern Abbey", of parts of *The Prelude*, of "Intimations of Immortality" and of the "Ode to Duty". And Stephen's implication is evident. The first Voice is very, very good; the second Voice is horrid.

The critical verdict embodied in J. K. Stephen's parody can be read between the lines of most nineteenth-century criticism of Wordsworth. Arnold's essay is only Stephen's poem writ large. Our grandfathers and great-grandfathers enjoyed and revered the sonnets, the odes, the natural descriptions, the flower-pieces and the poems about birds. They liked the poems about Lucy and Matthew, and such things as "Ruth" and "The Solitary Reaper". About *The Prelude*, on the other hand, they were lukewarm or undecided. Arnold, for example, thought it 'by no means Wordsworth's best work',[1] and Macaulay was depressed by 'the endless wildernesses of dull, flat, prosaic twaddle', as well as being shocked by the poem's politics ('to the last degree Jacobini-

---

[1] Preface (1879), p. xi.

cal, indeed Socialist').[1] And about most of the poems in *Lyrical Ballads*, except Coleridge's contributions, the Victorians preferred not to think at all. George Brimley, the Librarian of Trinity College, Cambridge, who wrote a sensible and well-informed appreciation of Wordsworth in *Fraser's Magazine* in 1851, says that the only people he had ever met who had had a good word to say for poems like "The Idiot Boy" were 'persons who were in some way connected with' Wordsworth.[2] No doubt Christopher Wordsworth, the poet's youngest brother who eventually became the Master of Trinity, had sometimes spoken up for *Lyrical Ballads* in the Combination Room as a matter of family loyalty.

One obvious point that emerges is chronological. The poems of Wordsworth that the nineteenth-century critics disliked were the early ones. For the *juvenilia*, such as *An Evening Walk* (which was most of it written 1788–9, though it was not published until 1793) and *Descriptive Sketches* (written 1790–2, published 1793), they had no good to say at all. And the only poem in the first edition of *Lyrical Ballads* (published 1798, though some of its contents were written in 1795, if not earlier) that they admired enthusiastically was the Tintern Abbey lines, which were composed after the other pieces in it. The poems that were liked best in the nineteenth century were those of Wordsworth's middle period, that is to say, those added to the second edition of *Lyrical Ballads* (1800) and those in *Poems in Two Volumes* (1807). It was the 1807 poems above all—especially the sonnets, the odes, the Scotch poems, and such things as "To the Daisy" and "To the Cuckoo"—that endeared Wordsworth to

---

[1] G. O. Trevelyan, *The Life and Letters of Lord Macaulay*, p. 541 of 1889 edition (28 July 1850). The entry in Macaulay's Journal must have been approximately contemporary with his remark recorded by Arnold that 'ten years earlier more money could have been raised in Cambridge alone, to do honour to Wordsworth, than was now raised all through the country' (Preface, p. v). As there were only three editions of Wordsworth's complete poetical works in the 1830s as against nine in the 1840s Macaulay's gloom was almost certainly unjustified. It looks as though it was his own interest in Wordsworth that had waned—coupled perhaps with a Cambridge man's wish to score off Oxford (which had not got much farther poetically by 1840 than Rogers or Campbell).

[2] *Essays*, ed. W. G. Clark (1905), p. 133.

the Victorian reader. In Palgrave's *Golden Treasury*, for example, of the forty-one poems by Wordsworth only two were drawn from the first edition of the *Lyrical Ballads*, and seven from the second, whereas twenty-five poems out of the forty-one had originally appeared in *Poems in Two Volumes*. The *Oxford Book of English Verse* presents a similar picture. As with Palgrave, Quiller-Couch's emphasis is on the poems of the middle period. If anything, indeed, in the forty years that separates the two anthologies, feeling against the early manner had hardened and the *Oxford Book* hasn't even one poem from the first edition of *Lyrical Ballads*.

The Two Voices, then, would seem to be Wordsworth's earlier manner and his later manner. The bad Voice is the poetry written up to July 1798 (the date of "Tintern Abbey"), the good Voice is the poetry written after that date. It is more difficult to identify the year when the "dotages" are supposed to begin. According to Arnold, the 'really first-rate work' was written in the decade 1798–1808.[1] But his selection does not adhere at all strictly to this *terminus ad quem*, more than a third of the poems included in it having actually been written after 1808. A modern Wordsworthian has suggested that the real dividing line between the great poems and the failures comes in 1815.[2]

The point of view expressed so piquantly in Stephen's lines has only to be stated in prosaic terms like these for its inherent improbability to become immediately apparent. The notion that the same poet will write complete drivel in June 1798 (when Wordsworth finished *Peter Bell*) and a sublime masterpiece in July is a paradox that would not normally merit serious consideration,

---

[1] Preface (1879), p. xii. Arnold's formula of the Golden Decade has had an astonishing success. It has been repeated recently by the two greatest Wordsworth scholars of our time—Ernest de Selincourt (in his edition of *The Prelude*, 1926, p. xlvi) and Helen Darbishire (*The Poet Wordsworth*, 1950, p. 3). But it will not stand a moment's examination. The poems written in 1797 include two that are as good as anything Wordsworth wrote later (*The Ruined Cottage* and "The Old Cumberland Beggar"), whereas the best that 1807 can show are "Song at the Feast of Brougham Castle" and parts of *The White Doe of Rylstone*. A much better formula would be Spring 1797 to Summer 1806. See Appendix II, p. 211 below ("Wordsworth's Poems: a Chronological List").

[2] Edith C. Batho, *The Later Wordsworth* (1933), p. 314.

unless overwhelming evidence was produced that this was a very special case with exceptional factors operating in it. The nearest, however, that we get to any rational explanation is the thesis of Wordsworth's intermittent inspiration. Arnold put it as follows:

> To give aright what he wishes to give, to interpret and render successfully, is not always within Wordsworth's own command. It is within no poet's command; here is the part of the Muse, the inspiration, the God, the 'not ourselves'. In Wordsworth's case, the accident, for so it may almost be called, of inspiration, is of peculiar importance. No poet, perhaps, is so evidently filled with a new and sacred energy when the inspiration is upon him; no poet, when it fails him, is so left 'weak as is a breaking wave'.[1]

Although Arnold does not seem to have realised it, the upshot of such an interpretation is far from complimentary. It turns Wordsworth into a psychological freak, a poetic Jekyll and Hyde, who is at one moment a genius and at the next an imbecile. And its *a priori* unlikelihood is surely considerable. A poet is distinguished from most other human beings by *superior* powers of mental and moral co-ordination and concentration. He is not more at the mercy of "accident" than most of us, but less so. To assume a lack of psychological continuity in the evolution of his personality is simply to melodramatise our own failures of comprehension. There will naturally be days when he is writing less well, but the failure will always be a relative failure only. It is only gradually over a period of years that artistic maturity is reached, and the complementary process of artistic degeneration is equally gradual. To assert, as Arnold in effect does, that Wordsworth used to follow up Monday's masterpiece with Tuesday's rubbish is to present him as a neurotic case, a victim of schizophrenia. And, as it happens, there is next to no evidence to support such an assertion. During the period of Dorothy Wordsworth's Grasmere Journal (1800–03) we know almost from day to

---

[1] Preface (1879), p. xxii. The quotation is from "A Poet's Epitaph", but the phrase, as Wordsworth uses it in that poem, has no connection with poetic inspiration. Indeed the whole notion of intermittent inspiration is Shelleyan rather than Wordsworthian.

day what poems Wordsworth was writing. They were not all equally good poems, of course, but none of them, I think, were bad poems, and there is certainly no suggestion whatever of that zig-zagging from the poetic heights to the poetic depths and back again that Arnold posits. What we do find during these years are changes from one poetic manner to another and back again, especially in 1802, but it must be emphasised that these were not changes from bad poetry to good poetry, or *vice versa*, but simply from one *genre* to another *genre*. Wordsworth wrote very good poems and less good poems in both his early and later manners, but I am not aware of the existence of one poem of his written after he reached poetic maturity in 1797 and before the gradual degeneration set in about 1805 that can be called a really bad poem. "Vaudracour and Julia" (1804), which Arnold thought the very worst poem Wordsworth ever wrote, has recently been discovered to have considerable merits. It is the later poems, such as the "Ecclesiastical Sonnets", the "Evening Voluntaries", the "Sonnets upon the Punishment of Death", *et hoc genus omne*, that are really bad. Empty, pretentious, humourless, clumsily expressed, often without any human feeling in them at all, they deserve all the abuse and ridicule they have had poured upon them.[1] But many years separate the worst of the "dotages" from the poems of the great period.

The theory of Wordsworth's intermittent inspiration marked a fundamental failure of appreciation. But the reason why most

---

[1] Edith C. Batho's *The Later Wordsworth* (1933), includes an attempted defence of the later poems, but as such it is a most unconvincing performance. She claims that Wordsworth's post-1815 production 'contains much that is good, some that is magnificent, and little that is positively bad' (p. 314), and as examples of the 'good things' she lists "Dion", the Duddon sonnets, "Mutability" and the King's College Chapel sonnets in the Ecclesiastical series, "Ethereal Minstrel", "The Triad", the Abbotsford sonnet, "Why art thou silent?", the lines on Charles Lamb, the "Extempore Effusion", the poem on a mountain-daisy ('So fair, so sweet'), and 'nearly all the poems of 1846'. Unfortunately no serious attempt is made to make these bold words good. There are, of course, good or goodish lines in most of the poems Miss Batho has listed, but only two of them can possibly be called 'magnificent'—the Duddon "After-thought" and the "Extempore Effusion". What her book, in its own way a most interesting one, establishes is that the later Wordsworth was a much more intelligent and honourable *man* than we had realised.

of the Victorian critics—there were honourable exceptions, like Dowden, who even defended the third stanza of "The Thorn"[1] —were not able to recognise the merit of Wordsworth's earlier manner was not simply defective literary taste. They were the victims of their historical position. The Victorian critics were too near the eighteenth century. Their hatred of Pope and all his works made it difficult for them to be fair to a poetry that was, in spite of important differences, basically Augustan. A realisation of the eighteenth-century nature of Wordsworth's early manner is, indeed, the clue to its proper understanding.

Arnold's objection to eighteenth-century poetry—an objection that colours every aspect of his critical theory—was that it was composed in the wits and not in the soul; that is, in modern terminology, in the conscious rather than in the subconscious mind. Now the only one of Wordsworth's poems in the first edition of the *Lyrical Ballads* that can possibly be said to have been composed in the soul is "Lines written a Few Miles above Tintern Abbey". And this, as we have seen, was a last-minute addition not at all in keeping with the rest of the volume. In the other poems the wits and the senses did most of the composing. At this period Wordsworth still had his eyes, metaphorically as well as literally, *on the object*—in a manner that often recalls Crabbe and Cowper, sometimes Thomson, and occasionally Pope. There is a sober factuality in many of these poems—*Peter Bell*, for example— that used to worry his Romantic critics, including even Coleridge. As Hazlitt walked back with him from Alfoxden one moonlight night in June 1798, 'He lamented', Hazlitt reports, 'that Wordsworth was not prone enough to believe in the traditional superstitions of the place, and that there was something corporeal, a *matter-of-factness*, a clinging to the palpable, or often to the petty, in his poetry.'[2] Arnold would have echoed Coleridge's lamentations. It is clearly the absence of the incorporeal in "The Sailor's Mother" that makes Arnold pronounce it without qualification

---

[1] *Transcripts and Studies* (1888), p. 145. The whole essay ("The Text of Wordsworth's Poems") is still well worth consulting.

[2] "My First Acquaintance with Poets." Hazlitt's essay, which was written 1822–3, is in *The Plain Speaker* (1826).

'a failure'. He contrasts it with "Lucy Gray", which must be one of the most incorporeal of all Wordsworth's poems, and which Arnold thought 'a beautiful success'.[1] But by any absolute scale "The Sailor's Mother" is obviously at least as good as "Lucy Gray"; Swinburne thought it better.[2]

Curiously enough Wordsworth's own note on "Lucy Gray" specifically contrasts 'the way in which the incident was treated and the spiritualizing of the character . . . with Crabbe's matter of fact style of treating subjects of the same kind'. This note was dictated in 1843, and its interest is not so much in the contrast it draws between Crabbe and Wordsworth himself as in the relevance of the contrast to his own case. Poems like "The Sailor's Mother" are very like Crabbe. The matter-of-fact style that Wordsworth dissociated himself from in his old age was exactly the style to which his friends had deplored his obstinate adherence forty years earlier. In July 1802, for example, Coleridge wrote to Southey that he had been startled by a 'daring humbleness of language and versification, and a strict adherence to matter of fact, even to prolixity' in some of Wordsworth's recent compositions. Coleridge may have been thinking of "The Sailor's Mother" itself, which dates from March 1802, or else of "Alice Fell", or "Beggars", or "Resolution and Independence", all of which had been written in the spring and early summer of 1802. But the conclusion he drew was not the Victorian conclusion— that such poems were *bad*. Coleridge did not go so far as Arnold. 'I rather suspect,' he confessed to Sotheby, 'that somewhere or other there is a radical difference in our theoretical opinions respecting poetry.'[3]

A radical difference in their theories of poetry—the phrase sums up the essence of the problem. For the difference that divided Wordsworth from Coleridge in 1802 was to all intents and purposes the difference between Wordsworth's earlier manner and his latter manner. It was the difference between the eighteenth century and the nineteenth century, between a poetry primarily of the conscious mind and a poetry primarily of the subconscious

---

[1] Preface (1879), p. xxii. [2] *Miscellanies* (1886), p. 127.
[3] Letter of 29 July 1802.

mind, between a literature conceived as social communication and a literature of individual inspiration.

It should now be possible to define the Two Voices more precisely and to raise once again the problem of their inter-relationship. J. K. Stephen's first Voice, that of the mountain torrent, is clearly the Romantic element in Wordsworth's poetry. It was natural for the Victorians to find it congenial as they were Romantics themselves, and now that we have more or less outgrown Romanticism it is natural for us to think it some-what over-rated. The second Voice—realistic, colloquial, detailed—disconcerted the Victorians because it was so unlike what they had come to expect poetry to be. They may not have realised its Augustan affiliations, but they recognised intuitively that this kind of poetry was the enemy of their kind of poetry. Today we can see that there is a place for both kinds. Wordsworth, however, is not at heart either an Augustan master or a Romantic master. The peculiarity of his poetry is that it oscillates between the two styles. In his best poems, early and late, the Two Voices act, as it were, as positive and negative poles, between which the spark of his poetic genius plays. The poems are Augustan *and* Romantic. And that means that their proper appreciation demands in the reader an equally sensitive response to two very different kinds of poetry. J. K. Stephen's response was only partial. He could appreciate "Intimations of Immortality", but he could not see what Wordsworth was getting at in *Peter Bell*, and so he wrote off the *Peter Bell* manner as the bleating of an old half-witted sheep. Today the opposite danger is perhaps more likely. We find it difficult to adjust ourselves to the reorientation of poetic values that is involved in a proper reading of such a poem as "Intima-tions of Immortality". The Romantic elements in Wordsworth tend to make us uneasy or sceptical. But unless we can make the necessary adjustment, the momentary suspension of disbelief, we shall not be able to understand Wordsworth's most original and most characteristic poems.

There is one critical admission that needs to be made. A corol-lary of the all-importance in Wordsworth's poetry of a combina-tion of Augustan and Romantic elements is that each element in isolation is often, perhaps usually, second-rate. To find whole passages of the very best Romantic poetry in Wordsworth is not at all easy. In Swinburne's essay on "Wordsworth and Byron", which is largely concerned with showing that Wordsworth and Byron are not as good Romantic poets as Coleridge and Shelley, only two lines are finally produced, after an exhaustive search, which are of the purest Romantic gold. They are

> For old, unhappy, far-off things,
> And battles long ago.

These lines from "The Solitary Reaper" are almost alone apparently in possessing the elixir of Coleridge, Shelley and Keats—'something', as Swinburne puts it, 'in the mere progress and resonance of the words, some secret in the very motion and cadence of the lines, inexplicable by the most sympathetic acuteness of criticism'.[1] There is the same scarcity of absolutely first-class Augustan poetry in Wordsworth. Crabbe, one feels, would always have put it with more precision; Cowper would never have been guilty of Wordsworth's elusiveness and obscurity. It is this lack of finish, by both Romantic and Augustan standards, that irritates the parodists. In a sense, they are right in being irritated—bad workmanship is always fair game—but to get too irritated is to exhibit a defective sense of proportion. A certain roughness about the edges—what Tennyson called the *thick-ankled* element in Wordsworth's verse[2]—does not seriously affect the quality of his most characteristic work.

The Two Voices, then, are (i) an essentially objective poetry, evincing a strong sense of social responsibility, but crude, naïve and often bathetic (the Augustan manner), (ii) an essentially subjective poetry, egocentric, sentimental and escapist, but often charming because of its spontaneity (the Romantic manner). And the great poems, on this hypothesis, are those which combine the two elements in Wordsworth's poetry in a new inclusive whole. Such a combination of the objective and the subjective, the Augustan and the Romantic, is achieved in the best passages

---

[1] *Miscellanies*, p. 127.
[2] *Tennyson. A Memoir. By his Son* (1897), II, 505.

in *The Prelude*, in the Lucy series, in "Michael", in "Resolution and Independence", and, if sometimes rather precariously, in a considerable number of other poems.

In Coleridge's terminology, these poems, which are Wordsworth's masterpieces, reveal the balance and reconcilement of opposite and discordant qualities. It will be remembered that, according to Coleridge's own account in *Biographia Literaria*, it was the impression that Wordsworth's recitation of his *Salisbury Plain* made on him in 1796 that started him off on the analysis of the poetic process that ended in this definition of the Imagination.[1] What had impressed him in Wordsworth's poem was precisely the fusion of the objective and subjective elements—'the union of deep feeling with profound thought; the fine balance of truth in observing, with the imaginative faculty in modifying, the objects observed; and above all the original gift of spreading the tone, the atmosphere, and with it the depth and height of the ideal world around forms, incidents, and situations, of which, for the common view, custom had bedimmed all the lustre, had dried up the sparkle and the dew drops'.

Unfortunately Coleridge's analysis of Wordsworth's later poems, which occupies the greater part of *Biographia Literaria*, was conducted in other terms, and he has not told us what the opposite and discordant qualities are that are balanced and reconciled in Wordsworth's best poems. In general no doubt they

---

[1] Ch. iv. Coleridge's memory played him false in one detail. Unless there was some unrecorded meeting later in the year he cannot have heard Wordsworth *recite* his *Salisbury Plain* in 1796. Azariah Pinney, the younger son of the owner of Racedown, wrote to Wordsworth on 25 Mar. 1796, 'I delivered it [*Salisbury Plain*] on my arrival here [Bristol] to Cottle and requested that Coleridge would inspect it, which he appears to have done with considerable attention for I understand he has interleaved it with white paper to mark down whatever may strike him as worthy of your notice and intends forwarding it to you in that form....' Clearly Coleridge made the acquaintance of the poem in manuscript. Azariah Pinney wrote to James Tobin on 12 Apr. 1796, 'His Salisbury Plain is so much altered that I think it may in truth be called a new poem—I brought it with me to Bristol—It is now at Coleridge's, by whom it has been attentively read and pronounced a very fine poem....' See Bergen Evans and Hester Pinney, "Racedown and the Wordsworths", *Review of English Studies*, Jan. 1932, pp. 12–13, 12. I owe the date of the letter to Tobin to the kindness of Lady Pinney who has allowed me to look through the Racedown MSS.

include those that Coleridge detected in *Salisbury Plain*—on the one hand, profound thought and the accurate observation of familiar incident and situations, on the other hand, deep feeling and the faculty of idealisation. But it is difficult to be satisfied with terms as general as these, and in any case Coleridge's account is manifestly incomplete. It needs supplementing with a first-hand analysis of some of the poems themselves. Once such an analysis has been accomplished, it may be possible to define more precisely the nature of the shift of emphasis in Wordsworth's poetry that undoubtedly occurred in the middle of 1798.

Three poems suggest themselves for analysis as typical and representative. They are "Goody Blake and Harry Gill", a poem that is often considered the extreme example of Wordsworth's objective manner; "There was a Boy", an attractive poem spoilt by the confusion of objective and subjective trends; and "She dwelt among the untrodden ways", the poem parodied by Hartley Coleridge, which is a triumphant example of controlled subjectivity.

III

"Goody Blake and Harry Gill" was probably the first to be written, as it is undoubtedly, to use Wordsworth's own word, the 'rudest', of the *Lyrical Ballads* proper. Its special interest is that it raises in an acute form the problem of the divergencies between eighteenth-century and nineteenth-century standards of poetic taste, and their repercussions on the criticism of Wordsworth's poetry. "Goody Blake" was a poem the nineteenth century could make nothing of. Most of Wordsworth's Victorian critics make no reference to it at all. One of the few who does is F. W. H. Myers, who was responsible for the Wordsworth volume in the "English Men of Letters" series, and his comment makes it clear why nobody else mentioned the poem. It was a poem, Myers says, 'justly blamed for triviality'.[1] In the days when the decisive criteria were the Grand Style and the Great Subject, this crude ballad of country life must have seemed a trifle altogether unworthy of Wordsworth.

---

[1] *Wordsworth* (1881), p. 33.

With Wordsworth's older readers, on the other hand—the men and women whose literary tastes had been formed and matured in the eighteenth century—it was one of his most popular pieces. It was, for example, the only one of Wordsworth's poems for which Crabbe evinced any enthusiasm. According to Wordsworth himself, Crabbe once said in his hearing that 'everybody must be delighted with that poem'.[1] Hannah More, a representative blue-stocking, threw up her hands in ecstasy when Cottle, the original publisher of *Lyrical Ballads,* read it aloud to her, and she insisted on its being read to her a second time.[2] Charles James Fox picked it out as one of the four best poems in either volume of the second edition of *Lyrical Ballads.*[3] It was actually reprinted in the *Ipswich Magazine* for April 1799, with a letter specially commending it to the attention of the farmers of Suffolk. Even the reviewers liked it. In the notice in the *Analytical Review* for December 1798 it is selected for special commendation and it is the only one of the poems to be quoted in its entirety. And it was a popular piece with the early anthologists. It is the only poem, for example, from *Lyrical Ballads* to be included in Sidney Melmoth's *Beauties of British Poetry* (1801) and in C. Earnshaw's *The Wreath* (circa 1805).

Today it is difficult to share either the disgust of the nineteenth century or the enthusiasm of the eighteenth century. A grotesque tale of an old countrywoman's curse and its serio-comic aftermath is not one the modern reader will easily like or dislike very much, at any rate at the first glance. But there is more to the poem than meets the casual eye, and a careful reading suggests at least two good reasons why Crabbe, Hannah More, and Fox thought so highly of it. It is *alive,* and it *rings true.* The impression that a reading of it leaves today is that, within its limits and in spite of the crudity of the expression, we have here something extraordinarily convincing and dramatic. The moonlight on the stubble, with Harry lurking behind the elder-bush and Goody

---

[1] See Wordsworth's letter to Alaric Watts, 16 Nov. 1824.

[2] See Cottle's *Reminiscences* (1847), p. 260.

[3] Fox's letter, written 25 May 1801, was printed by Christopher Wordsworth in *Memoirs of William Wordsworth* (1851), I, 171.

filling her apron with the sticks from Harry's hedge, provides an excellent opening scene. Harry's jumping out, with a triumphant 'I've caught you then at last', as he grabs the old woman's arm and shakes her, produces an effective climax. And then comes the peripeteia, as Goody drops the sticks and kneels in prayer on them 'To God that is the judge of all':

> She pray'd, her wither'd hand uprearing,
> While Harry held her by the arm—
> 'God! who art never out of hearing,
> 'O may he never more be warm!'
> The cold, cold moon above her head,
> Thus on her knees did Goody pray,
> Young Harry heard what she had said,
> And icy-cold he turned away.

No doubt this is tragi-comedy rather than tragedy. There is a strong dash of the grotesque, if not of farce, both in Harry's chattering jaws and teeth ('Like a loose casement in the wind') and in the layers of waistcoats and blankets in which he has to be wrapped, once the curse has fallen. But Wordsworth's grotesquerie has respectable eighteenth-century antecedents—Fielding and Smollett on one side, Hogarth and Rowlandson on another. And behind it there is genuine human feeling. Wordsworth has identified himself to a quite remarkable degree with this simple old woman and her lifelong struggle to keep warm:

> 'Twas well enough when summer came,
> The long, warm, lightsome summer-day,
> Then at her door the *canty* dame
> Would sit, as any linnet gay.

Goody's difficulties came on with the winter. She lived in Dorset,[1] where the coal had to come round by sea, and she depended—as Wordsworth and his sister had to some extent depended during their two winters at Racedown Lodge in that county—on the firewood she could pick up in the fields and woods near her solitary hut:

---

[1] Only true of the early editions. In 1820 'This woman dwelt in Dorsetshire' becomes 'Remote from sheltering village-green', and the reference to the high price of coal is also deleted.

Oh joy for her! when e'er in winter
The winds at night had made a rout,
And scatter'd many a lusty splinter,
And many a rotten bough about.

What is so admirable is Wordsworth's attitude to Goody
Blake. There is not a trace of condescension in it. In this he is
better than the Augustans proper. Goldsmith and Cowper would
either have sentimentalised the old woman or turned her ever
so slightly into a figure of fun. Nor is there any exploitation of
her distress to demonstrate Wordsworth's superior sensibility or
keener social conscience. This is impersonal poetry, in the sense
that a whole social order is expressing itself through the medium
of the poem. Wordsworth was able to take for granted in his
readers a common social philosophy, of which the fundamental
tenet was that Christian ethics must determine social relationships.
Goody Blake could appeal to God against Harry Gill, because
Harry, the stickler for property rights, was *wrong*. It is above all
the ethical implications of the poem that relate it to the Augustan
tradition. If on the surface "Goody Blake and Harry Gill" is a
somewhat crude imitation of the street ballads of the eighteenth
century, at bottom it is, I believe, a not altogether unworthy
descendant from *Gulliver's Travels* and *Tom Jones*.

It is this that makes Fox's commendation of "Goody Blake"
particularly interesting. Charles James Fox represented eighteenth-
century culture at its best. He was, as his secretary John Bernard
Trotter has testified, 'master of all the best of the ancient and
modern poets', Virgil and Pope being perhaps his favourites. In
spite of a certain weakness for poetic rhetoric Fox always re-
sponded to pathos in poetry if it was genuine. 'The tenderness
of Mr. Fox's heart', Trotter noted, 'manifested itself by his
always dwelling in poetry, with peculiar pleasure upon domestic
and affecting traits of character, when happily portrayed by the
author.'[1] It was to this side of Fox that Wordsworth's early
poems appealed. At Coleridge's suggestion complimentary

---

[1] *Memoirs of the Latter Years of the Right Honourable Charles James Fox* (3rd
edition, 1811), pp. 91–2.

copies of the 2nd edition of *Lyrical Ballads* had been despatched,
with appropriate covering letters, to the Duchess of Devonshire,
Wilberforce (who was a friend of Wordsworth's uncle William
Cookson), Sir Bland Burgess, Mrs. Jordan the actress, and a
number of other notabilities, including Fox. As is the way with
eminent recipients of the works of unknown poets, most of the
great and the good did not bother to reply. But Fox did, in a
friendly and sensible letter. He had read, he says, the whole of the
two volumes—and with particular attention the two poems
Wordsworth had mentioned in the letter to him (they were
"Michael" and "The Brothers"). But the poems he liked best
were not these two but "We are Seven", "Goody Blake", "The
Idiot Boy" and "The Mad Mother" (the poem that begins 'Her
eyes are wild'). By nineteenth-century standards it was an
inexplicable selection. These are precisely the poems that Swinburne was later to label 'doleful examples of eccentricity in
dullness'. Not one of the four was included by Palgrave (who
was guided and assisted, it must be remembered, by Tennyson)
in *The Golden Treasury*. And "We are Seven" was the only one
to be admitted into Arnold's *Poems of Wordsworth*. The oddity of
Fox's selection, by nineteenth-century standards, is increased when
it is realised that among the poems he must have read and passed
over were the Lucy and Matthew poems, "Tintern Abbey",
"There was a Boy", "Nutting" and "Ruth", as well as
"Michael" and "The Brothers".

Of the four poems commended by Fox "Goody Blake and
Harry Gill" is much the closest to the eighteenth-century tradition. It springs from the same world, *mutatis mutandis*, as Carey's
"Sally in our Alley", Hogarth's prints, George Lillo's plays, and
Smollett's novels. But almost purely Augustan and objective
though the poem is, its distinction lies in something that has been
added to the eighteenth-century tradition. In its most elementary
form we have here already that combination of objectivity and
subjectivity which is the Wordsworthian hallmark. Wordsworth
has identified himself too fully with Goody—her poverty and
loneliness and susceptibility to cold—not to raise the reader's
suspicion that a fellow-feeling for another social outcast is at the

back of the poem. The Augustans, the sentimentalists as much as the realists and the satirists, remained *outside* the characters they depicted. Though it is easy to overlook the fact in the general grotesqueness of the poem, Wordsworth has, in however small a way, got *inside* Goody Blake.

IV

"There was a Boy", the second poem that it is proposed to analyse in detail, combines the best and the worst of Wordsworth's middle period. If "Goody Blake and Harry Gill" is a poem that has not had justice done to it, "There was a Boy" is a poem whose defects are still too often glossed over. There is really no excuse for its last nine lines:

> This boy was taken from his mates, and died
> In childhood, ere he was full twelve years old.
> Pre-eminent in beauty is the vale
> Where he was born and bred: the church-yard hangs
> Upon a slope above the village-school;
> And, through that church-yard when my way has led
> On summer-evenings, I believe that there
> A long half-hour together I have stood
> Mute—looking at the grave in which he lies!

For once Jeffrey and the *Edinburgh Review* were completely justified in their sarcasms. It must be remembered that the one thing we know about the dead boy is that he was an expert in imitating the hooting of an owl; 'and for the sake of this one accomplishment', Jeffrey comments, 'we are told, that the author has frequently stood mute, and gazed on his grave for half-an-hour together!' The remark occurs in a review of Crabbe's *Poems*.[1] As Jeffrey rightly says, the last nine lines are the sort of sentimental nonsense from which Crabbe is absolutely free. He does not point out, as in fairness he should have done, that the rest of the poem is far superior to anything in Crabbe. Coleridge's comment

---

[1] *Edinburgh Review*, Apr. 1808.

on the lines immediately preceding the sentimental conclusion is
well known: 'That

> Uncertain heaven received
> Into the bosom of the steady lake

I should have recognised anywhere; and had I met these lines
running wild in the deserts of Arabia, I should instantly have
screamed out "Wordsworth".'[1] And almost the whole of the first
part of the poem is typical of Wordsworth at his very best. What
immediately impresses the modern reader is the extraordinary
vividness with which the scene is conjured up. It is this aspect of
the poem which has recently attracted Aldous Huxley. In an
entertaining passage in *Texts and Pretexts* Mr. Huxley has described
the boy

> hooting and hooting with the indefatigable persistence of childhood,
> while the yet more persistent, because even less grown-up, owls
> hallooed and screamed their answer: hoot! halloo! hoot, hoot,
> halloo!—while the echoes bounced back and forth from wall to wall
> of the mountains—hour after hour; boy communing with bird and
> both profoundly, indescribably happy; happy with the deep mind-
> less happiness of living creatures rejoicing in their life; hour after
> hour, until either some infuriated adult came out with a stick to stop
> the din, or else, in a silence, as Wordsworth has described, the child
> was suddenly made aware again of his forgotten self-consciousness,
> his momentarily obliterated mind and, along with these, of the outer
> world and of its strangeness.[2]

But who was the boy who is presented so vividly? The
actuality of the description makes the question inevitable. In its
context in Book V of *The Prelude* the boy certainly appears to have
been one of Wordsworth's schoolfellows at Hawkshead School.
And Wordsworth's own note on the passage seems to confirm this: 'This practice of making an instrument of their own

---

[1] Letter to Wordsworth, 10 Dec. 1798.

[2] *Texts and Pretexts* (1932), p. 156. Though Huxley has misinterpreted lines
16-25, he realises that the Boy was a poetic fiction and that 'it was really little
William himself who stood there at the lake's edge . . .'. The MS. which proves
that he was right was only described by de Selincourt in the 1932 re-issue of his
edition of *The Prelude*.

fingers is known to most boys, though some are more skilful at it than others. William Raincock of Rayrigg, a fine-spirited lad, took the lead of all my schoolfellows in this art.' Raincock did not die young and so cannot be Wordsworth's 'Boy', but a search through the Hawkshead Parish Register has produced one boy, a certain John Vickars, who died about the right time and at about the right age.[1] *Faute de mieux* it seemed that the distinction must go to the otherwise unknown Vickars. The recent discovery, however, of an early draft of this passage has disposed of John Vickars's claim to immortality. The Boy, it seems, was Wordsworth himself. The early MS. has 'I' and 'my' instead of 'he' and 'his', and there is, of course, no sentimental conclusion. In this early draft the poem is autobiography pure and simple. The change from the first to the third person was, therefore, from fact to fiction, and its later insertion in the autobiographical *Prelude* represented, however innocently, an attempt to pass fiction off as fact. The contrast between this sort of thing and the conscientious factuality of "Goody Blake and Harry Gill" (which versifies an actual case recorded in a medical treatise by Erasmus Darwin) is a significant pointer to the direction of Wordsworth's evolution.

It is not difficult to reconstruct the poem's evolution. The first draft was written at Goslar in Germany, in the late autumn or early winter of 1798, at the same time as a number of other autobiographical passages in blank verse dealing with Wordsworth's childhood. These fragments were the nucleus round which *The Prelude* was eventually constructed. When Wordsworth returned to England in 1799 he decided to bring out a second edition of *Lyrical Ballads* expanded into two volumes. The second volume, it was arranged, was to contain the poems written in Germany or later, and among the material available for it were these early fragments of *The Prelude*. In the end he selected two of the fragments—"Nutting" and "There was a Boy". Presumably the

---

[1] See Eric Robertson, *Wordsworthshire* (1911), p. 67. Vickars died on 28 July 1782. He is described in the Register as 'a Charity Boy from Cragg', and he may have been one of the ten Blue Coat boys who were educated free at Hawkshead School.

latter was thought to finish rather abruptly and so an obituary
conclusion was concocted to tie up the loose ends. This coda
was obviously written in the coldest of cold blood; it is a piece of
mere literary carpentry and nothing else.[1] The poem's insertion,
sentimental conclusion and all, in Book V of *The Prelude*, as
though the Boy was an actual schoolfellow of Wordsworth's,
dates from 1804.

When Wordsworth reprinted the lines in 1815 in the first
collected edition of his poems, the poem was made to lead off the
section devoted to 'Poems of the Imagination'. The reason for
this prominence is explained in a passage in the Preface, which
throws some light on Wordsworth's original motives, as far as he
was still conscious of them, in writing the poem :

> I dismiss this subject with observing—that, in the series of Poems
> placed under the head of Imagination, I have begun with one of the
> earliest processes of Nature in the development of this faculty.
> Guided by one of my own primary consciousnesses, I have presented
> a commutation and transfer of internal feelings, co-operating with
> external accidents, to plant, for immortality, images of sound and
> sight, in the celestial soil of the Imagination. The Boy, there intro-
> duced, is listening, with something of a feverish and restless anxiety,
> for the recurrence of those riotous sounds which he had previously
> excited; and, at the moment when the intenseness of his mind is
> beginning to remit, he is surprised into a perception of the solemn
> and tranquillizing images which the Poem describes.

The best commentary on this pronouncement is an anecdote
recorded by De Quincey. One night he and Wordsworth had
been waiting by the road-side for the carrier from Keswick, and,
as the cart didn't come, Wordsworth had put his ear to the road
to try if he could hear the sound of the approaching wheels. As

---

[1] The earliest version of the conclusion is in a red leather pocket-book of
Dorothy Wordsworth's now in the Wordsworth Museum (MS. 18A) which
de Selincourt does not seem to have used. The diction of this version is more
perfunctory if less glossily sentimental than in the final text:

> And there along that bank when I have passed
> At evening, I believe that near his grave
> A full half-hour together I have stood,
> Mute,—for he died when he was ten years' old.

he got up, having heard nothing, he noticed a star shining brightly on the horizon. He then turned to De Quincey and made the following extremely revealing statement:

> I have remarked, from my earliest days, that, if under any circumstances the attention is energetically braced up to an act of steady observation, or of steady expectation, then, if this intense condition of vigilance should suddenly relax, at that moment any beautiful, any impressive visual object, or collection of objects, falling upon the eye, is carried to the heart with a power not known under other circumstances. Just now, my ear was placed upon the stretch, in order to catch any sound of wheels that might come down upon the lake of Wythburn from the Keswick road; at the very instant when I raised my head from the ground, in final abandonment of hope for this night, at the very instant when the organs of attention were all at once relaxing from their tension, the bright star hanging in the air above those outlines of massy blackness fell suddenly upon my eye, and penetrated my capacity of apprehension with a pathos and a sense of the infinite, that would not have arrested me under other circumstances.[1]

The psychological process described to De Quincey is evidently, in the light of the comments of the 1815 Preface, the basic material of "There was a Boy". This at any rate is what the poem is supposed to be about. The process, it will be noted, falls into three phases. The first phase is one of intense anticipatory concentration on an expected sound or sight. Can he hear the carrier? Will the owls answer? The second phase introduces a relaxation of the attention. The carrier can't be heard. The owls won't answer. The third phase, following immediately on the second, involves the sudden impingement on the consciousness of a different and unexpected sense-impression. Instead of hearing the carrier, Wordsworth sees the star. Instead of hearing the owls, the Boy hears the waterfalls and sees the rocks and the woods and the reflection of the sky in the lake. To this third phase Wordsworth obviously attributed a special significance. The sound of

---

[1] *Recollections of the Lake Poets*, ed. E. Sackville-West (1948), p. 144. This is one of the many passages that De Quincey omitted when revising the articles in *Tait's Magazine* (where the *Recollections* were originally printed 1834–9), for the Collected Edition of his works.

the waterfalls penetrated 'far into' the Boy's 'heart'. In 'the celestial soil of the Imagination' images of sound and sight were planted for 'immortality'—the same 'immortality' no doubt as that celebrated in the great Ode.[1] Finally a 'sense of the infinite' had been carried to the 'heart' with a 'power' not known under other circumstances.

What Wordsworth meant by such terms as 'heart', 'power' and 'Imagination' is made clear by the account of the behaviour of the Boy's visual impressions. What we are told is that the visible scene 'Would enter unawares into his mind'. A mind into which things enter without its being conscious of their entry can only be the subconscious mind. The term did not exist in Wordsworth's time, but it is clear that he intended the gist of the poem to be the subconscious influence on the personality of beautiful natural scenery.

In all this there was no doubt much psychological acuteness. Wordsworth was as good an observer of mental phenomena as of physical phenomena. What is disturbing, however, is the emphasis he lays upon the mental characteristics that he has observed. Our interest is invoked for the Boy solely because his physical surroundings have imprinted themselves on his subconscious mind as a result of his failure to get the owls to respond to his shouts. Why this psychological phenomenon should be expected to interest us poetically in the Boy is not clear. It certainly does not seem to provide an adequate motive for Wordsworth spending half an hour looking at the Boy's grave—particularly as the Boy was really, it appears, Wordsworth himself.

In its original autobiographical form, "There was a Boy" had represented a piece of psychological self-analysis. Wordsworth was apparently trying to explain to himself how it was that the imagery of the mountains, waterfalls, lakes etc., of the Hawkshead neighbourhood had come to assume a special importance in his mind. Why was it, when he was writing poetry, that these images kept recurring? The episode of the owls suggested a possible explanation. He had discovered as an adult that the relaxation of

---

[1] In Wordsworth 'immortal' and 'immortality' usually mean 'infinite', 'infinity'. They are regularly used in this sense in *The Excursion*.

the attention might, in certain circumstances, induce a feeling of almost mystical ecstasy. Perhaps as a boy he had experienced unconsciously what the adult experienced consciously. The hypothesis would seem to explain the curious power these natural images exercised over him.

Wordsworth may have felt that speculations of this nature, though of absorbing interest to himself and to people like Coleridge (the quality of the writing proves that), could not be expected to interest his ordinary readers. The possibility suggests a respectable reason for the change of person and the tacking on of the sentimental conclusion in the printed version. But if this is so, Wordsworth had underrated the intelligence of his readers. What excites us in "There was a Boy" is not the would-be-pathetic contrast between the living Boy and the grave in the churchyard. Nor is it the psychological discovery Wordsworth believed he had made. The poem's distinction derives from its vivid recreation of the lost world of childhood. For Wordsworth this recreation was only a by-product apparently of the process of psychological self-analysis; for us it is poetically all that counts.

What it all amounts to is that "There was a Boy" is not one poem but three poems. In the first place there is the poem in the third person and with the sentimental conclusion, the poem that Jeffrey made fun of and Fox ignored. We can perhaps call this poem the Elegy in a Lake District Churchyard. Its only interest, considered as a poetic whole, is the chasm that it indicates between what really interested Wordsworth in 1800 and what he thought his readers would be interested in. Such a chasm did not exist when Wordsworth wrote "Goody Blake and Harry Gill", only two years earlier, and its emergence must no doubt be considered either an effect or a cause of the progress towards subjectivity. The second poem in "There was a Boy", or more strictly the second poetic level, is the psychological case-history. Unlike the sentimental first level this was not something superimposed later when publication approached. Wordsworth's interest in the associationist psychology of David Hartley was genuine, and the Preface to the second edition of *Lyrical Ballads* announces in so many words that the principal purpose he had in mind when writing these poems, including presumably "There was a Boy", was 'to illustrate the manner in which our feelings and ideas are associated in a state of excitement'. It is difficult, however, to take such a statement at its face value. The emotional core of the poems has no connection whatever with Hartleian psychology, and it seems possible that the psychology merely provided a framework within which Wordsworth was able to express feelings and intuitions of which he was not wholly conscious. What one may call the third poem in "There was a Boy", the extraordinarily vivid and moving description of one of those 'glad animal movements' of boyhood referred to in "Tintern Abbey", is almost certainly an example of this sort of unawareness. What he imagined to be an illustration of the process by which ideas and feelings are associated was really, it seems fair to say, an attempt on the part of the adult Wordsworth to re-establish a connection with his own boyhood. It was, in particular, the Boy's relationship with wild nature that Wordsworth was trying to recapture, and the poem records with a beautifully articulated precision two balanced phases in that relationship—an active phase and a passive phase. In the active phase, as the Boy blows his mimic hootings, the rocks and islands seem almost to come to life (it is they who knew the Boy, not the Boy who knew them), and even the stars begin 'To move along the edges of the hills'. Then, as the Boy and the owls relapse into silence, a passive phase supervenes and there is a lifeless, almost gravitational coalescence of Boy, torrents, rocks, woods and lake. The poetic materials here are subjective enough in all conscience, but they are recorded with a quite remarkable objectivity. The approach is almost clinical (this was perhaps where Hartley came in useful), until we reach the climax of the poem, the line and a half that so impressed Coleridge:

> and that uncertain heaven received
> Into the bosom of the steady lake.

The coalescence of Boy and landscape has now become a coalescence of sky and lake, with the sky entering 'Into the bosom' of the lake just as the 'visible scene' had entered unawares 'into' the

Boy's mind. The implied correlation of 'bosom' and 'mind' is suggestive and idiosyncratic. As Coleridge recognised, the lines are peculiarly Wordsworthian and it will be legitimate to turn to another passage from *The Prelude* to elucidate them. The passage that suggests itself is the discussion in the second book of the process by which a baby on his mother's breast

> Is prompt and watchful, eager to combine
> In one appearance, all the elements
> And parts of the same object, else detach'd . . .
> In one beloved presence, nay and more,
> In that most apprehensive habitude
> And those sensations which have been deriv'd
> From this beloved Presence, there exists
> A virtue which irradiates and exalts
> All objects through all intercourse of sense.
> No outcast he, bewilder'd and depress'd;
> Along his infant veins are interfus'd
> The gravitation and the filial bond
> Of nature, that connect him with the world.[1]

I am not suggesting a specific connection between the two passages. In "There was a Boy" Wordsworth isn't likely to have intended anything as definite or theoretical as the later passage. But, if there is some connection, however slight, it seems to follow that the image of 'The bosom of the steady lake' takes us behind Wordsworth's boyhood to his infancy. The poem that began, half-consciously, as an attempt to re-establish a connection with his own boyhood ends up, or so it seems, in what was probably a wholly unconscious continuation of the process from boyhood into infancy. The urgency of the need to effect some such psychic continuity with his younger selves is guaranteed by the quality of the poetry.

V

"There was a Boy" fails as a poem, in spite of the brilliance and suggestiveness of many of its details, because it is chaotic. The three poems into which it is only too easily divisible co-exist

---

[1] *Prelude*, II, ll. 242–64.

but do not cohere. Between the facile sentimental elegy, the acute psychological document and the profound fragment of subjective autobiography the connections are accidental rather than essential. The root of the discrepancy is that there is no common or consistent attitude to objective reality. Regarded as the protagonist of a piece of pre-romantic sob-stuff it doesn't matter who the Boy was or whether he ever existed at all, but regarded as a piece of evidence towards a psychological law the Boy must obviously have been a real person, about whose identity and *bona fides* there can be no doubt at all. With "Goody Blake and Harry Gill" we know where we are. The poem carries the sub-title 'A True Story', and the 'Advertisement' prefixed to the first edition of *Lyrical Ballads* explains that it was 'founded on a well-authenticated fact which happened in Warwickshire'. If challenged Wordsworth would have been able to point to the section 'Mutable Madness' in Darwin's *Zoonomia; or, the Laws of Organic Life*, where the whole extraordinary story is related in sober prose. But, because we can't be certain whether the Boy did or didn't die young, and whether he is Wordsworth or a school-friend of Wordsworth's or a figment of Wordsworth's imagination, we haven't the same confidence in "There was a Boy". And this applies to the poem's third or autobiographical level too. At this level poetic symbolism has come in to complicate the critical problem. Did the stars, for example, only seem to 'move along the edges of the hills' (an optical illusion), or did they really move within the closed symbolic reality of the poem? Either interpretation is possible, and the reader, reduced to guessing, finds himself a little puzzled and a little irritated.

"She dwelt among the untrodden ways", though only written a few weeks after the first draft of "There was a Boy", suffers from none of these indecisions and anomalies. It is a better poem very largely because it defies and excludes phenomenal reality with an even greater scrupulousness than "Goody Blake and Harry Gill" respected it. In this poem the poetic constituents are wholly symbolic and the documentary framework has completely disappeared. But it is a controlled subjectivity, intellectually sophisticated and almost mathematically coherent:

She dwelt among the untrodden ways
 Beside the springs of Dove,
A Maid whom there were none to praise
 And very few to love:

A violet by a mossy stone
 Half hidden from the eye!
—Fair as a star, when only one
 Is shining in the sky.

She lived unknown, and few could know
 When Lucy ceased to be;
But she is in her grave, and, oh,
 The difference to me!

"The Song of Lucy", as Charles Lamb called it—when first published, in the second edition of *Lyrical Ballads*, it was actually headed "Song", a title Wordsworth dropped later—was Lamb's special favourite among the poems added in 1800.[1] It was no doubt the poem's hallucinatory quality that endeared it to him. His favourite poem in the first edition had been "The Ancient Mariner", and the two poems are not nearly so dissimilar as a superficial reading might suggest. But the dreamlike quality of Coleridge's poem comes from the incidents, whereas in Wordsworth's poem the effect derives from a special use of language. Put very crudely Wordsworth's method here is to combine positive and negative ideas so that they cancel each other out: in the resulting confusion of common-sense criteria the reader finds himself according a momentary credibility to a non-rational reality. A simple example of the method is the paradox propounded by the last two words of the poem's first line. How can *ways* be *untrodden*? It is the process of treading that creates and maintains a way. No doubt we *can* take *untrodden* as meaning 'only occasionally trodden', but this is not what the line actually says. What it says is that Lucy lived among ways that were not, strictly speaking, ways at all. There are two similar verbal contradictions in lines 3–4 and 9–10. If there were a very few who loved Lucy there cannot have been, literally, *none to praise* her. And if she had

---

[1] See his letter to Wordsworth, Feb. 1801.

really *lived unknown* how could there be even a few who knew when she ceased to be? The contradictions are unobtrusive and it isn't difficult to make certain silent corrections which make Wordsworth's statements completely intelligible. By *praise* a public eulogy of some sort may have been intended, such as Lucy's simple neighbours would have been incapable of. And by *unknown* Wordsworth may have meant that she was unknown to the wider world, a social nobody. The qualifications are easy enough to insert, but it is obvious, once these surface contradictions are pointed out, that qualifications of some sort do in fact have to be inserted. The meanings are not actually in Wordsworth's text. Simple though the poem may appear to be, it is not just a series of straightforward statements.

The immediate effect of the verbal contradictions is to undercut, as it were, the statements with which they are associated. If they are disregarded—if, that is, the reader confines his attention to the common-sense meaning of these three sentences without considering the form of its expression—a picture emerges of two incompatible worlds, one public and one private. The public world is traversed by well-trodden ways, its values are not love but praise, and the penalty that it holds over its members is to be unknown. The private world, on the other hand, has so few inhabitants that its ways are the merest tracks, its modes of communication are so intimate that praise is something of which it is incapable, and to be unknown outside its own little circle is a condition that it takes for granted. In other words, if the verbal contradictions are disregarded we are left with a crude and almost vulgar statement of the case for a Rousseauist escapism. God made the country and man made the town. In fact, however, to disregard the verbal contradictions is to misread the poem—they are after all a prominent part of its text—and once registered their effect is to blur the rigid outlines of the antithesis by an implicit criticism of all linguistic distinctions. If it is possible to use language so loosely that *untrodden* need not mean 'not trodden', that *love* cannot connote *praise*, and that *unknown* obtains a positive sense ('known to a few'), *and yet be completely intelligible*, the neighbouring oppositions and collocations of grammar and logic naturally also tend to become discredited. Both the private and the public worlds retreat into a common unreality for the reader, who emerges with the impression that the boundaries between them are less absolute and perhaps less important than the surface meaning of these three sentences had suggested.

Some such interpretation of the function of the verbal contra-dictions in this subtle and elusive poem is suggested by the behaviour of the imagery in the crucial second verse. The role of this imagery as a sort of fulcrum is established by the repetitions in the third verse of phrases from the first verse—'She lived' repeats 'She dwelt', 'few' repeats 'very few', and the sentence-patterns are similar—which provide a frame, as it were, for the syntactically dissimilar second verse. The poem's success derives from and turns upon the half-hidden violet and the single star. It is significant, therefore, that there is also a contradiction between the surface function of the violet and the star and the actual impression that they create in the reading of the poem. Superficially the violet and the star are antithetic opposites, like the public and the private worlds of the other verses. Indeed, it looks as though the half-hidden violet is intended to symbolise Lucy's insignificance in the public world, and the single star to represent her supreme importance in the private world. In the actual reading, however, the images behave in a much less logical way. The simplest way to put it is to say that the two images turn out to be one image. The reader begins by looking *down* at the violet and then *up* at the star, and in the process the two juxtaposed images form themselves into a single landscape—presumably a twilight one when it would be particularly difficult to distinguish the violet from the mossy stone. The merging of the two images has a further symbolic consequence. In some sense, if it was only a superficial one, the violet symbolised Lucy and so did the star—and with the two images now forming the terminal extremes of this tremendous new image Lucy inevitably comes to occupy the whole interval between them. Lucy *is* the whole evening scene. The symbolic aggrandisement of Lucy and the sublimity that it confers upon her react upon the poem's conclusion, and it is their combination that converts the near-bathos of the last line

3

into 'the most perfect pathos', as Keats called it, according to his friend Bailey.[1] But the sublimity and the pathos are in a sense by-products. What "She dwelt among the untrodden ways" seems to be *saying*, as a poem, is that the distinctions of the intellect, the water-tight compartments in which we keep violets and stars, our public lives and our private lives, need to be broken down in the interests of a higher reality. It is only as a symbol of this higher reality that Lucy achieves poetic coherence. Whatever other meanings attach themselves to her are adventitious or secondary. It follows that, in so far as the poem has a central meaning, it is not a poem about human love or human death so much as about the nature of human knowledge. In the strictest sense of the term, it is a metaphysical poem.

The method employed with the poem's words and images is repeated in the central symbol. There is the same technique of arousing and disappointing the reader's rational expectations. The antithetical opposites collide and disintegrate, and their place is taken by a more inclusive, more impalpable whole. The process is applied to Lucy in the first line of the poem. Here we seem to have a human being ('She dwelt')—who is not, however, a human being. Instead of living in a house she lives *among* ways that are not really ways—which suggests a bird rather than a girl (a suggestion that receives irrational, and therefore in this context significant, reinforcement from the river-name *Dove* in the next line). Is she perhaps, like the nightingales, skylarks and cuckoos of the later Romantics, a symbol of the poetic afflatus? And in that case is her death Wordsworth's first symbolic acknowledgement of the drying-up in himself of the capacity of ecstatic response to wild nature? Such an interpretation, however, is immediately contradicted by the capitalisation of *Maid* in the third line. If she is holier than other maidens Lucy, it is clear, is not primarily a bird. The merging of the two opposed images in the second verse brings with it a further implication. If Lucy can span the whole evening landscape from the violet at our feet to the immensely distant star, she must almost be a nature-spirit, a supernatural creature. The human being, an English girl (her name proves

---

[1] H. E. Rollins, *The Keats Circle* (1948), II, 276.

that) whom the poet had loved, returns in the last verse. Unlike
a nature-spirit she has died, unlike a bird she is in a grave. But the
final Lucy, when the poem's conclusion has been reached, is not
a human being or a bird or a saint or a nature-spirit. She is not
even a synthesis of these human and non-human beings. The
contradictory symbols cancel each other out, just as the positive
and negative concepts have on the verbal level and the opposed
images on the level of imagery. The total effect of these devices
is to create in the reader's mind the impression that Lucy exists
on a plane of reality to which such contradictory categories do not
apply. The suspension of disbelief is complete. Even Lucy's early
and unexplained death is not entirely tragic. In the irrational
context of the poem it is right that she should die, just as it was
right that the Ancient Mariner's guiltless companions should die
while he himself survived. In Wordsworth's closed but completely coherent subjective world the values of everyday life are
as irrelevant as the logic of common sense.

VI

The analyses that have been attempted in the preceding
sections were embarked upon with two objects in view. One was
to see if it would be possible to expand or fill in the acute but
somewhat schematic account Coleridge gives in *Biographia
Literaria* of the impression Wordsworth's early poems made on
him. What struck him, it will be remembered, about *Salisbury
Plain*, when he got to know it in 1796, was 'the union of deep
feeling with profound thought; the fine balance of truth in
observing, with the imaginative faculty in modifying, the objects
observed, and above all the original gift of spreading the tone,
the atmosphere, and with it the depth and height of the ideal
world around forms, incidents and situations, of which, for the
common view, custom had bedimmed all the lustre, had dried up
the sparkle and the dew drops'. With the analyses of three poems
completed in some detail it should now be possible to determine
how far Coleridge's account of *Salisbury Plain* is relevant to
Wordsworth's poetry in general, if not to that poem itself (which

has not been printed, except for a long extract in *Lyrical Ballads*, in the form in which Coleridge knew it).

The second objective proposed in the analyses was to define more closely the character of the change that Wordsworth's poetry seems to undergo in the summer of 1798. A complete answer is obviously not possible on the basis of three short poems, one of which was written three or four months before the change is thought to have occurred, but the nature of the problem should be clearer.

Coleridge makes two assertions about *Salisbury Plain* in the sentence under discussion. One is that the separate poetic constituents of the poem are divisible into two antithetic categories—on the one hand, (i) deep feeling, (ii) imaginative modifications of phenomenal reality, (iii) refreshing idealisations; on the other hand, (i) profound thought, (ii) accurate observations, (iii) everyday *dramatis personæ*, incidents and setting. Coleridge's other assertion is that the six opposed qualities achieve 'union' and 'balance'. In other words, the poem is both emotional and rational, in equal quantities of each, the writing is both fanciful and realistic, and the subject-matter is at the same time idealised and sordid. Both of Coleridge's assertions are exaggerated, of course, especially as applied to *Salisbury Plain*, a promising but very imperfect poem, but they do point out, with accuracy and discrimination, what might be called the intentions of Wordsworth's poetry. A few of his poems, like "The Old Cumberland Beggar", Book II of *The Prelude* and "Resolution and Independence", may even be said to unite all the six constituents in a more or less perfect balance. In most of the poems, however, including some of the best ones, one or more of Coleridge's constituents will generally be found to be missing, and it is not always possible to talk of a 'union' or 'balance' between those that are not.

None of the three poems analysed conforms precisely to Coleridge's formula. There is no 'deep thought' in "Goody Blake and Harry Gill" and little or no idealisation in it either. And perhaps the only 'modifying' touch contributed by Wordsworth's imagination to the poem is the simile describing Goody in

summer—'as any linnet gay'. "There was a Boy", on the other
hand, seems to have all the separate qualities distinguished by
Coleridge, but they are certainly not in a state of union or balance.
And though "She dwelt among the untrodden ways" does
achieve union and balance and possesses most of Coleridge's
other constituents, there is little realistic observation in it in the
ordinary sense. It is not clear either that if 'deep thought' covers
the psychological law promulgated in "There was a Boy" it
should also include the rational irrationality of "She dwelt among
the untrodden ways". A label as vague as all that is almost useless.
This is not to deny that the formula provides an excellent point
of departure. As a general description of the most characteristic
features of Wordsworth's poetry it is probably the best that has so
far been advanced. But obviously it must not be pressed too hard.
It is not much help certainly when one tries to define what the
essential difference is between the poems written before July 1798
and those written after it.

The special problem that "Goody Blake and Harry Gill"
raised was the nature and degree of Wordsworth's own involve-
ment in the poem. On the face of it the poem is a straightforward
translation of Erasmus Darwin's prose into the idiom of the
contemporary street-ballad. It ends on a highly didactic note:

> Now think, ye farmers all, I pray,
> Of Goody Blake and Harry Gill.

And Wordsworth's own statements about the poem and poems
like it suggest that what he was most concerned about in writing
them was to illustrate a psychological principle. What impresses
and interests the reader, however, is the emotional authenticity of
Goody Blake. We believe in her misery in the cold weather and
we share her hatred of Harry for condemning her to more of it.
The poem is good, or at any rate fairly good, because we cannot
help identifying ourselves momentarily with Goody. But if the
reader identifies himself in this way with the poor old woman the
writer must have done so too. Why then does Wordsworth try
and fob us off with the lesson the poem will teach farmers or its
psychological interest? We are left in a state of slightly resentful
bewilderment.

The curious thing is that the poems written after July 1798 raise almost identical problems. Some of them have already been discussed in the case of "There was a Boy". It is not simply that the reader cannot help asking if the Boy is a real boy or not, and if he is real whether he is the young Wordsworth or a school-friend of his. There is also the question of the relationship of the irrelevant sentimental conclusion to what precedes it, and the further difficulty about the psychological law that the poem is apparently illustrating—a difficulty similar in kind to that raised by "Goody Blake and Harry Gill" but more embarrassing in "There was a Boy" because the psychological aspect is so much more prominent.

"She dwelt among the untrodden ways" is also a puzzling poem, but its puzzles are more fundamental. It does not really matter who Lucy is, though the question is a natural one to ask. What is really disturbing is the ultimate implication of Words-worth's poetic method in the poem. Its success, as we have seen, derives from what can only be called a kind of linguistic perver-sity. Matthew Arnold once described the Lucy poems and their companions as having 'no style'—a curious comment on the face of it since every poem must possess a style of its own if it is to succeed as poetry. But Arnold's phrase does in fact describe Wordsworth's use of language in "She dwelt among the un-trodden ways". By manipulating his words, metaphors and symbols so that they create the illusion of cancelling each other out, he was able to suggest a more inclusive and a more rarefied meaning than it was possible to express directly. But the poetry lay *between* the words. In a phrase like 'oh! The difference to me!' the pathos comes from the inexpressibility of the emotion that is nevertheless expressed. And so, if style is the perfection of language in its normal uses, Wordsworth's use of language here is the negation of style. In order to hint at meanings behind language he has had to discredit and break down the ordinary apparatus of language. Carried to its logical conclusion the process amounts to an attack upon poetry itself, since language is the medium of poetry and a poem is inconceivable without it.

It should be obvious by now that Wordsworth's change of

poetic manner in the summer of 1798 cannot be explained in merely literary terms. Coleridge's formula and the simplified version of it that I have presented, in which Wordsworth's Augustan and Romantic 'Voices' are proposed as complements of each other, are useful introductory devices. To the reader who is only beginning to get to know his way about Wordsworth's poetry they may perhaps be recommended as convenient and reasonably reliable signposts. But they do not answer the questions that arise the moment one starts looking at all closely at particular poems. These questions, the real puzzles, all go back to Wordsworth himself. The mixture of autobiography and fiction, the confusion of conscious, semi-conscious and subconscious meanings, the superimposed layers of social propaganda and anarchic nihilism—all this sort of thing can only be sorted out and explained in terms of Wordsworth's own state of mind when he wrote his poems. To a greater degree than with any other major English poet his reader needs continuous extraneous assistance— not so much to clear up *minutiæ* of interpretation as to understand the whole poetic attitude, what Wordsworth is getting at in the widest sense. This is because his poems do not derive their vitality so much from the common literary tradition, as Milton's, Tennyson's and Eliot's do, or from the common literary audience, as Chaucer's, Dryden's and Auden's do, as from Wordsworth himself. They are exceptionally personal poems, almost all of them directly or indirectly autobiographical. It follows that a sympathetic understanding of the oblique personal confessions and the indirect autobiographical allusions in the poems must necessarily be preceded by a general knowledge of the outlines of Wordsworth's life. We cannot read Wordsworth properly until we have got to know Wordsworth. And this means not only the external Wordsworth, the gaunt, rather unlikeable figure who went to school and to Cambridge, who travelled, had an illegitimate daughter, settled at Grasmere and married. It also means the internal Wordsworth who loved and suffered and feared. It is becoming clearer every day, with the progress of modern Wordsworthian studies, that it is the internal, emotional Wordsworth who really matters. The critics and biographers have paid too much attention in the past to Wordsworth's ideas, to his political theories, his adoption and rejection of Godwinism, his enthusiasm for Hartley's associationism, his attacks upon poetic diction, and his idealisation of the Westmorland 'statesmen'. I am not sure that any of these interests, real though they were, affected his poetry very much. Their elucidation has only a marginal relevance, in my experience, to the difficulties and obscurities of the poems themselves. Wordsworth was not primarily a thinker but a feeler. The determining events of his career and the sources of all that is essential in his poetry were the personal tragedies, the anguished decisions, the half-conscious half-animal terrors and ecstasies, and *not* the discoveries of the intellect.

The importance of the subjective elements in Wordsworth's poetry will not, on this hypothesis, require further emphasis. Since the poems are either the direct or the symbolic expression of his personal feelings, moods and intuitions their interpretation must depend upon a reconstruction of the evolution of the affective undercurrents of his personality. It will be necessary therefore to try and define states of mind of which Wordsworth was not wholly conscious himself, which he sometimes mis-understood or tried to suppress. The evidence, of course, is always inadequate and sometimes non-existent. I have often had to guess and no doubt I have often guessed wrong. But there is no alternative. If Wordsworth's poetry is to go on being read it must be *understood*, fully and consciously. As it becomes more remote in time the reader can no longer count on the unconscious compre-hension, the instinctive fellow-feelings, on which the Victorian reader could draw. And the venture is eminently worth while—even if we

> must tread on shadowy ground, must sink
> Deep—and, aloft ascending, breathe in worlds
> To which the heaven of heavens is but a veil.

Chapter Two

THE FATHER OF THE MAN[1]

My heart leaps up when I behold
   A rainbow in the sky:
So was it when my life began;
So is it now I am a man;
So be it when I shall grow old,
   Or let me die!
The Child is father of the Man;
And I could wish my days to be
Bound each to each by natural piety.

I

WORDSWORTH was thirty-one when he wrote those now almost too familiar lines. Apparently they summed up for him, then and later, the whole process of growing up. The special doctrinal importance that he attached to them is shown by their being prefixed to the section of his poetical works devoted to "Poems referring to the Period of Childhood". The last three lines also reappear as an epigraph to "Intimations of Immortality", the poem that expounds the consolatory function of "Recollections of Early Childhood".

A childhood in which the element of continuity is provided by rainbows has an uncomfortable sound. But by ordinary standards Wordsworth's childhood was exceptionally discontinuous. This was perhaps one of the reasons why he came to ascribe an almost mystical importance to rainbows, stars, clouds, winds, mountains, lakes and woods, and the animals, vegetables and minerals associated with them. In a world in which human satisfactions

---

[1] The exigencies of my 're-interpretation' may sometimes obscure the external facts of Wordsworth's life and the historical order in which his poems were written. For the benefit of the sceptical or bemused reader I have added two Appendixes, pp. 205–21 below—a 'Time-Table of Wordsworth's Movements up to 1800', and a chronological list of the poems to the end of 1815.

did not recur, they recurred. Natural piety may have been at
bottom a substitute for the emotional security of a happy family
life. With nobody left to love him, or to be loved by him,
Wordsworth fell in love with nature. According to his own
statement, at any rate, it was on a basis of this passionate delight
in the natural scenery of the Lake District that his adult life was
eventually built—"Love of Nature leading to Love of Mankind",
to quote the title of Book VIII of *The Prelude*.

The first seven years of Wordsworth's life were probably
happy enough. In retrospect, and in acute contrast with the years
that followed them, they may well have seemed blissfully happy.
Generalising from his own nursery experiences, he summed up
his memories of those early years in the great "Ode". Heaven lay
about him in his infancy. Or so at any rate it seemed to the mature
Wordsworth a great many years later.

What the infantile heaven was like, he has described in part of
Book I of *The Prelude*:

> Oh! many a time have I, a five years' Child,
> A naked Boy, in one delightful Rill, . . .
> Made one long bathing of a summer's day,
> Bask'd in the sun, and plunged, and bask'd again
> Alternate all a summer's day, or cours'd
> Over the sandy fields, leaping through groves
> Of yellow grunsel, or when crag and hill,
> The woods, and distant Skiddaw's lofty height,
> Were bronz'd with a deep radiance, stood alone
> Beneath the sky, as if I had been born
> On Indian Plains, and from my Mother's hut
> Had run abroad in wantonness, to sport,
> A naked Savage, in the thunder shower.[1]

That was Cockermouth in Cumberland, his 'sweet Birthplace',
as he called it, where William Wordsworth came into the world

---

[1] *Prelude*, I, ll. 291–304. All quotations are from the 1805 text. The 1850 revision is a deplorable affair. In his classic edition (1926) de Selincourt, though
recognising the general superiority of the earlier version, seems to me to exag-
gerate the poetical merit of many of the later changes. On inspection they will
almost always be found to be only superficial improvements—emptily elegant
phrases, pretty-pretty images, pseudo-profundities.

on 7 April 1770. The 'delightful Rill' was a mill-stream attached
to the river Derwent, which ran immediately behind the Wordsworths' house, then as now the largest in the little town. John
Wordsworth, the father, was the agent of the first Earl of Lonsdale, who was the owner of one of the largest estates in the north-
west of England, and by middle-class standards the Wordsworths
were comfortably off. A by-product perhaps of this material
prosperity was the freedom allowed to the children. They did not
see much of their father, a busy and silent man, and it was the
mother,

> who was the heart
> And hinge of all our learnings and our loves . . .[1]

Anne Wordsworth was a kind and sensible woman, who imposed few restrictions on the children's activities. On one
occasion, for example, a butterfly hunt ended up in the little
William exploring all by himself the pitch-black dungeon in the
ruins of Cockermouth Castle.[2] Generally, however, he had a
companion on the bird's-nesting and butterfly-catching adventures in his sister Dorothy, who was the nearest to him in age of
the five Wordsworth children. Such as it was, the difference in
their ages at this time—Dorothy was some twenty months the
younger—may have emphasised a fundamental difference of
temperament:

> A very hunter did I rush
> Upon the prey:—with leaps and springs
> I followed on from brake to bush;
> But she, God love her! feared to brush
> The dust from off its wings.[3]

In the poems celebrating this period of his life, Wordsworth
keeps returning to the contrast between his own wildness and the
gentleness of Dorothy. It sounds an innocent enough wildness in
all conscience. But Wordsworth tells us in his *Autobiographical
Memoranda*—the objective record dictated in his old age which

---

[1] *Prelude*, V, ll. 257–8.
[2] "Address from the Spirit of Cockermouth Castle."
[3] "To a Butterfly."

supplies an invaluable complement to the earlier and more or less subjective autobiography of *The Prelude*—that his mother confessed to a friend of hers that the only one of her children whose future caused her any real anxiety was William. He will be memorable, she said, either for good or for evil.[1]

William's wildness was what we should now call 'vitality'. Almost every boy goes through a naughty stage round about the age of seven, and William's greater naughtiness was simply the corollary of his greater vitality. De Quincey, who knew Wordsworth very well indeed (his *Recollections of the Lake Poets* is much the best biography of Wordsworth), was struck by the strength of what he called his 'animal appetites'. The observation occurs in the detailed and fascinating account that De Quincey gives of Wordsworth's physical appearance:

> The nose, a little arched, is large; which, by the way (according to a natural phrenology, existing centuries ago amongst some of the lowest amongst the human species), has always been accounted an unequivocal expression of animal appetites organically strong. And that expressed the simple truth: Wordsworth's intellectual passions were fervent and strong: but they rested upon a basis of preternatural animal sensibility diffused through *all* the animal passions (or appetites) . . .[2]

There is plenty of other evidence to confirm the general accuracy of De Quincey's impression. The flame of life burned more strongly in Wordsworth than in most of his contemporaries. For one thing, even as a boy, he was apparently never ill. John Wordsworth's accounts give details of payments to doctors and nurses for the other children, but never for William, and in later life, except for headaches and a mysterious pain in the side that may have been connected with the later eye-trouble, he retained

---

[1] The *Autobiographical Memoranda* were dictated in Nov. 1847. They will be found in the second chapter of Christopher Wordsworth's *Memoirs of William Wordsworth* (2 vols. 1851)—one of the few bright spots in that dreary compilation. (Another oasis is Sir John Taylor Coleridge's reminiscences in Vol. II of Wordsworth's conversations with him in 1836.)

[2] *Recollections of the Lake Poets*, ed. E. Sackville-West, p. 122.

the same immunity from disease. Another and more familiar example of Wordsworth's exceptional vitality are his feats of pedestrianism. Even as an old man, Wordsworth thought nothing of walking thirty miles a day. One summer afternoon, according to George Brimley,[1] 'the coach met Mr. Wordsworth and stopped; and a young lady inside who was going on a visit to the poet, put her head out to speak to him. "How d'ye do?" said he—"how d'ye do! Mrs. Wordsworth will be delighted to see you. I shall be back in the evening. I'm only going to tea with Southey."' Southey lived a good fifteen miles away, with hardly a yard of level ground all the way! De Quincey once calculated that by the time they were sixty-five years old the Wordsworthian legs had traversed 175,000 to 180,000 English miles.

The boy's naughtiness, it is obvious, was a sheer superfluity of animal spirits. Properly handled, as his mother was handling it, there was nothing to worry about. The evil potentialities that she detected in him can safely be ascribed to the imaginations of her father and her mother, who never liked or understood their young grandson. Indeed, if his mother was Wordsworth's good angel, Mr. and Mrs. Cookson of Penrith were undoubtedly his bad angels. Their influence on Wordsworth's life, and so on his poetry, is of incalculable importance, and it will be worth recording what little is known about this unamiable couple.

William Cookson was the principal mercer, or draper, in the little Cumberland town of Penrith. His chief distinction in the eyes of his fellow-townsmen was that he had married 'above himself'—his wife being the heiress of a minor 'county' family, the Crackanthorps of Newbiggen Hall, Westmorland. In character he seems to have been a typical *petit bourgeois*—Philistine, snobbish, puritanical and avaricious. His elder son, Christopher, who lived with his parents and helped in the shop, was a chip of the same block, perhaps indeed an even more disagreeable specimen than his father. And Mrs. Cookson, if less actively detestable, shared most of her husband's characteristics.

An analysis of the family accounts makes it clear that the young Wordsworths spent much of their time, perhaps half of it

---

[1] *Essays*, p. 157.

altogether, with these grandparents at Penrith.[1] It is significant, however, that whereas there are several ecstatic references to Cockermouth in *The Prelude*, the childhood days at Penrith receive no mention at all either there or in the other poems. The omission suggests that Wordsworth preferred not to remember his visits to Penrith.[2] As long as his mother was alive, the oppressive pseudo-gentility of the draper's shop may not have mattered much, but her sudden death in March 1778 changed the whole of Wordsworth's world. Henceforth, until he went up to Cambridge in 1787, it was the Cooksons, and to a lesser degree his morose and broken-hearted father—who, however, died in 1783—who ruled his world. The sudden shock of the transition from the mildness of his mother's authority to the tyranny of the Cooksons left a profound impression on Wordsworth. The boy's high spirits seem to have been immediately diagnosed as wickedness and drastic steps were taken to suppress them. And the sense of isolation and incomprehension was intensified by the removal of his ally and playmate Dorothy to far-distant Halifax in Yorkshire, where she passed into the care of a kindly cousin of their mother's. Wordsworth did not see her again for over nine years.

In Book I of *The Prelude*, looking back at the years following his mother's death and his separation from Dorothy, Wordsworth expresses his astonishment that he survived them without loss of mental balance:

> Ah me! that all
> The terrors, all the early miseries,
> Regrets, vexations, lassitudes, that all
> The thoughts and feelings which have been infus'd
> Into my mind, should ever have made up
> The calm existence that is mine when I
> Am worthy of myself![3]

---

[1] See Gordon Wordsworth, "The Boyhood of Wordsworth", *Cornhill Magazine*, Apr. 1920, p. 414.

[2] The one exception is the moving account of the little Wordsworth's finding himself alone on the site of the murderer's gibbet (*Prelude*, XI, ll. 279–316), which was by the Border Beacon near Penrith. But the exception only confirms the rule since this episode did not occur in the town but on the heaths above it.

[3] *Prelude*, I, ll. 355–61.

One or two anecdotes have survived to show what the 'early miseries' were like in practice, and how Wordsworth reacted to them. Their significance as the background against which his nature-mysticism developed has not, I think, been sufficiently stressed by his biographers.

Above the shop, which was at the top of the Penrith market place, there was a large drawing-room, though it is typical of the Cookson *ménage* that the carpet was only laid down there on special occasions. Its walls were covered with family portraits, no doubt of the Crackanthorps and their connections, and it was in this so-called drawing room of his grandfather's that the young William made his first protest against the social order. He and his brother Richard, who was two years the older, had been whipping tops on the uncarpeted floor, when William stopped abruptly and said to Richard, pointing at one of the ancestresses, 'Dare you strike your whip through that old lady's petticoat?' Richard, who was to grow up into a dilatory London solicitor, with the family tree as his one hobby, refused the challenge. 'No, I won't', he said. 'Then', said William, poising the lash before an enormous hooped petticoat in one of the portraits, 'here goes!' For which the poet added, when telling the story seventy years later, 'no doubt, though I have forgotten it, I was properly punished'.[1]

Another Penrith episode is also recorded by Wordsworth in the *Autobiographical Memoranda*. 'I was of a stiff, moody, and violent temper,' he says, 'so much so that I remember going once into the attics of my grandfather's house at Penrith, upon some indignity having been put upon me, with an intention of destroying myself with one of the foils which I knew was kept there. I took the foil in hand, but my heart failed. . . .'[2] It would be interesting to know what the indignity was that had been put upon him on this occasion. When relating these episodes Wordsworth added a significant comment. 'But possibly,' he said,

---

[1] *Memoirs of William Wordsworth*, I, 9. Mrs. Moorman, who has examined the family accounts, tells me that Uncle Kit presented Wordsworth's father with a bill for £75 at Whitsun 1779 for expenses incurred in connection with William. Perhaps one item in this formidable figure was 'To family portraits destroyed'?

[2] *Ibid.*

'from some want of judgment in punishments inflicted, I had become perverse and obstinate in defying chastisement, and rather proud of it than otherwise.'

It was while living with the Penrith grandparents that Wordsworth attended his first school, where his future wife Mary Hutchinson, a daughter of the Penrith tobacconist, was a schoolfellow. A somewhat exclusive establishment, it was kept by Anne Birkett, who is described as 'a remarkable personage, who had taught three generations, of the upper classes principally, of the town of Penrith and its neighbourhood'.[1] To the segregation from the lower classes, the sub-shopkeeper stratum, that this tribute suggests may perhaps be ascribed, in part at any rate, the almost total ignorance of folk-lore and folk-song displayed in Wordsworth's poetry. Their absence differentiates it sharply from the poetry of his contemporaries in Scotland and the north of England. Burns and Hogg—the latter Wordsworth's exact contemporary, who had grown up only some seventy miles from Cockermouth and Penrith—and their English counterpart Robert Anderson of Carlisle (whose *Poems on Various Subjects* was published in the same year as *Lyrical Ballads*) were the products of an essentially popular culture. Their poems sprang from and were addressed to a popular audience; Wordsworth's were not. 'Well you see, blessed barn,' a Grasmere farmer told Canon Rawnsley, by way of explaining why none of his neighbours read the poet's works, 'there's pomes and pomes, and Wudsworth's was not for sec as us.'[2] This verdict is confirmed by a writer in the *Westminster Review* for January 1855, who had heard, he says, the "Reed Robin" of Anderson 'sung in an outhouse upon the Fells to a party of sporting dalesmen by a country lad in a manner that moved both performer and audience to tears'. Wordsworth's poems, however, were not loved or sung in this way:

The writer of the "Lyrical Ballads", even in his own beloved lake country, has not superseded its native uncouth melodists; the maker

---

[1] *Memoirs of William Wordsworth*, I, 17.

[2] "Reminiscences of Wordsworth among the Peasantry of Westmorland", *Transactions of the Wordsworth Society*, VI (1884). The Reminiscences are also to be found in Rawnsley's *Lake Country Sketches* (1903), pp. 12–13.

and enricher of that district, just as Scott was of the country around the Trosachs, he is spoken of with great respect and reverence by all his countrymen, but he is never sung. Intensity, gracefulness, learning, and philosophy seem to be far from advantages to him who would become the people's poet . . .[1]

Wordsworth's unawareness of the popular poetic tradition was the price paid for the pseudo-gentility of the draper's shop. At the time when the young Walter Scott was drinking in old Border ballads, songs and legends at his grandmother's knee at Sandy-Knowe, the young Wordsworth's grandmother was no doubt instructing her grandchildren in the surpassing grandeur of the Crackanthorps of Newbiggen Hall. Except in the servile soul of Richard the seed did not sink deep, but for the rest of his life William at any rate was never entirely at ease in the company of his social inferiors. It was not snobbery, but a consciousness of the immensity of the gap that separated the rich and the poor. A broadside version of "We are Seven" that was published about 1820 has the alternative title, "The Little Maid and the Gentleman". One point certainly of the poem is that the two interlocutors live in different social worlds, the Little Maid with her own peculiar system of arithmetic, the Gentleman with his. And between these two worlds no communication was possible:

> 'But they are dead; those two are dead!
> 'Their spirits are in heaven!'
> 'Twas throwing words away; for still
> The little Maid would have her will,
> And said, 'Nay, we are seven!'

It is evident that there was a similar failure of communication between the young Wordsworths and even the more amiable adults of Penrith. Indeed in both "We are Seven" and the "Anecdote for Fathers", the poem preceding it in *Lyrical Ballads*, it is clearly Wordsworth's recollection of his own difficulties in making contact with the alien, if not hostile, world of 'grown-ups' that enables him to present the child's point of view so sympathetically.

Things got even worse for the young Wordsworths after their

---

[1] *Op. cit.*, pp. 43–4.

father's death in 1783. Owing to his long absences on business they had never seen much of him, and beyond the fact that he made William learn a lot of Spenser, Shakespeare and Milton by heart, we know little or nothing of his relations with his children. There is a well-known passage in Book XI of *The Prelude* which describes Wordsworth's impatience at the delay in the appearance of the two horses that were to carry him and his brothers back to Cockermouth for the Christmas holidays. Ten days later, on 30 December, John Wordsworth died, and

> The event
> With all the sorrow which it brought appear'd
> A chastisement . . .[1]

—a statement which suggests that it was the effects resulting from his father's death which were felt to be the real disaster. John Wordsworth may not have been regretted by the children very much in and for himself. A sense of guilt can, indeed, be detected because of the gap between what William did feel and what he knew he ought to have felt. As he put it in *The Vale of Esthwaite*, one of his earliest poems, where the episode of the long wait for the horses is also introduced:

> I mourn because I mourned no more.
> Nor did my little heart foresee
> She lost a home in losing thee.
> Nor did it know, of thee bereft,
> That little more than Heaven was left.[2]

John Wordsworth's death was certainly not the emotional disaster for the children that his wife's death had been. Apart from the two passages just referred to, there is not a single allusion of

---

[1] *Prelude*, XI, ll. 368–70.

[2] Except for an 'Extract' of 14 lines, very much re-written, that Wordsworth included among his "Poems written in Youth", *The Vale of Esthwaite* was first printed by de Selincourt in Vol. I of his edition of *The Poetical Works* (1940). The lines in the passage quoted are numbered by de Selincourt 433–7. Unfortunately de Selincourt did not print the whole of the surviving text of the poem. Some interesting additional extracts were transcribed by Wordsworth into the leather-bound notebook (MS. D.C., I, 4), which includes fair copies of all the early poems he wished to preserve in 1787.

any kind to his father in the whole of Wordsworth's poetical works. In so autobiographical a poet the omission is tantamount to a confession of indifference, if not of active dislike. Financially, however, John Wordsworth's death was a calamity for his children. Instead of being left with a modest competence, as they might reasonably have expected, they found themselves with very little indeed that they could count on. Most of their father's savings, it transpired, had gone in more or less forced loans to Lord Lonsdale, his half-mad employer, who now refused to pay them back. And nearly twenty years were to pass before the sum involved, some £5,000 was refunded by the second Earl (the 'good Earl', as he was called locally, to distinguish him from his predecessor the 'bad Earl'). Some of Wordsworth's later revolutionary fervour can no doubt be attributed to a natural resentment at Lonsdale's dishonesty and the series of legal chicaneries by which he succeeded in evading the payment of one penny to the Wordsworths until he died.

A vivid picture of life in and behind the draper's shop is to be found in the letter Dorothy wrote to a Halifax friend, when she was summoned back to Penrith to help in the house:

I was for a whole week kept in expectation of my Brothers, who staied at school all that time after the vacation began owing to the ill-nature of my Uncle who would not send horses for them because when they wrote they did not happen to mention them, and only said when they should break up which was always before sufficient. This was the beginning of my mortifications for I felt that if they had had another home to go to, they would have been behaved to in a very different manner, and received with more chearful countenances, indeed nobody but myself expressed one wish to see them. At last however they were sent for, but not till my Brother Wm had hired a horse for himself and came over because he thought someone must be ill; the servants are every one of them so insolent to us as makes the kitchen as well as the parlour quite insupportable. James has even gone so far as to tell us that we had nobody to depend upon but my Grandfr, for that our fortunes we[re] but v[ery sma]ll, and my Brs can not even get a pair of shoes cleaned without James's telling them they require as much waiting upon as any *gentlemen*, nor can I get a thing done for myself without absolutely entreating it as a [fav]our. James happens to be a particular favorite [with] my Uncle Kit, who has taken a dislike to my Br [and] never takes any notice of any of us, so that he thinks [whi]le my Uncle behaves in this way to us he may do anything. We are found fault with every hour of the day both by the servants and my Grandfr and Grandmr, the former of whom never speaks to us but when he scolds, which is not seldom. I daresay our fortunes have been weighed thousands of times at the tea table in the kitchen and I have no doubt but they always conclude their conversations with 'they have nothing to be proud of.' [1]

This was the draper's shop as Dorothy found it in July 1787 after nine years' absence. She was fifteen when she wrote this letter. By this time William was seventeen, John (the sailor brother who was drowned in 1805) fourteen, and Christopher, who was to grow up to be the Master of Trinity College, Cambridge, thirteen. Richard, the eldest, had already settled in London. By then, of course, the young Wordsworths were old enough, or nearly old enough, to look after themselves. It is the years immediately following their mother's death in 1778 and their father's death in 1783 that do not bear contemplation. 'Many a time', Dorothy tells her friend, 'have Wm, Jn, C, and myself shed tears together, tears of the bitterest sorrow, we all of us, each day, feel more sensibly the loss we sustained when we were deprived of our parents. . . . [We] always finish our conversations which generally take a melancholy turn, with [w]ishing we had a father and a home.'

Dorothy did not have to wait long before she was able to escape from Penrith again. On her serene and sunny disposition the gloomy tyranny of the Cooksons left little or no impression. But William had been exposed for a much longer period and at a more defenceless age to the grandparents and Uncle Kit, who

---

[1] This undated letter to Jane Pollard is the earliest of Dorothy's letters to survive. All quotations both from her letters and from Wordsworth's are from de Selincourt's edition (6 vols. 1935–9). The one serious fault I have to find with this superb piece of editing is that de Selincourt neglected the numerous letters by Wordsworth that are only extant in print—in Victorian biographies, *Notes and Queries*, etc. It is true that most of the printed letters belong to the second and non-creative half of Wordsworth's life and have little biographical value.

had become one of the children's two legal guardians on their father's death (the other was Uncle Richard Wordsworth, a customs official at Whitehaven). The mark left on his proud and sensitive nature was profound and indelible.

The 'early miseries' are a psychological fact of the first importance to an understanding of Wordsworth's character. Positively, they help to explain the passionate attachment that he felt not only for Dorothy but also for his brother John. John's loss in the *Abergavenny*, an East-Indiaman that went down in the Channel in 1805, was the one real tragedy of Wordsworth's adult life. There is a special pathos in a phrase that he used in a letter to Richard at the time: 'God keep the rest of us together! the set is now broken.'[1] Their common misfortunes had been a bond that tied the young Wordsworths much more closely together than most brothers and sisters.

But the negative importance of the 'early miseries' was perhaps even greater. They help as much as anything to explain why Wordsworth, for good and for bad, was not as other men are. One direct consequence of the denial of an outlet to the boy's affections and energies in the draper's shop was the intense *Wanderlust* from which he was never free. Wandering, he once said, was his *passion*, and this rapturous pedestrianism is the subject of an eloquent paragraph in Book XII of *The Prelude*:

> Oh! next to one dear state of bliss, vouchsafed
> Alas! to few in this untoward world,
> The bliss of walking daily in Life's prime
> Through field or forest with the Maid we love, . . .
> Oh! next to such enjoyment of our youth,
> In my esteem, next to such dear delight
> Was that of wandering on from day to day . . .[2]

Even falling in love, it will be seen, was conceived by Wordsworth in terms of country walks. It is significant that his poetry too was almost all of it composed on his feet. 'Nine-tenths of my verses', he calculated towards the end of his life, 'have been

---

[1] The letter is dated 11 Feb. 1805.
[2] *Prelude*, XII, ll. 127–37.

murmured out in the open air.'[1] And the quasi-mystical experiences described in *The Prelude*—the climb to the raven's nest, the crossing of the Alps, losing his way as a child where the murderer had been hanged, the ascent of Snowdon, for example—all occurred to him when walking, running or climbing. His comment on the character of the 'Wanderer' in *The Excursion* was that, if he had himself been born in a class which would have deprived him of a liberal education, being strong bodily he would almost certainly have taken to the 'way of life . . . in which my Pedlar passed the greater part of his days'.[2] His lifelong interest in books of travel was perhaps another aspect of the same obsession.

The open road provided Wordsworth with an escape-route from Penrith. That is, I suppose, the psychological explanation of his *Wanderlust*. The escape was from human authority—in the embodiment of a bad-tempered draper in a drab little provincial town—to whatever was non-authoritarian, non-urban, non-human. Penrith is just outside the Lake District proper, and its physical and spiritual opposite was mountains and lakes. Their consolatory function derived from their difference from Penrith. In its origins, at any rate, Wordsworth's religion of nature was just as negative as his *Wanderlust*. There is a revealing phrase in "Lines written a Few Miles above Tintern Abbey" which suggests that the mature Wordsworth was at least partly aware of the negative character of his early attitude to natural beauty. When describing his adolescent feeling for nature he says that he was

> more like a man
> Flying from something that he dreads, than one
> Who sought the thing he loved.

This can only mean that the nature-worship of the first visit to Tintern, which had been only a repetition of what he had felt as a youth in the Lake District, was based on and secondary to the

---

[1] I.F. note on the second "Ode to Lycoris". (The I.F. notes are those dictated to Isabella Fenwick, at her request, in 1843. Primarily a record of the occasions on which the various poems were written, they are also a repository of much important biographical information.)

[2] See the beginning of the I.F. note on *The Excursion*.

fear of man. The mysterious 'something' that he dreaded was perhaps a quasi-personification of the social order represented for him by Uncle Kit and the grandparents, though it may well have been accompanied and reinforced by supernatural sanctions.

A particularly illuminating example of this emotional attitude is the episode of the stolen boat in Book I of *The Prelude*. The huge cliff that seemed to stride after the skiff is clearly a reflection of the boy's guilty conscience. 'It was an act', he says of the taking of the boat, 'of stealth And troubled pleasure.' But it is difficult to believe that the temporary unauthorised loan of a boat can have induced so profound and memorable a sense of guilt. Something more was obviously involved. The fact that the lake where the episode took place was Ullswater seems to provide the clue: Wordsworth was spending the night at Patterdale *on his way back to Penrith.* It was apparently the first day of the summer holidays and no doubt he was proceeding by easy stages from Hawkshead School, where he was thoroughly happy, to the prison-house of the draper's shop. Is it not possible that, without fully realising what he was doing, the boy had been trying to escape into the silence and solitude of the night from the gaol he was due to enter the next day? In that case the menacing cliff must be seen as a subconscious symbol of adult authority. Here in fact in alarming physical form was that 'something' which he dreaded and from which his instinct was to fly.

In his self-analysis in *The Prelude* Wordsworth lays particular stress on the contribution of fear to his natural piety. In an interesting passage in Book I, for example, a distinction is drawn between the 'gentlest visitations' with which Nature may educate a specially 'favor'd Being' (he seems to have had Dorothy in mind here) and the 'Severer interventions' employed in his own case. He was disciplined, he says, by 'pain and fear'. Nature's instructions were sometimes milder, but that was 'rarely in my boyish boys'. Generally speaking his initiation into the religion of nature was painful and alarming.

There was certainly a neurotic element in Wordsworth's attitude to nature. His ecstatic, terrified absorption in natural scenery is worlds away from the healthy delight of Chaucer and

Shakespeare in the processes of vegetable and animal growth. Wordsworth's nature—'rocks and stones and trees', rivers and mists, winds, stars and rainbows—is curiously uncreative and dead. Was it perhaps primarily a mirror in which his subconscious mind could reflect itself? Things can often be said in terms of 'nature', through the intervention of a symbol, that cannot be said, or even thought, directly and objectively.

II

Wordsworth's response to natural scenery did not remain merely neurotic. In time the subjective identification with nature was counter-balanced by an objective, almost connoisseur's interest in nature as the Picturesque. The Two Voices begin to make themselves heard. That they do is attributable as much as anything to his eight years at Hawkshead Free School. The lessons at the Penrith Dame's School had been followed by a period at Cockermouth Grammar School, where Wordsworth learnt little or nothing. In 1779, however, Richard and William were sent as boarders to the distant village of Hawkshead, where a sixteenth-century Archbishop of York had founded a small school. (In its palmiest days there were never more than a hundred pupils.) Thenceforth it was only during the summer and Easter holidays that the Wordsworth boys had to endure the purgatory of Penrith. The month at Christmas, a lesser evil, was generally spent with Uncle Richard at Whitehaven.

Luckily for the Wordsworths Hawkshead was all that Penrith was not. The teaching was good, if the range of subjects was limited (English, Latin, Greek, Writing and Arithmetic) and before and after school hours there were practically no restrictions on the boys' activities. Wordsworth's account of their excursions by foot, on horseback and by water in Books I and II of *The Prelude* is confirmed in almost every detail by a poem written by a school friend of his, one Charles Farish, whose *The Minstrels of Winandermere* describes a summer expedition of a party of Hawkshead schoolboys to Bowness. Farish's narrative is interspersed with lyrical pieces, supposed to be sung by the different boys, one of which seems to have been written as early as 1783,

that is, in the middle of Wordsworth's school career. This poem
is called "The Vacation", and a few verses from it will be worth
quoting:

> 'Go'! is the word, when each enraptur'd boy
> Rushes impetuous from the rattling seats:
> Hark to the shouts that speak the general joy:
> See with what transport every bosom beats.
>
> Not with more joy the weary Trojans spied,
> The shore deserted and disburthen'd main:
> Not with more joy their gates they open'd wide
> And pour'd impatient myriads on the plain . . .
>
> So here in knots by Esthwaite's pleasing lake,
> The playful youths their different sports pursue;
> Some rouse the trembling hare, some beat the brake,
> And force the unwilling lapwing into view.
>
> With oary arms some press the wrinkling deep,
> While each young breast with emulation burns;
> Some teach the flatted pebble how to sweep
> Above the waves, and sink and rise by turns.
>
> Others their brows with flowery wreaths entwine,
> And bid the rocks re-echo to their cry,
> Or throw with nicer art the waving line,
> And slowly trail the imitated fly.[1]

'Esthwaite's pleasing lake' is the small lake now known as
Esthwaite Water, which lies between Hawkshead and Lake
Windermere. For Wordsworth, as for Farish's schoolboys, it was
the scene or the occasion of most of his boyish sports. With the
possible exception of the 'ducks and drakes' (Wordsworth was

---

[1] *The Minstrels of Winandermere* was published in 1811 and, to judge by the
poems' style, most of its contents cannot have been written much earlier. "The
Vacation" is the one exception. As the lines quoted demonstrate the poetic
manner here is that of Goldsmith or Gray rather than Southey or Scott. The
poem describes the emotions of a boy who is leaving Hawkshead (it is the end
of his last term) and for whom the beginning of the holidays is the end of his
happy schooldays. Farish left Hawkshead in 1783 when he went up to Cambridge,
and it is a reasonable guess that he wrote "The Vacation" in the interval between
school and university.

always clumsy with his hands),[1] his amusements out of school hours seem to have been identical with those catalogued by Farish. There was, however, one important difference. It was that Wordsworth generally amused himself, if we can trust the evidence of *The Prelude*, by himself. When he went bird's-nesting it was on his own. During the skating season, he would break away from the others. And he was certainly unaccompanied when in the autumn evenings he went the guilty round of his woodcock snares:

> On the heights
> Scudding away from snare to snare, I plied
> My anxious visitation, hurrying on,
> Still hurrying, hurrying onward; moon and stars
> Were shining o'er my head; I was alone,
> And seem'd to be a trouble to the peace
> That was among them.[2]

Presumably this was the phase of 'coarser pleasures' and 'glad animal movements' that is referred to in "Tintern Abbey" as preceding the 'dizzy raptures' of his 'thoughtless youth'. The intercourse that he held with the eternal Beauty was still, at ten years old, an unconscious one. Even at this time, however, the face of Nature occasionally spoke rememberable things to the young boy. Indeed, his education in Natural Piety, if we may trust the description of the process in *The Prelude*, seems to have been essentially towards an ever greater consciousness of the feelings the natural scene aroused in him, and a more and more

---

[1] 'I doubt whether he was ever on a horse in his life. For I recollect that Hartley Coleridge, in criticising one of his poems—"Lucy" I think—said that a certain verse, in which the poet described himself as riding, was spoiled for him (H. C.), because the idea of Mr. Wordsworth on horseback was utterly incongruous. The only feat I remember his performing in the way of sport, was endeavouring to catch what he thought to be a trout, by tickling it, but which when he hauled it on shore, to his horror proved to be a toad!' (Edward Whately, "Personal Recollections of the Lake Poets", *The Leisure Hour*, 1 Oct. 1870, p. 653). Whately was quite wrong, of course, in thinking Wordsworth never rode a horse. As a boy and a young man he was often on horseback, but it seems to be true that he was a very indifferent rider (see H. D. Rawnsley, *Lake Country Sketches*, 1903, p. 135).

[2] *Prelude*, I, ll. 318–24.

sophisticated appreciation of the causes of those feelings. The protective armour with which it endowed him proved its strength, according to his own account, in the difficult period of puberty, which coincided with his father's death:

> For now a trouble came into my mind
> From unknown causes. I was left alone,
> Seeking the visible world, nor knowing why.
> The props of my affections were remov'd,
> And yet the building stood, as if sustain'd
> By its own spirit! All that I beheld
> Was dear to me, and from this cause it came,
> That now to Nature's finer influxes
> My mind lay open, to that more exact
> And intimate communion which our hearts
> Maintain with the minuter properties
> Of objects which already are belov'd. . . .[1]

The morbidity of the state of mind described in these lines is mitigated by the movement towards objectivity implied in the new interest in the minuter properties of the visible world. This new addiction to detail and

> manifold distinctions, difference
> Perceived in things, where to the common eye,
> No difference is . . .[2]

would seem to have been altogether healthy. It can no doubt be connected with Wordsworth's sudden discovery of poetry a short time before his father died. A more immediate cause, however, was a discovery of another kind that he made at the age of fourteen on the road between Hawkshead and Ambleside. The sun was setting at the time and its effect, he noticed, was to make the boughs of an oak that happened to be between him and the sun stand out much more distinctly than they did by day. 'The moment', he said later, 'was important in my poetical history; for I date from it my consciousness of the infinite variety of natural appearances which had been unnoticed by the poets of any

---

[1] *Prelude*, II, ll. 291–302.   [2] *Ibid.*, II, ll. 318–20.

age or country, so far as I was acquainted with them; and I made a resolution to supply, in some degree, the deficiency.'[1] The moment was not less important, I suspect, in Wordsworth's psychological history. It marked the end, for the time being at any rate, of the extreme subjectivism of his earlier relationship to the physical world. How extreme that subjectivism had been can be seen from a passage in Wordsworth's note on "Intimations of Immortality". 'I was often unable', he says, 'to think of external things as having external existence, and I communed with all that I saw as something not apart from, but inherent in, my own immaterial nature. Many times while going to school have I grasped at a wall or tree to recall myself from this abyss of idealism to the reality.'

The cottage where he lodged when at school was at Colthouse,[2] a little hamlet half a mile from the school buildings, and only a very dreamy boy could have achieved these abysses of idealism in the ten minutes' walk. But Wordsworth was a very dreamy boy indeed. Towards the end of his life, he told Bonamy Price, the Oxford economist, that there had been a time when he had to push against something that resisted to be sure there was anything outside himself. When making these avowals to Price, he suited the action to the word by clenching the top of a five-barred gate that they happened to be passing, and pushing against it with all his strength. 'Such natural spontaneous idealism', Price commented, when describing the incident later, 'has probably never been felt by any other man.'[3]

The link with the external world was re-established, or at least strengthened, as a result of the excited interest Wordsworth now began to take in poetry:

---

[1] I.F. note on *An Evening Walk*. Helen Darbishire has seen a notebook in which Wordsworth and his school friends recorded similar picturesque 'moments' (*Wordsworth*, 1953, p. 12).

[2] The Tysons, with whom Wordsworth lodged, were certainly living in Colthouse in 1784, when Hugh Tyson died. Ann Tyson also died there. The probability is that Wordsworth lived with them at Colthouse throughout his schooldays. See Oliver de Selincourt, *Review of English Studies*, Oct. 1945, pp. 329–30.

[3] See Price's letter to William Knight, 21 Apr. 1881. The letter is printed in Knight's edition of *The Poetical Works* (1883), IV, 58.

> Thirteen years
> Or haply less, I might have seen, when first
> My ears began to open to the charm
> Of words in tuneful order, found them sweet
> For *their own sakes*, a passion and a power;
> And phrases pleas'd me, chosen for delight,
> For pomp, or love.[1]

By some odd accident the first poem to arouse his youthful enthusiasm was the "Ode to Wisdom" of Dr. Johnson's blue-stocking friend Elizabeth Carter. This was a favourite anthology piece in the later eighteenth century, and its character can be gauged from its first verse:

> The solitary bird of night
> Thro' the pale shades now wings his flight
> And quits the time-shook tow'r,
> Where, sheltered from the blaze of day,
> In philosophic gloom he lay,
> Beneath his ivy bow'r.

Miss Carter's metre, which is that of his own "Ruth", must have remained tucked away at the back of Wordsworth's memory, but for her matter the adult Wordsworth can have had little sympathy or respect. Miss Carter was soon supplanted, however, by Gray and Goldsmith, who provided the models for the poems that he began to write when he was fourteen and fifteen. Unlike the better-known English schools, Hawkshead School did not go in for verse-composition in Latin and Greek, and exercises in English verse took their place. Wordsworth's earliest original compositions, "The Pleasures of Change" and "The Summer Vacation", were both 'a task imposed by my master'. These exercises have not survived. They were succeeded by the lines on the bicentenary of the School, 'written as a school exercise at Hawkshead anno ætatis 14', which was published by Wordsworth's nephew after his death. 'The verses were much admired', Wordsworth says, and their success, which incidentally was thoroughly deserved (the rhetoric is very spirited), 'put it into my head to compose verses from the impulse of my own mind'.[2]

---

[1] *Prelude*, V, ll. 575–81.   [2] *Memoirs of William Wordsworth*, I, 10.

The man who commissioned these early poems of Wordsworth's was the Rev. William Taylor, who was the headmaster of Hawkshead School from 1782 to 1786, when he died at the early age of 32. Taylor can be compared with Beaupuy and Coleridge as one of the decisive influences in Wordsworth's intellectual life. It was almost certainly Taylor's kindly interest that reconciled Wordsworth to the claims of human authority, and Taylor's death, in Wordsworth's penultimate year at Hawkshead, made a great impression on the sixteen-year-old boy. There is a well-known passage in Book X of *The Prelude*, in which Wordsworth has described how eight years later, in August 1794, he came across Taylor's grave in the churchyard at Cartmel. The boys had been called into his bedroom, one by one, to say goodbye to the dying man. 'My head will soon lie low', he said to Wordsworth. The passage ends:

> He loved the Poets, and if now alive,
> Would have loved me, as one not destitute
> Of promise, nor belying the kind hope
> That he had form'd, when I at his command,
> Began to spin, at first, my toilsome Songs.[1]

Taylor was the original of Wordsworth's Matthew, the loveable old schoolmaster in the poem of that name and its two sequels ("The Two April Mornings" and "The Fountain"). An element of fantasy has entered into these poems, but the relationship that they depict between Matthew and his young friend undoubtedly reflects the terms Wordsworth had finally been on with Taylor. Whether Taylor did or did not really write

> those witty rhymes
> About the crazy old church-clock,
> And the bewildered chimes.[2]

it is clear that he must have been a most original and attractive man. Politically, to judge by the progressive opinions expressed by Wordsworth in the bicentenary lines, Taylor was certainly a Whig, perhaps even a potential Radical.

It would be to claim too much for Taylor to say that he made

---

[1] *Prelude*, X, ll. 511–15.   [2] "The Fountain", ll. 70–2.

Wordsworth into a poet. What he did was to introduce the boy to poetry and to teach him an abhorrence of poetic slovenliness. The scrupulous, not to say fussy, attention to the details of poetic craftsmanship that kept the mature Wordsworth revising and re-writing his poems was, I suspect, a habit of mind derived from Taylor. Taylor's own literary predilections can be guessed from his dying instruction that the last verse of Gray's "Elegy" was to be inscribed on his tombstone. Gray had been in residence at Pembroke College only a year or two before Taylor came up to Emmanuel, and he clearly represented a *ne plus ultra* of poetry for Taylor as for so many of his contemporaries. Wordsworth was later to revolt against Gray, but for what may be called the School of Gray—poets like Collins, Dyer, Akenside, Beattie, Langhorne and Mickle—he retained to the end an uncritical affection which may be attributed to Taylor's influence. The album of "Poems and Extracts" that he presented to Lady Mary Lowther, a daughter of the 'good' Lord Lonsdale, in 1819 is almost entirely made up, except for thirty pages devoted to Lady Winchilsea (an early 'discovery' of Wordsworth's own), of this so-called pre-romantic poetry.

Beattie's *Minstrel* was, it seems, the poem that exerted the greatest influence on the young Wordsworth. It took the place in his poetical education that Bowles's *Sonnets* occupied in Coleridge's. Here was a *contemporary*, 'perhaps not many years older than himself, surrounded by the same circumstances, and disciplined by the same manners', as Coleridge put it,[1] who must often have seemed to Wordsworth to be giving poetical utterance to his own unspoken thoughts. Beattie's 'Edwin' was the son of a Scotch shepherd, a nature-lover from childhood, who on every possible occasion

> to the forest sped;
> Or roam'd at large the lonely mountain's head;
> Or, where the maze of some bewilder'd stream
> To deep untrodden groves his footsteps led,
> There would he wander wild, till Phoebus' beam,
> Shot from the western cliff, released the weary team.[2]

---

[1] *Biographia Literaria*, ch. i.   [2] *The Minstrel*, Bk. I, stanza xvii.

In its own heavy-handed way, *The Minstrel* is a sort of *Prelude*,
in Spenserian stanzas instead of blank verse but also dealing with
the 'Growth of a Poet's Mind'. And Edwin's poetry was also
nature-poetry:

> From Nature's beauties variously compar'd
> And variously combin'd, he learns to frame
> Those forms of bright perfection, which the bard,
> While boundless hopes and boundless views inflame,
> Enamour'd consecrates to never-dying fame.[1]

Dorothy wrote to a friend a little later that 'the whole character
of Edwin resembles much what William was when I first knew
him—after my leaving Halifax'.[2] It is not impossible that William
at this time was to some extent consciously modelling himself on
Beattie's hero.

The reconciliation with the human world that Taylor, and the
English poets to whom Taylor had introduced him, had begun,
was carried one step further by John Fleming, a fellow schoolboy,
'then passionately loved', according to *The Prelude*, with whom
Wordsworth used to circumambulate the little lake of Esthwaite
Water before school started,

> Repeating favourite verses with one voice,
> Or conning more . . .[3]

Fleming's father was a Mr. Raincock who had been a customs
official in London, and no doubt an aroma of London culture
hung about the Raincock home at Rayrigg Hall, near Windermere. Altogether four of the boys were at Hawkshead with
Wordsworth, one of them being that William Raincock who was
so good at imitating owls. John, however, had changed his name
from Raincock on becoming the heir of a member of the ancient
local family of Fleming, and a certain social superiority to the rest
of his schoolfellows, including Wordsworth, is indicated by the
'Esq.' added to his name in the leaving volume he presented to

---

[1] *The Minstrel*, Bk. II, stanza lviii.
[2] Dorothy Wordsworth to Jane Pollard, 10 July 1793.
[3] *Prelude*, V, ll. 588–9.

the school library. Wordsworth's own leaving volume, which was shared with three other boys who were going on to Cambridge with him, is simply inscribed 'William Wordsworth of Cockermouth'.[1] De Quincey got the impression that as a boy Wordsworth had been 'austere and unsocial . . . in his habits; not generous; and not self-denying'.[2]

Only one anecdote, however, survives of his schooldays (apart from those recorded by Wordsworth himself in *The Prelude* and elsewhere):

> When he was a boy at school at Hawkshead, he was even then distinguished above his fellows in verse writing. One day a boy, much older than himself, asked him to take a walk with him, which seemed an act of great condescension, but it soon appeared that the boy had an object in view, for he presently addressed to him, in his north country dialect, the following question: 'How is it, Bill, thee doest write with such good verses? Doest thee invoke Muses?'[3]

Fleming, who was older than Wordsworth, left Hawkshead in June 1785. By that time Wordsworth's inner wounds had begun to heal, and some sort of a balance had been achieved between the subjective and the objective worlds. It is to the years 1785 and 1786 that he seems to look back in *The Prelude* as the period when his love of nature was deepest and purest. But the balance was a precarious one and it was soon upset. Into the vacuum created by Fleming's departure to St. John's College, Cambridge, and by Taylor's death in June 1786, a new and disturbing influence entered in the form of the beautiful Mary of Esthwaite Water.

All that is known about Mary is what can be read between the lines of some of Wordsworth's earliest poems. Professor de Selincourt, who was the first to print these poems, was under the impression that the Mary they concern was Mary Hutchinson, Wordsworth's future wife. Mary Hutchinson was living at Penrith at this time, and an earlier minor flirtation with her in the

---

[1] After his father's death Wordsworth had no real right to describe himself as 'of Cockermouth'. Was it perhaps a gesture of defiance directed against Penrith?

[2] *Recollections of the Lake Poets*, p. 142.

[3] Edward Whately, "Personal Recollections of the Lake Poets", *The Leisure Hour*, 1 Oct. 1870, p. 653. One of Southey's nephews was told the same story by Wordsworth himself (see Knight's *Life of Wordsworth*, I, 38).

holidays need not be ruled out. (There is a reference to her in an early text of *The Prelude* as 'the maid To whom were breathed my first fond vows'.[1]) But Mary Hutchinson cannot be the Mary of "Reynolds, come, thy pencil prove", "Beauty and Moonlight" and "A Ballad" (de Selincourt's title for a poem in ballad form that has no title in the MS.), if the incidental information provided by these poems is to be given any weight. Mary of Esthwaite Water had jet-black hair and an ivory-white complexion (whereas Mary Hutchinson's complexion, according to De Quincey, was fair and her hair dark-brown)[2]; she lived in 'Esthwaite's Vale', *i.e.* at Hawkshead or in its neighbourhood (whereas the Hutchinsons were at Penrith all the time until 1789); and she had a father who was still alive (whereas Hutchinson *père* had died in 1785). Accordingly to "A Ballad" the Mary of these poems lived in a house near a bridge, and her bedroom window overlooked Esthwaite Water. She was, no doubt, the daughter of one of Wordsworth's humble neighbours at Colthouse.

Of the three 'Mary' poems, the two written first do not call for special comment. "Beauty and Moonlight" is a poem of considerable promise. Years later Wordsworth gave a copy of it to Coleridge, who then worked it up into the familiar "Lewti", the scene being changed from 'Winander's stream' to Circassia. This poem and "Reynolds, come, thy pencil prove" (an accomplished adaptation from Anacreon) suggest nothing more serious than the healthy calf-love of adolescence. It is different with "A Ballad", a curious poem which was perhaps intended as an elaborate private joke. If so, it is a joke that leaves a decidedly nasty taste in the mouth. Mary, it seems, is dying from a broken heart. Her lover William has broken his promise to her, and Mary sees him laughing gaily with other girls. As she lies dying, she reflects upon the situation:

> Heaven told me once—but I was blind—
> My head would soon lie low;
> A Rose within our Garden blew
> Amid December's snow.

---

[1] See de Selincourt's edition of *The Prelude* (1926), p. 440.
[2] *Recollections of the Lake Poets*, p. 114.

> That Rose my William saw—and pluck'd,
>   He pluck'd and gave it me;
> Heaven warn'd me then—ah blind was I—
>   That he my death would be.

A glove that William had given her is then brought to her bedside. She sees it, sighs and expires:

> The next day to the grave they went,
>   All flocked around her bier;
> Nor hand without a flower was there
>   Nor eye without a tear.

There is not a hint of irony or the mock-heroic in the whole poem, though it is impossible to believe that Mary has really died. What purpose the fiction was supposed to serve is not clear. Was William hoping to minimise his own defection by a sentimental exaggeration of Mary's distress? Some such an interpretation is suggested by the Chattertonian "Dirge sung by a Minstrel" which accompanies "A Ballad" in the small quarto notebook bound in brown calf into which Wordsworth copied his schoolboy poems. In its first form, this poem commemorated the death of a boy, but the final version substitutes a girl, the poet's love, who is presumably Mary, though the actual name is not given. There is the same uncomfortable mixture of reality and literary fantasy as in "A Ballad":

> List! the bell-Sprite stuns my ears
> Slowly calling for a maid;
> List! each worm with trembling hears
> And stops for joy his dreadful trade.

It would be uncritical to make too much of the Mary affair. I cannot believe, for instance, that Mary of Esthwaite Water was the prototype of Wordsworth's Lucy. In so far as Lucy had any human original she was, almost certainly, Dorothy Wordsworth. But there is at any rate a significant parallel between the fiction of Mary's and Lucy's early deaths. Sooner or later apparently Wordsworth *had* to kill the thing he loved, even though it was only in poetry.

What went wrong in this early love-affair it is impossible even
to guess. If "A Ballad" is to be trusted, the fault was on Wordsworth's side and not on Mary's. Some time between August 1786,
when Wordsworth wrote "Reynolds, come, thy pencil prove",
and March 1787, the date of "A Ballad", something occurred to
make Mary less desirable in his eyes. But what it was we shall
probably never know. The immediate effect of the Mary affair,
however, is not in doubt. Its psychological repercussions can be
seen without the possibility of mistake in *The Vale of Esthwaite*,
a long poem in octosyllabics that was written, according to the
leather-bound notebook, 'at Hawkshead in the Spring and
Summer of 1787', that is, in the months immediately following
the composition of "A Ballad".

In some respects *The Vale of Esthwaite* is an eminently Wordsworthian poem. A passage headed "Evening Sounds" in the
selections from the poem transcribed into the leather-bound notebook reveals a precocious precision in the use of language:

> The ploughboy by his gingling wain
> Whistles along the ringing lane,
> And, as he strikes with sportive lash
> The leaves of thick o'erhanging ash,
> Wavering they fall; while at the sound
> The blinking bats flit round and round.

There is an admirable objectivity in these lines, which show the
young poet conscientiously carrying out his programme of
recording 'the infinite variety of natural appearances'. The
parallel passage in *The Minstrel*, a catalogue of morning sounds,
is certainly no better than Wordsworth's vignette. The wavering
descent of the leaves of the ash is, indeed, an observation of a
more delicate order altogether than anything in Beattie's poem.
The special interest of the passage in Wordsworth's poetic evolution is that this cool and detached notation, which represents an
enormous advance on the accomplished rhetoric of the earlier
poems, is accompanied by whole paragraphs that are almost
hysterical. The advance in objectivity here seems to have been
made possible only by an almost simultaneous regression into

extreme subjectivity elsewhere in the poem. For side by side with such eye-on-the-object writing as the "Evening Sounds" are pages and pages of flesh-creeping supernatural 'horrors'. The poet is apparently making a tour of the country round Esthwaite Water, and after noting realistically a young shepherd and his dog, he suddenly finds himself, though it is only noon, in 'Superstition's glades':

> And hark! the ringing harp I hear
> And lo! her druid sons appear.
> Why roll on me your glaring eyes?
> Why fix on me for sacrifice?

And this sort of thing keeps on recurring. Although there was literary precedent enough for such Gothic terrors, Wordsworth's supernatural seems to me to have a nightmare quality that is not literary at all. Obviously, I should say, he was really frightened. The old subjectivism had apparently returned, if in a new form. It was supernatural fears very like these that he had felt when he stole the boat at Patterdale or took the woodcocks out of other people's snares. There can be little doubt that a guilty conscience played a part in those childish terrors, and his betrayal of Mary— if he did betray Mary—may have had similar psychological consequences.

Taylor was dead by the time the Mary affair got under way and for the months of March, April and May 1787, Wordsworth had no one to turn to for advice or consolation. But in June Fleming returned from Cambridge for the Long Vacation, and in July the Wordsworth boys were reunited with Dorothy in the Penrith shop. Towards the end of *The Vale of Esthwaite* there are, as it happens, sentimental tributes to both Fleming and Dorothy. The lines to Dorothy seem to suggest—a point of great psychological interest—that she now resembled his boyish memory of his mother:

> Sister, for whom I feel a love
> Which warms a Brother far above,
> On you, as sad she marks the scene,
> Why does my heart so fondly lean?

> Why but because in you is given
> All, all, my soul would wish from Heaven?
> Why but because I fondly view
> All, all that Heav'n has claimed, in you.

Fleming is complimented in more rhetorical terms:

> While bounteous heaven shall Fleming leave
> Of Friendship what can me bereave?
> Till then shall live the holy flame,
> Friendship and Fleming are the same.

Curiously enough, though Wordsworth went to the same college at Cambridge as his friend, Fleming seems, at this point, to pass out of his life. There is not one reference to him in either Wordsworth's letters or poems until *The Prelude*, when:

> our minds,
> Both silent to each other, at this time
> We live as if those hours had never been.[1]

Perhaps Fleming had been associated in some way with Mary and was made to share her exclusion? Whatever the reason Dorothy's lively interest in her brother and the excitements of Cambridge soon drove both Mary's lovely face and Mary's shortcomings, whatever they were, out of Wordsworth's head. The poetry that he was to write in 1788 proves this. And there was to be only an occasional return to the nightmare horrors of *The Vale of Esthwaite* until another love-affair went wrong, again somewhat mysteriously, six years later.

III

Wordsworth became a member of St. John's College, Cambridge, in October 1787, and took his B.A. in January 1791. Although his correspondence makes it clear that he made many firm friends at Cambridge, none of them has recorded the impression that he made upon his contemporaries there. The one surviving item of evidence, apart from the extremely subjective

---

[1] *Prelude*, II, ll. 356–8. Fleming went into the Church and became the Vicar of Rayrigg. He died, 'not in good circumstances' (see Wordsworth's letter to Robert Jones, 30 Mar. 1835), in 1835.

portrait that he drew of his first year in Book III of *The Prelude*, is a passage in the review of *An Evening Walk* that appeared in the *Gentleman's Magazine* for March 1794. The anonymous reviewer, who has not been identified, writes that he saw Wordsworth once or twice, 'while I was his contemporary at Cambridge':

> The only time, indeed, that I have a clear recollection of having met him, I remember his speaking very highly in praise of the beauties of the North; with a warmth indeed which, at that time, appeared to me hardly short of enthusiasm. He mentioned too, which appears also from the present poem, that he had received the whole of his education in the very bosom of the Lakes, at a small seminary, which has produced of late years in our University several names which have done it very considerable credit.

It is interesting to learn that Wordsworth was already, at Cambridge, a propagandist for the Lake District—so much so, indeed, as to seem to this casual acquaintance to have been guilty of that 'enthusiasm' which to the eighteenth century, with its philosophy of *nil admirari*, was almost the sin of sins. A less polite word for 'enthusiasm' was madness. And, as it happens, this was the precise term, Wordsworth tells us, that some of the undergraduates applied to his habit of conducting private conversations with himself:

> Such sympathies would sometimes shew themselves
> By outward gestures and by visible looks.
> Some call'd it madness. . . .[1]

He had already formed those habits of ambulatory composition aloud which were later to fascinate and alarm his Grasmere neighbours. Apparently he wrote next to no verse his first year, but during his second and third winters at Cambridge it was his practice, he says, to retire after dark into the College gardens, where he continued to pace up and down its 'Groves And Tributary walks' in the throes of poetic composition, until the Porter's bell called him in at nine o'clock.[2] An odd way this of spending the winter evenings! It is not surprising that his second

---

[1] *Prelude*, III, ll. 145-7.   [2] *Ibid.*, VI, ll. 81-2.

cousins at Halifax were beginning to call him that 'eccentric young man'.[1]

The principal poetical product of the Cambridge years was *An Evening Walk*, a poem of 446 lines in heroic couplets, which, though not published until 1793, was most of it written, according to Wordsworth's own account, in 1788 and 1789. At least two stages can be distinguished in the process of the poem's composition. About half of it appears to have been written in the period July 1788–June 1789. At this stage the poem consisted of a series of descriptions of Esthwaite Water and the immediate surroundings of Hawkshead, which may be regarded as a continuation, and in part perhaps a re-writing, of the more objective passages in *The Vale of Esthwaite*.[2] The principal technical difference is that the latter was in octosyllabic couplets, a distant descendant of Dyer's *Grongar Hill*, whereas *An Evening Walk* was in decasyllabic couplets reminiscent of Goldsmith. Almost everything that is good in the poem is to be found in this first draft. It includes the moving account of the beggarwoman and her two children (based on, but much better than, the description of the soldier's widow in Langhorne's *Country Justice*) and the two really brilliant catalogues of the sounds heard respectively before and after sunset. These passages should no doubt be connected with the self-dedication to poetry that Wordsworth records in Book IV of *The Prelude*, which deals with his first "Summer Vacation" (nine weeks of it spent at Hawkshead, though for part of the time he was at Penrith with Dorothy or staying with his Wordsworth relations):

---

[1] See de Selincourt's *Dorothy Wordsworth* (1933), p. 50.

[2] An unbound quarto notebook in the Wordsworth Museum (MS. D.C., I, 7) contains early drafts of several passages of *An Evening Walk*. The longest of these passages, the basis of ll. 255–326 in the first edition, has the figure 106 entered against its last line. This suggests that there may have originally been 60 lines that are now lost preceding l. 255. The passage describes the misfortunes of a soldier's widow and may have been intended at this stage as a separate poem. The other passages are descriptive fragments, some of them partly based on *The Vale of Esthwaite*. The real trouble with *An Evening Walk* in its final form is that the framework into which the earlier fragments have been fitted is a mere piece of machinery and the fragments, where the poetry is to be found, have no essential connection with each other.

> I made no vows, but vows
> Were then made for me; bond unknown to me
> Was given, that I should be, else sinning greatly,
> A dedicated Spirit.[1]

The modern reader may find it difficult at first to adjust himself to *An Evening Walk*. His first impression is likely to be how 'literary' it all is. The poem's second paragraph, for example, begins as follows:

> Fair scenes! with other eyes, than once, I gaze,
> The ever-varying charm your round displays,
> Than when, erewhile, I taught, 'a happy child',
> The echoes of your rocks my carols wild.

Why, the reader will wonder, is 'a happy child' in inverted commas? The phrase is sufficiently commonplace, and, if it has been borrowed, it would seem unnecessarily scrupulous to feel it incumbent to acknowledge the loan in this way. And as a matter of fact, when Wordsworth reprinted the poem in 1820, he did leave the inverted commas out. But the Wordsworth of 1820 was a very different person, with a very different poetic theory, from the undergraduate who wrote the poem. In the original text the inverted commas were a tribute to a contemporary poet whom Wordsworth admired and with whose works he took it for granted his readers would also be familiar. Although none of Wordsworth's editors seems to have identified it, there can be no doubt, I think, that an allusion is intended here to Charlotte Smith's Sonnet V "To the South Downs":

> Ah! hills belov'd!—where once, an happy child,
>   Your beechen shades, 'your turf, your flowers among',
>   I wove your blue-bells into garlands wild,
>   And woke your echoes with my artless song.

It will be noticed that Mrs. Smith had the same addiction to inverted commas. In her case the quotation—this time from Gray —is acknowledged in the elaborate notes at the end of her volume. Notes and inverted commas were a necessary part of the apparatus

---

[1] *Prelude*, IV, ll. 341–4.

of poetry in the 1780's. It was a particularly 'literary' moment in the history of English poetry, the decadent twilight of the Augustan tradition, and by the time he had completed the second draft of *An Evening Walk*, Wordsworth was as 'literary' as any of them. But the notes and quotations were all added *after* the poem proper had been completed, and they do not affect its essential value.

Wordsworth is unlikely to have acquired his intimate knowledge of Charlotte Smith's *Elegiac Sonnets* before 1789, since his copy (now in the Wordsworth Museum, Grasmere) is the fifth edition, which was only published in that year. For his topographical notes he depended on James Clarke's *A Survey of the Lakes*, of which the edition he used, the second, also appeared in 1789. Another book he cites in a note is William Gilpin's *Observations relative chiefly to Picturesque Beauty made . . . in Several Parts of Great Britain, particularly the Highlands of Scotland*, which was published in the same year. (Gilpin was a relative of his Hawkshead and Cambridge friend, Charles Farish, and for some years Wordsworth took his views on the Picturesque with great seriousness.) In view of all this, and the fact that no book published after 1789 is used or referred to, it seems probable that the poem assumed its existing form in 1789–90. The device of the letter—it is nominally *An Epistle; in Verse, Addressed to a Young Lady, from the Lakes of the North of England*—can only have begun to have any reality in the Long Vacation of 1789, when Dorothy, the 'Young Lady' of Wordsworth's title, had left the Lake District for Lincolnshire and Wordsworth was back at Hawkshead or staying with his various relations. It was presumably in the course of its transformation into a poetic epistle that the poem's range was extended to include Windermere, Grasmere, Rydal, and other places even further afield. Unfortunately, whenever Wordsworth deserts Esthwaite Water, the writing loses most of its precision and brilliance. This difference in poetic quality between the descriptions of the Hawkshead district and those of other parts of the Lake District is perhaps another example of that subjective accompaniment which his best objective writing seems to have demanded. As in *The Vale of Esthwaite*'s "Evening

Sounds" the impersonal description was apparently only made possible by its emotional context and associations.

An Evening Walk belongs to a *genre* much cultivated in the eighteenth century, that of the 'loco-descriptive poem', of which the best-known representative today is probably Pope's *Windsor Forest*. The guide-book elements are, however, its least successful parts. What gives the poem its value today is the delicacy and detail of some of the descriptions. It is impossible not to be reminded of Dorothy Wordsworth's future journals in such a passage as the following:

> The whistling swain that plods his ringing way
> Where the slow waggon winds along the bay;
> The sugh of swallow-flocks that twittering sweep,
> The solemn curfew swinging long and deep;
> The talking boat that moves with pensive sound,
> Or drops his anchor down with plunge profound;
> Of boys that bathe remote the faint uproar,
> And restless piper wearying out the shore;
> These all to swell the village murmurs blend,
> That soften'd from the water-head descend.

There is a verbal precision here that is perhaps more Tennysonian than Wordsworthian. The 'talking boat' is particularly brilliant —the perfect epithet for the chatter of the little lake waves against the boat's side. The ten lines are typical of the poem as a whole because of their combination of realistic observation, the eye and the ear on the object, with literary reminiscence. The 'whistling swain', for example, comes from Milton's "L'Allegro" by way of Gray's "Elegy" and Beattie's *Minstrel*. The 'slow waggon' is also from Beattie. The odd word 'sugh' is from Burns's "Cotter's Saturday Night", but indirectly through Gilpin's book on the Highlands, which provides an explanation of Burns's word ('the sound which the wind makes, when it is resisted'). And the 'solemn curfew' descends from "Il Penseroso", again via Gray and Beattie. This curfew is certainly a bit disconcerting. There had been no curfew in the Lake District, as far as I know, since the Middle Ages. As much is equally true, of course, of most of the rest of England and Scotland, but the curfews of Milton,

Gray and Beattie, if equally anachronistic, are less disturbing, because their settings are so patently unrealistic. Gray's country churchyard is not really that of Stoke Poges in Buckinghamshire so much as the Never-Never-Land of the Latin pastoral tradition. But Wordsworth's catalogue is rooted in reality. The village murmurs are descending from his own Hawkshead, beyond which there was, as the old maps show, a real Water Head Hill. We can even identify the spot where Wordsworth was standing as he segregated and defined the separate noises of the summer evening. The internal allusions all point to what was then a strip of common on the east side of Esthwaite Water, which is described in the later "Lines left upon a Seat in a Yew Tree, which stands near the lake of Esthwaite, on a desolate part of the shore, commanding a beautiful prospect". 'This spot', according to Wordsworth's own note on the yew-tree poem, 'was my favourite walk in the evenings during the latter part of my school-time.'[1]

A real place, real sights, real sounds. In this context the curfew must be admitted to have been a mistake. Here, if only momentarily, there is a clash between the Two Voices. The talking boat was *objective*, it had an existence in time and space; the solemn curfew, on the other hand, was *subjective*, the memory of a mental event experienced in the pages of a book. In 1794, when Wordsworth was preparing a revised edition of the poem, the couplet became

> The sugh of swallow flocks that twittering pass,
> The clamorous land-rail quaking in the grass.

which is an improvement in as far as it gets rid of the curfew, though 'pass' is less vivid than 'sweep'. The substitution of a natural noise (the landrail's cry) for a social phenomenon (the curfew) has, moreover, a profounder significance. It is a symptom of the difference between the Wordsworth of the Cambridge period and the Wordsworth who emerged from the crisis-year of

---

[1] According to Knight (*The Poetical Works* (1882), I, 108) local tradition placed Wordsworth's yew on the east side of the lake about three-quarters of a mile from Hawkshead. Robertson (*Wordsworthshire*, p. 92) has confirmed the tradition from an examination of the local Enclosure Award (1799).

1792–3. For there can be no doubt, in spite of the Mary episode, that at Hawkshead and Cambridge the neurosis inflicted by Penrith had begun to disappear. Taylor and Fleming had initiated a process of reconciliation with society which such friends as Farish, Robert Jones (with whom Wordsworth shared a momentous walking-tour through France, the Italian Lakes, Switzerland and the Rhineland in his last Long Vacation), Basil Montagu, William Mathews and others continued. In spite of his eccentricities he had made plenty of friends at Cambridge, which was already emerging from its mid-century intellectual torpor. A more accurate picture probably of the spirit, if not the letter, of his life at Cambridge than Book III of *The Prelude* is that provided by his brother Christopher's diary there. Christopher's entry for 5 November 1793, is particularly interesting because it introduces Coleridge (who came up eight months after Wordsworth went down) as well as *An Evening Walk* and its successor *Descriptive Sketches* (the two poems were both published early in 1793):

> Tuesday Nov. 5. Roused about nine o'clock by Bilsborrow and Le Grice with a proposal to become member of a literary society: the members they mentioned as having already come into the plan, Coleridge, *Jes.*, Satterthwaite, Rough, and themselves, *Trin.* C , and Franklin, *Pembroke.* Heard Allen's dissertation on K. William; was to have gone to Coleridge's to wine, to consult on the plan, had I not been engaged at home with the Howeses and Strickland. Went with them to the coffee-house. On my going out met Bilsborrow: returned back with him. Soon after came in Le Grice, Coleridge and Rough. Got all into a box and (having met with the Monthly Review of my Brother's Poems), entered into a good deal of literary and critical conversation on Dr. Darwin, Miss Seward, Mrs. Smith, Bowles, and my Brother. . . . Coleridge talked Greek, Max. Tyrius he told us, and spouted out of Bowles. At nine o'clock called on Satterthwaite, and sat awhile with him.[1]

That was, I suppose, a typical day in the life of a Cambridge undergraduate with literary interests. When he was writing *The*

---

[1] Extracts from Christopher Wordsworth's diary are printed in his *Social Life at the English Universities in the Eighteenth Century* (1874), pp. 587 ff.

Prelude, some fourteen years after his university days had ended, Wordsworth looked back with regret on the number of hours he had spent in just this fashion:

> We saunter'd, play'd we rioted, we talk'd
> Unprofitable talk at morning hours,
> Drifted about along the streets and walks,
> Read lazily in lazy books. . . .[1]

But the regrets were almost certainly afterthoughts. At the time he may well have enjoyed the literary and critical conversations at least as much as his brother. We have one glimpse, the only one that has survived, of such a conversation in a note that Wordsworth added to a line of *Guilt and Sorrow*, when the poem was published in 1842. The note reads: 'From a short MS poem read to me when an undergraduate by my schoolfellow and friend, Charles Farish, long since deceased. The verses were by a brother of his, a man of promising genius, who died young.'[2] There may well have been similar interchanges. Farish must surely have read Wordsworth the poem on Hawkshead School quoted earlier in this chapter, and no doubt Wordsworth retorted by 'spouting' bits of *An Evening Walk* at him. These are the habits of undergraduate poets. And it is impossible to doubt that the eccentric country youth benefited by such humanising contacts.[3]

An Evening Walk itself is evidence that he did. No doubt it is primarily a poem of natural description, but men and the works of men are not excluded in the way that they were to be in some of his later poems. There is, for example, a whole paragraph on a slate quarry. And in the passage describing the sounds of evening

---

[1] *Prelude*, III, ll. 251–4.

[2] The note is appended to l. 81. The promising poet was probably Charles Farish's elder brother John Bernard Farish. Charles eventually became a Fellow of Queens'. In 1793 as the University Proctor he had to rebuke Coleridge for clapping his hands during the trial of William Frend, who had written an anti-Pitt pamphlet, in the Vice-Chancellor's Court. See E. K. Chambers, *Samuel Taylor Coleridge* (1938), p. 21.

[3] Wordsworth's contacts with senior members of the University seem to have been distant and occasional. He did well in the College examinations at the end of his first term, but contented himself in his second and third years with taking papers only in the subjects that interested him. The details will be found in a paper by E. A. Benians in *The Eagle* (the St. John's College magazine), Aug. 1950.

that has already been quoted the waggon and the swallows, the bathing boys and the sandpiper, come in happily and naturally side by side. There is the same mixture of the human and the non-human in the last and best lines of the poem. This is another catalogue of the sounds that were to be heard on and near Esthwaite Water, but evening has now become night:

> All air is, as the sleeping water, still,
> List'ning th' aëreal music of the hill,
> Broke only by the slow clock tolling deep,
> Or shout that wakes the ferry-man from sleep,
> Soon follow'd by his hollow-parting oar,
> And echo'd hoof approaching the far shore;
> Sound of clos'd gate, across the water born,
> Hurrying the feeding hare thro' rustling corn;
> The tremulous sob of the complaining owl;
> And at long intervals the mill-dog's howl;
> The distant forge's swinging thump profound;
> Or yell in the deep woods of lonely hound.

It would be difficult to praise this passage too highly. The blend of pastoral artifice and realistic observation is almost perfect. This is what, in their various ways, Pope and Lady Winchilsea, Thomson and Dyer, Collins and Cowper, and a hundred minor poets, from Sir John Denham with his *Cooper's Hill* (1642) to William Crowe with his *Lewesdon Hill* (1788), had been feeling their way to for the last century and a half. That Wordsworth had done it as well as the best of them, while he was still in his teens, is a really remarkable case of literary precocity.

The echoes from Thomson ('aëreal'), from Beattie (the clock and the hare both come out of *The Minstrel*), and his own earlier poems (the 'hollow-parting oar' is a condensation of a line in an early unpublished sonnet—'Of unseen oar parting with hollow sound')[1] don't really matter in this kind of poetry. Or rather, they are part of the point of this kind of poetry. The object of the

---

[1] The sonnet, which begins 'when slow from pensive twilight's latest gleam', is in MS. D.C., I, 4, p. 104. The phrase 'hollow sounding' is also used in *The Vale of Esthwaite*, l. 226, and may be an echo of 'The hollow-sounding bittern', in Goldsmith's *Deserted Village*, l. 44.

pastoralist is to extend poetry's range without abandoning the terri-
tory that has already been won for it. The fact that he is adding
new phrases and images to a common store presupposes the continuous utility of the diction and imagery that have already proved
their poetic qualities. It is an essentially civilised art, therefore,
adapting for its own day and audience a cultural tradition that
reaches back through the Renaissance to Rome, Alexandria and
primitive Greece.

And the æsthetic conformity implies a social conformity.
When he wrote those last lines of *An Evening Walk*, Wordsworth
was, in fact, though he may not actually have realised it, singing
the praises of the social order in which he had been brought up.
Penrith had been almost forgotten and almost forgiven. The next
step, logically, would have been a country curacy where, with
Dorothy as his housekeeper, he could settle down into a useful
and respectable adult life. And, as it happens, this is precisely the
prospect that he dangles before himself towards the end of his
poem—a cottage for the two of them:

> How fair it's lawn and silvery woods appear!
> How sweet it's streamlet murmurs in mine ear!
> Where we, my friend, to golden days shall rise,
> 'Till our small share of hardly-paining sighs
> (For sighs will ever trouble human breath)
> Creep hush'd into the tranquil breast of Death.

Dis aliter visum. The curacy that an influential relative offered
at Harwich could not be taken up for the time being, as the age
for admission to Anglican orders was then twenty-three. To fill
in the time he decided to become a travelling tutor, a rich young
man's bear-leader on the Grand Tour. But to qualify himself for
such a post it was necessary first of all to spend a winter in France
learning the language. The decision was a casual and half-hearted
one. 'It will at any rate be very useful to him', Dorothy wrote to
her friend at Halifax, 'and as he can live at as little expenses in
France as in England (or nearly so), the scheme is not an ineligible
one.'[1]

---

[1] Dorothy Wordsworth to Jane Pollard, 7 Dec. 1791.

Dorothy's prophecy was only partly fulfilled. As far as the cost of living went, the France of 1791–2 did not prove very different from contemporary England. In other respects, however, the gulf was approximately that which divides *Cranford* from *Wuthering Heights*. In France Wordsworth stepped out of the Picturesque into Passion, and with him English poetry moved from the lawns and pleasances of the Augustans into the whirlpools of Romanticism.

Chapter Three

STURM UND DRANG

I

WORDSWORTH did not land at Dieppe until 27 November 1791. The packet-boat's departure was delayed by contrary winds, and he had had therefore to kick his heels in Brighton for the four preceding days. Fortunately Charlotte Smith, the author of the *Elegiac Sonnets*, lived in Brighton, and a call by her young admirer was received 'in the politest manner'.[1] Mrs. Smith even provided him with an introduction to another feminine bestseller, Miss Helen Maria Williams, who was then living at Orleans.[2] The delay also enabled Wordsworth, always a dilatory letter-writer, to catch up with his arrears of correspondence. One of the letters that he wrote from Brighton—to his Cambridge friend William Mathews, an unstable young man with literary ambitions who was the brother of a then celebrated mimic and comedian—happens to have survived.[3] Though not by any means a good letter—few if any of Wordsworth's letters can be called

---

[1] Wordsworth to Richard Wordsworth, 19 Dec. 1791.

[2] Wordsworth's editors, including even de Selincourt, persist in attributing to him a deplorable "Sonnet on seeing Miss Helen Maria Williams weep at a Tale of Distress", which was published in *The European Magazine*, Mar. 1787, above the signature Axiologus. The excuse for this attribution is that Coleridge later addressed some hexameters 'Ad Vilmum Axiologum', the word being presumably an attempt to find a Græco-Latin equivalent for 'Wordsworth'. No doubt somebody of the name of Wordsworth *was* responsible for the sonnet, but it was certainly not William Wordsworth, who did not meet Miss Williams until 1820. Wordsworth is not an exceptionally rare name. *The Gentleman's Magazine* records the marriage of a John Wordsworth in 1783 and an H. Wordsworth ('of Ivy-lane') in 1784. Perhaps one of them was the original Axiologus? The terms in which Wordsworth refers to Helen Maria Williams in the letter of 1791—'Miss Williams, an English Lady'—do not suggest that he had been writing sentimental sonnets about her four years before.

[3] Wordsworth to William Mathews, 23 Nov. 1791.

good letters—it throws an unconscious light on the character of Wordsworth at twenty-one that is decidedly interesting.

He is, he tells Mathews, tolerably happy now, though his character is, he realises, fluid and in need of discipline. 'I am doomed to be an idler through my whole life. I have read nothing this age, nor indeed did I ever.' He ends by apologising for the 'outrageous egotism' of his letter, and hopes that his winter at Orleans will effect 'some improvement, which God knows I stand in sufficient need of'.

It is not difficult to relate the character painted in this letter— egocentric, but with no firm outlines to the egotism, self-deprecatory, but not quite to the point of self-criticism—to that revealed in the early poems. The irrational, almost hysterical subjectivity displayed in the supernatural episodes of *The Vale of Esthwaite* has been outgrown. Four and a half years have elapsed since Mary of Esthwaite Water passed out of his life, and contact has now been resumed with ordinary every-day human beings. There are no ecstasies now, but their place has been taken by a condition of uninterrupted placidity. 'I am tolerably happy.' The prolonged convalescence is clearly approaching its end and he will soon be ready to take his place in the world of action. For the moment, however, he is still the passive adolescent, a young man to whom things happen, for whom action is essentially just a momentary reaction to external stimulus. *An Evening Walk* had been to all intents and purposes little more than a series of un-related sense-impressions. The single items in the catalogue were on the whole beautifully done, the notation of sound being par-ticularly delicate, but the relationship between one paragraph and the next, even sometimes between one line and another, was often arbitrary and forced. The young poet could see and hear, but he could not organise. In terms of subject-matter anything that could be seen or heard in the course of an evening walk in the Lake District was grist to his poetic mill. In terms of emotional attitude the necessitating condition was simply the pleasure that a man of culture and sensibility can be expected to feel in the face of nature—'How pleasant' (l. 97), 'Not undelightful' (l. 127), 'I love to mark' (l. 141), 'I love . . . to stray' (l. 195), 'Sweet are

the sounds' (l. 301). There is no contrast of moods, no development of attitude. Even the structural device of a letter to the
distant Dorothy is perfunctory, the greater part of the poem not
being in letter-form at all.

A recognition of this condition can perhaps be read into
Wordsworth's confession 'I am doomed to be an idler through
my whole life'. By an idler he meant, I suppose, a man without
purpose or consistency, a drifter with the tide, a shuttlecock of
circumstance—the exact antithesis, that is to say, to the man of
action. The most disquieting thing perhaps in the letter to
Mathews is the way he takes it all for granted. And this passivity
is not to be temporary but lifelong; it is not voluntary but the
effect of 'doom'. Altogether it was not, it will be agreed, a very
promising frame of mind in which to take up residence in a
foreign country undergoing a revolution.

The situation, indeed, was ominously similar to that in which
Wordsworth had found himself six years before. There is even
a similarity in his attitude to nature. The healthier and happier
relationship to the real world that Taylor and Fleming and the
discovery of poetry had combined to promote, had been reflected, it will be remembered, in a new interest in 'the infinite
variety of natural appearances'. With a certain solemnity the
young Wordsworth had dedicated himself to the recording in
verse of the *details* of landscape. The discovery of the Picturesque,
which Wordsworth made shortly before he and Jones made their
prolonged tour of the Alps, came to very much the same thing.
Instead of detail, however, it was now lightings and colours that
had become a matter of absorbing, almost technical interest. He
now owned two of Gilpin's elaborate and expensive works on
Picturesque Beauty, and since his return from the Continent in
October 1790 he had actually begun a poem on the tour that was
to be called "Picturesque Sketches". (The title was changed later
and it was eventually published, early in 1793, as *Descriptive
Sketches*.)

But there was an important difference. Wordsworth was now
a man of twenty-one, and not a boy of fifteen. He was therefore
approaching, if he had not already reached, sexual maturity. And

there are one or two indications that he was by no means at this time the 'solemn and unsexual man' Shelley later accused him of being. Consider, for example, the account of the girls of Como and the 'voluptuous dreams' they inspired in his and Jones's hearts, that comes near the beginning of *Descriptive Sketches*:

> Those lips, whose tides of fragrance come, and go,
> Accordant to the cheek's unquiet glow;
> Those shadowy breasts in love's soft light array'd,
> And rising, by the moon of passion sway'd.

When Wordsworth reprinted the poem in 1820, these lines were left out. But their expurgation then only emphasises their significance in 1791.

It is difficult not to attach a similar significance to a sentence in an early letter of Dorothy's. Wordsworth had spent the preceding Christmas with her at their Uncle William's vicarage in Norfolk, and she had been delighted then, she tells a friend, with his 'violence of Affection if I may so term it which demonstrates itself every moment of the Day when the Objects of his affection are present with him, in a thousand almost imperceptible attentions to their wishes, in a sort of restless watchfulness which I know not how to describe, a Tenderness that never sleeps, and at the same time such a delicacy of manners as I have observed in few men'.[1] A dangerous young man, one would say, if there were unattached feminine hearts in the vicinity. In Norfolk the object of this violent and persistent affection had been only a sister. But Dorothy was not able to accompany him to Orleans, and there her place was taken by a very different young woman, who was to provoke a far more serious crisis than the one Mary of Esthwaite Water precipitated.

In November 1791, the French Revolution was still in its first phase. Louis XVI had ratified the new National Constitution in September, and the foreign interventions, which were to be the prelude to the Reign of Terror, did not start until the following spring. In the meantime, to the informed English observer, a constitutional monarchy more or less on the English pattern must

---

[1] Dorothy Wordsworth to Jane Pollard, 16 Feb. 1793.

have seemed the likeliest outcome. At this time English opinion was still on the whole favourable to the Revolution. To most of the intellectuals, including the group of young Cambridge men settled in London with whom Wordsworth had been associating after taking his degree at the beginning of the year, a political millenium must have seemed to be heralded:

> Bliss was it in that dawn to be alive,
> But to be young was very heaven!

The famous passage in *The Prelude* was published separately, before the rest of the poem, under the heading "French Revolution as it appeared to Enthusiasts at its Commencement". In a general way Wordsworth must certainly be included among those enthusiasts, although in 1791 his political enthusiasms and indeed all his political views were almost entirely second-hand. When he and Jones had landed at Calais the preceding year on their way to the Alps, they had found the whole nation, as he wrote to Dorothy at the time, 'mad with joy in consequence of the revolution'.[1] But, although, when sailing down the Rhône, the two Englishmen fraternised with some delegates from the ceremony at Paris of 14 July (the day on which the King, the Assembly and the National Guard had renewed the civic oath), their attitude had remained detached, almost that of sightseers. 'It was a most interesting period to be in France', the letter to Dorothy continues, 'and we had many delightful scenes, when the interest of the picture was owing solely to this cause.' The tepidity of these political comments contrasts with the excitement with which he records the scenery they had been enjoying. 'I am a perfect enthusiast', he wrote, 'in my admiration of Nature in all her various forms.' In the terminology of *The Prelude*, the hour of Man had not yet struck But the transformation of the enthusiast for Nature into the enthusiast for the Revolution was soon to be accomplished.

The first letter from Orleans was reassuring. 'We are all perfectly quiet here.' He has found cheap and comfortable

---

[1] Wordsworth to Dorothy Wordsworth, 6 Sept. 1790.

lodgings, which he is sharing with some cavalry officers and a young Parisian. The upper classes, he reports, are all against the Revolution and the lower classes are all for it. His French is improving, but he is not yet able to speak it 'with decent accuracy'. Unfortunately Miss Williams has left Orleans. One French family, however, with whom he has scraped an acquaintance, he finds 'very agreeable'.

This letter to his brother Richard was written on 19 December 1791. The next letter of Wordsworth's that survives is one to Mathews, written from Blois on 17 May 1792. A reconstruction of the critical five months between the two letters must be largely a matter of guesswork. There are, however, two certainties. By May Wordsworth had become the intimate friend of Michel Armand Beaupuy, the one officer with republican sympathies in the garrison at Blois—to whom he *may* have been introduced by those cavalry officers, his fellow-lodgers at Orleans. And by May a certain Annette Vallon, who *may* have been a friend of that agreeable family at Orleans (her favourite brother lived there), was two months with child by the young Englishman. The association of the events is certainly not a coincidence. Together they mark Wordsworth's attempted entrance into the adult world of social responsibilities:

> Not in Utopia, subterranean fields,
> Or some secreted island, Heaven knows where!
> But in the very world, which is the world
> Of all of us,—the place where in the end
> We find our happiness, or not at all! [1]

The portrait of Beaupuy fills some of the best-known pages in *The Prelude*. Except in the one detail of the date of his death (which occurred in 1796 and not, as Wordsworth thought, in 1793), modern research has found little of consequence to add to the account of Beaupuy, and it has amply confirmed the intelligence and disinterestedness Wordsworth ascribed to him. He

---

[1] "French Revolution, as it appeared to Enthusiasts at its Commencement", ll. 35–40.

could have had no better tutor in democratic political theory.
When he arrived in France he did not know, as he tells us,

> Whence the main Organs of the public Power
> Had sprung, their transmigrations when and how
> Accomplish'd . . .[1]

and this ignorance was not confined to constitutional history. In
the widest sense, he was politically uneducated. When he made
his way to Paris, however, in the autumn, he found no difficulty
in associating on equal terms not only with English Jacobins like
the younger James Watt, but also with at least one of the Girondist
leaders—Jacques-Pierre Brissot. It would not be an exaggeration
to say that the long walks he and Beaupuy took along the
Loire and in the woods round Blois *transformed* Wordsworth
intellectually.

But Wordsworth is unlikely to have made Beaupuy's acquaintance until about February 1792, when he transferred his quarters
from Orleans to Blois. By that time he was almost certainly
already in love with Annette Vallon. Indeed, the change of
residence is only explicable on the supposition that Annette's visit
to her brother was now over and that she had therefore to return
to Blois, where the Vallon home was. In other words, the intellectual transformation was subsequent to the emotional transformation. Wordsworth would probably not have become an active
political revolutionary, if the barriers of his passivity had not been
previously overthrown by sexual passion. Beaupuy was only an
effect, the cause was Annette.

Who then was Annette Vallon? What sort of a person was it
that was able to break through the guard of Wordsworth's
egotism and prudence?

Wordsworth has not answered these questions himself in so
many words, but he has supplied a half-answer in a tale told in
The Prelude. When he came to describe his 'Residence in France'
in Books IX and X, he made no direct reference whatever to the
Annette episode. Instead, however, he inserted the long tragic
tale of Vaudracour and Julia, which is obviously intended to

---

[1] *Prelude*, IX, ll. 102–4.

provide a sort of parallel to his own love-affair. The actual
writing, it must be admitted, except in one passage, is greatly
inferior to most of the rest of *The Prelude*, but as veiled autobiography this curious story, told him as fact, he says, by Beaupuy
and other first-hand witnesses, is not without interest.[1]

Vaudracour was a young nobleman, Julia was a bourgeoise,
though 'from Parents sprung Not mean in their condition', and
Vaudracour's father would not consent to their marriage. But
they were deeply in love, and 'whether through effect Of some
delirious hour', or trusting 'To Nature for a happy end of all',
they slept together, with the result that Julia

> without the name of Wife
> Carried about her for a secret grief
> The promise of a Mother.

Unknown to Vaudracour, Julia was removed by her parents to
another town when the baby's birth approached, but Vaudracour
succeeded in finding where she had gone and followed her. On
his father learning that he was now determined to marry Julia,
he instructed three ruffians to seize Vaudracour, who however
killed one of the men and then gave himself up to the authorities,
who put him into prison. He is finally released on condition that
he abandons Julia. There are various brief reunions, but soon after
the child is born Julia is made to enter a convent and in due
course Vaudracour goes out of his mind.

These are the bare bones of the story. As its melodramatic
middle and end cannot conceivably have been duplicated in any
way in Wordsworth's relations with Annette, it is presumably
in the opening phase of the story that the resemblance lies. If this
is so, Annette's decided social inferiority to Wordsworth would
seem to be a necessary consequence. And what is known of her
family does make it unlikely that Wordsworth's relations would
have smiled on the match. Her father, who was dead, had been
a barber-surgeon, and this was the occupation of her two older

---

1 Wordsworth's real source seems to have been *Letters Written in France, in the
Summer of 1790* (1790), by that Helen Maria Williams to whom Charlotte Smith
had given him an introduction in 1791, though they did not actually meet until
1820. See F. M. Todd, *Modern Language Review*, XLIII (1948), 456–64.

brothers. The younger brother was a notary's clerk at Orleans, and Annette herself can have had little or no education. Two of her letters have recently been discovered, and the grammar and spelling are extremely shaky, the punctuation non-existent. Additional objections, in the eyes of the Wordsworths and the Cooksons, would have been her religion and her ignorance of English. These seem the legitimate deductions to be drawn from Wordsworth's use of the Vaudracour and Julia story as a veiled parallel to his own love-affair. In both cases, social disparity, in the widest sense of the words, was the mainspring of the tragedy. It is possible that in retrospect Annette's nationality may have seemed a greater obstacle than her middle-class origins. In Book XII of *The Prelude* there is an eloquent eulogy of young love that recalls the account of Vaudracour's feelings for Julia:

> The bliss of walking daily in Life's prime
> Through field or forest with the Maid we love,
> While yet our hearts are young, while yet we breathe
> Nothing but happiness, living in some place,
> Deep Vale, or anywhere, the home of both,
> From which it would be misery to stir. . . .[1]

The proviso in the fifth line here is interesting. A happy love-affair is only possible apparently within a single community, 'the home of both'. It would seem to follow that a love-affair in which the homes of the lovers are in different districts cannot be a happy one. *A fortiori* a mixed marriage would be even more disastrous.

The account of Vaudracour and Julia was written some thirteen years after Wordsworth met Annette. It must not be mistaken for Wordsworth's feelings at the time. Its interest is the implicit verdict of the mature Wordsworth—recently married to Mary Hutchinson—on the youthful Wordsworth. A contributory factor to the verdict may have been the month at Calais that Wordsworth and his sister spent with Annette and Caroline, their illegitimate daughter, in 1802. They had not seen each other for nearly ten years, and at the reunion, about which very little is

---

[1] *Prelude*, XII, ll. 129–34.

known (except that Wordsworth wrote a great many sonnets during the four weeks on other topics), Annette may well have seemed much more foreign than when they first met.

In retrospect, then, Wordsworth almost certainly regretted the affair. A marriage with Annette would have been 'impossible'. But in 1792 he may well have thought otherwise. It is certain that he had promised Annette to marry her. A letter that she wrote to him on 20 March 1793, when Wordsworth had returned to England, assumes throughout that it is only a matter of time before he is back in France and they can get married. No doubt he had thought it would be easier to secure a post unencumbered with a French wife, and that was why he returned to England alone early in December 1792, just before Caroline was born. But the post eluded him, and on 1 February 1793 England and France were at war, a state of affairs which continued uninterruptedly until the Peace of Amiens in 1802. Although an occasional letter got through, it would have been difficult for anybody with Wordsworth's modest means to have slipped across the Channel, married Annette and brought her back to England. The question of marriage was apparently tacitly dropped on both sides. Later Wordsworth contributed—not ungenerously—to Caroline's dowry.

There is little to add, as far as the external history of the love-affair goes. Caroline was christened in the Cathedral at Orleans on 15 December 1792, the baptismal entry running as follows: 'Anne Caroline Wordswodsth, fille de Williams Wordswodsth, Anglois, et de Marie Anne Vallon'. Wordsworth was represented at the ceremony by André Augustin Dufour, a legal official for the Orleans district, whom he had empowered to act for him. Dufour's wife was the godmother, and the godfather was Paul Vallon, Annette's brother. It has been suggested that the Dufours were that agreeable family Wordsworth had mentioned in his letter to his brother the previous December. The fact that Caroline was born at Orleans and not at Blois provides one more parallel to "Vaudracour and Julia".

It is possible that, like Julia, Annette did not inform her lover as to her movements. If so, Wordsworth, like Vaudracour, must soon have found out, as he left Blois for Orleans early in September. No doubt by then Annette's pregnancy would have begun to be conspicuous. From Orleans Wordsworth went to Paris, presumably *en route* for England, though he may, perhaps, have hoped to secure a post there. He stayed in Paris from the end of October to the beginning of December.

It remains to assess the impact of the affair on Wordsworth. Apart from "Vaudracour and Julia", with its lyrical picture of Vaudracour's happiness:

> Arabian Fiction never fill'd the world
> With half the wonders that were wrought for him.
> Earth liv'd in one great presence of the spring,
> Life turn'd the meanest of her implements
> Before his eyes to price above all gold,
> The house she dwelt in was a sainted shrine,
> Her chamber-window did surpass in glory
> The portals of the East, all paradise
> Could by the simple opening of a door
> Let itself in upon him. . . .

Apart from this passage, which can certainly be taken as autobiographical, the only relevant documents are Wordsworth's letter to Mathews of 17 May 1792 and the long letter intended for Dorothy that Annette enclosed with the undelivered letter to Wordsworth written on 20 March 1793. Annette's letter, in spite of its breathless sentimentality, is most moving. She can only think of her dear William and her darling Caroline. There is not even a distant hint of reproach or recrimination, and her manifest disinterestedness—there are no requests for money or help of any kind whatever—is impressive, almost heroic. In the years of separation that followed Annette became a sort of Scarlet Pimpernel, assisting in the escape of dozens of aristocrats out of France. The whole story is told in Émile Legouis's admirable little book *William Wordsworth and Annette Vallon* (1922). The fundamental magnanimity of Annette's letter under all its sentimental silliness makes it easy to believe in the courage and determination she was soon to show in this 'Underground Movement' against the Republic and Napoleon. Wordsworth had fallen in love—though

I am not sure that he realised it—with a very remarkable woman. One passage in the letter must be quoted in full (the accentuation has been normalised and punctuation supplied). Annette is repeating here on paper her outpourings to the three-months old Caroline. Their excursions with the pram have apparently taken them past the convent where Annette had gone to school: 'Je parle à Caroline comme si elle entendois; je lui dit: "Regarde, ma fille; c'est ici le couvent où a été élevée ta mère, où souvent avec ton père nous nous sommes attendries en pensant à ces jours heureux de l'innocence où tu es actuellement. Conserve la longtemps, ma Caroline, si tu veux être heureuse; sois toujours sourde aux cris des passions; ne connois jamois d'autres sentiments que l'amour pour ton père, ta tante et ta mère." '[1] The implications of this piece of good advice given to the unconscious Caroline can hardly have been missed by Dorothy. Unlike her mother, Caroline is urged to be deaf to the cries of passion. Annette has brought her unhappiness on herself by allowing her passion to overcome her innocence. It is all her own fault. *William is not to blame.* When Dorothy alluded to the affair in a letter to Jane Pollard, her most intimate woman friend, her comment on William's behaviour is also surprisingly mild: '. . . though I must confess that he has been somewhat to blame, yet I think I shall prove to you that the excuse might have been found in his natural disposition. "In truth he was a strange and wayward wight fond of each gentle etc. etc." That verse of Beattie's *Minstrel* always reminds me of him. . . .' Beattie's Edwin was a dreamy youth, essentially, like the young Wordsworth, a man to whom things happen and not by any means the master of circumstance. It is clear, I think, that the leader in the affair must have been Annette. For one thing she was four years older than Wordsworth, twenty-five to his twenty-one when they met. And in any case it would have been difficult for Wordsworth, who was not exactly a lady's man even in England, to have taken the initiative in a language with which, according to his nephew, 'at that time he had a very imperfect acquaintance'.[2]

The problem then, to put it baldly, is not of Annette's seduction

---

[1] Legouis, p. 130.　　　　[2] *Memoirs of William Wordsworth*, I, 72.

by Wordsworth, but of Wordsworth's seduction by Annette. Why did Wordsworth allow himself to be seduced? What was it about Annette that he found so difficult to resist?

"Vaudracour and Julia" is no help here. The poem tells us something about Vaudracour's character—he was another Edwin, passive and futile—but little or nothing about Julia's. Wordsworth's letter to Mathews, however, is most illuminating —especially perhaps in the contrasts it presents to the letter written from Brighton. In the Brighton letter Wordsworth had seen himself doomed to be an 'idler' all his life. Now, in May 1792, he is the prophet of 'resolution': 'You have still the hope that we may be connected in some method of obtaining an independence. I assure you I wish it as much as yourself. Nothing but resolution is necessary. The field of Letters is very extensive, and it is astonishing if we cannot find some little corner, which with a little tillage will produce us enough for the necessities, nay even the comforts of life.'[1] The letter goes on to discuss in a thoroughly practical way the possibilities of a literary career for both of them. 'I assure you again and again that nothing but confidence and resolution is necessary.' The optimism and self-confidence may strike one as naïve, but the progress Wordsworth had made in the confrontation of reality is really remarkable. The passive man was in process of becoming the active man. This cautious young northerner seems to have caught fire from Annette's gallic recklessness.

There is no direct reference to Annette in the letter to Mathews, though it is impossible not to connect her with Wordsworth's reason for not writing sooner. Since his arrival in Blois, he writes, 'day after day and week after week has stolen insensibly over my head with inconceivable rapidity'. He was still expecting to enter the Church in the following winter or spring. 'My uncle, the clergyman', he says, 'will furnish me with a title.' The uncle, incidentally, was the extremely respectable William Cookson and this confidence in avuncular assistance suggests that Wordsworth was still unaware of Annette's pregnancy. The same conclusion can perhaps be drawn from another item of news included

---

[1] Wordsworth to William Mathews, 17 May 1792.

in the letter: their mutual friend Jones, Wordsworth's old companion in the Alps who was now a clergyman, was to have joined him at Blois. In the end Jones didn't come, but if he had, Annette would presumably have been introduced to him as Wordsworth's *fiancée*. Her pregnancy, however, could hardly have failed to put a severe strain on the clerical morality even of the easy-going Jones.

The sense in which Annette was the prelude to Beaupuy should be clear by now. In falling in love with Annette Wordsworth had broken down the barriers of his egotism. As lovers first of all, and then as parents, he and Annette found themselves committed to a social role. It was natural for the next step to be an enquiry into their duties to their neighbours and into the nature of this society in which they had now become involved. And the concurrence of the French Revolution with his own private revolution made a further extension of Wordsworth's social commitments inevitable. The good lover became the good father, the good father became the good citizen. It is possible that ideally an interval of mental and moral digestion should have intervened. Wordsworth's political philosophy might have stood the test of time better if he had *not* looked at mankind through the spectacles of his love for Annette. 'Beaupuy and Wordsworth' Dicey has complained, 'were in 1792 democrats who hoped to obtain every kind of socialistic reform by means which would have met with the approval of zealous individualists.'[1] But an over-idealistic political philosophy can hardly be regretted in the lover of twenty-two.

By the time Wordsworth reached Paris, at the end of October 1792, the French Revolution was rapidly approaching its climax. The Tuileries had been stormed on August 9th, and the king made a prisoner on the 10th. In the panic of the September massacres (2–4 September) over 3,000 Royalists had been taken from prison and killed, but the victory of Valmy on September 20th turned the tide against the allied invaders and on the 22nd France was proclaimed a Republic. With the moderates in a majority in

---

[1] A. V. Dicey, *The Statesmanship of Wordsworth: an Essay* (1917), p. 32. I have borrowed this quotation from de Selincourt's edition of *The Prelude*, p. 570.

the new Assembly Wordsworth could reasonably describe himself, in the account of those five weeks in Paris in *The Prelude*, as
arriving 'enflam'd with hope'.[1] It is almost certain that he knew
Brissot, the Girondist leader, who had many English friends,
including Charlotte Smith, and one of the hopes with which he
arrived inflamed may well have been for a minor political post.
Except on this supposition it is difficult to see why he should have
lingered in Paris for so long, instead of proceeding directly to
London.[2] Some lines in *The Prelude* suggest that Wordsworth
would certainly have liked to have taken an active part in the
political struggle:

> An insignificant Stranger, and obscure,
> Mean as I was, and little graced with power
> Of eloquence even in my native speech,
> And all unfit for tumult or intrigue,
> Yet would I willingly have taken up
> A service at this time for cause so great,
> However dangerous.[3]

One quite influential friend that he made in Paris was the younger
James Watt, the son of the inventor, who was a prominent
member of the Jacobin Club and had by his personal intervention
prevented a duel between Danton and Robespierre earlier in the
year. A glimpse of this association is provided in the report of
Wordsworth's conversation one day in 1841 that we owe to a
young friend of Watt's: '. . . he went on to Paris at the time
of the Revolution in 1792 and 1793, and was "pretty hot in it",
but he found Mr. Watt there before him, and quite as hot in the
same cause. They then both began life as ardent [and he adds,
thoughtless] radicals'.[4]

---

[1] *Prelude*, X, l. 38.
[2] A more prosaic possibility is that he had to wait all this time for his passport.
The Foreign Office records are full of complaints about the difficulty English
travellers in France had in getting passports in 1792. See for details F. M. Todd,
Modern Language Review, XLIII (1948), pp. 456–64.
[3] *Prelude*, X, ll. 131–7.
[4] J. P. Muirhead, "A Day with Wordsworth", *Blackwood's Magazine*, Jan.
1927, p. 733.

Watt was certainly 'pretty hot in it'. Early in 1793 he and Thomas Cooper actually carried the British flag in a Jacobin procession, for which they were magisterially censured by Burke in the House of Commons. But it is difficult to believe that Wordsworth was much more than an interested spectator. At any rate the post never materialised, and in his own words in *The Prelude*:

> In this frame of mind,
> Reluctantly to England I return'd,
> Compell'd by nothing less than absolute want
> Of funds for my support, else . . .
> I doubtless should have made a common cause
> With some who perish'd, haply perish'd, too . . .
> With all my resolutions, all my hopes,
> A Poet only to myself. . . .[1]

It is interesting to find the word 'resolution' turning up here again. Brissot and several other prominent Girondists were guillotined in October 1793, and it is within the bounds of possibility that Wordsworth might have shared their fate if they had made use of his services. It is more difficult to believe that, even if the poet had perished, two at any rate of his poems would not have been published. *An Evening Walk* had been more or less completed by 1790. Its successor *Descriptive Sketches* had been occupying a large part of his time since then, and a letter to his brother Richard dated 'Blois September 3' contains the specific statement that he expected to be in London in October 'about my publication'. It is true, as he wrote to Mathews some eighteen months later, the principal motive in the projected publications was self-advertisement—'as I had done nothing by which to distinguish myself at the University, I thought these little things might shew that I could do something'.[2] If a bread-and-butter job had turned up in Paris, the necessity for the advertisement would have disappeared. But, as nothing was to be had in Paris, it had become more than ever necessary to inform the English literary world of his talents, so that he could secure the reviewing

---

[1] *Prelude*, X, ll. 189–200.
[2] Wordsworth to William Mathews, 23 May 1794.

and miscellaneous journalism on which it would be possible to marry. The first object, then, on his return to London in December was to find a publisher for the two poems. This was more important even than seeing Dorothy and explaining his position to her. Everything, indeed, seemed to depend on the success of the poems. If they were well received, he could count on a career as a writer or journalist and the question of entering the Church, a career Wordsworth was never enthusiastic about, need not arise. It would be a simple matter to return to France and marry Annette—or so it must have seemed—and they could then settle down in England with no one knowing that Caroline was born before their marriage. Dorothy would, of course, join them, and they would then all four live happily ever after. The daydream can be reconstructed with a painful probability.

A publisher *was* found without difficulty. The obvious man was Johnson of St. Paul's Churchyard, a well-known radical and friend of radicals (including Blake, Tom Paine, and Mary Wollstonecraft), and the publisher of the influential *Analytical Review*. Apparently Johnson liked the poems, and he must have agreed to bring them out immediately, as they duly made their appearance early in 1793 in two thin quartos. But the rest of the programme went disastrously awry.

The storm that Wordsworth had been proposing to ride very nearly engulfed him. Unlike Vaudracour he did not go out of his mind, though his friends seem to have feared for his sanity at one moment. Their remedy, Dorothy told De Quincey, was the quaint one of playing cards with him. In later life, De Quincey says, cards 'could have had as little power to interest him, or to cheat him of sorrow, as marbles or a top'.[1] But in the period of crisis through which he passed from January to June 1793, any distraction may well have been welcome. The whole of these six months of concentrated failure, frustration, and disappointment were spent in London, and when his 'sense of distress' was at its worst, his London friends played cards with him *every single night*. 'So it was,' De Quincey concludes, 'for my information could not be questioned; it came from Miss Wordsworth.' The

---

[1] *Recollections of the Lake Poets*, ed. E. Sackville-West, p. 170.

anecdote is an interesting one. If it illustrates vividly how unhappy Wordsworth was at this time it also shows that he had a few friends at any rate who believed in him and in his future. Those constant unidentifiable London card-players were the first Wordsworthians.

II

The first disappointment was the poems. Nobody bought either *An Evening Walk* or *Descriptive Sketches*. Nobody seemed to take any interest in the two poems. The reviews were a long time in appearing, and when they did come out most of them were either hostile or contemptuous. The notices in *The Analytical Review* were the first to appear, and it might have been thought that one of Johnson's publications would at least have been polite to others from the same house. A radical journal too ought to have liked the long and eloquent apostrophe to Freedom, written at Orleans the preceding October, with which *Descriptive Sketches* ends. But the reviewer in *The Analytical Review* did not like either poem and said so. Except for a 'picturesque passage' in *An Evening Walk*, which is quoted *in extenso*, he found nothing to praise and a good deal to censure. The style in particular seemed to him obscure and inflated, as indeed it is, especially in the more rapidly and carelessly written *Descriptive Sketches*.

A similar verdict was pronounced later in the year by *The Critical Review* and *The Monthly Review*. It is possible that Wordsworth's poems may have seemed rather old-fashioned to the London literati. The provinces certainly liked them better. A literary society at Exeter is said to have held them in high esteem, and they were extolled at Derby by Erasmus Darwin and Anna Seward. Cambridge also thought well of them. The probable explanation is that, though the poetry of the School of Gray was still fashionable outside London, in London itself the sentimental simplicities of the Della Cruscan School were now preferred. Beattie's *Minstrel* was already becoming *vieux jeu*. A reviewer in the February number of *The Analytical Review*, the same literary hack, probably, who was to disparage Wordsworth in the March issue, found the simplicity of Lamb's eccentric friend George

Dyer a pleasant relief from the usual 'laboured elegance, which produces obscurity'. It was not long, indeed, before Wordsworth came to much the same conclusion himself. His final judgment on the two early poems was expressed in a letter of 1801: 'They are juvenile productions, inflated, and obscure, but they contain many new images, and vigorous lines.'[1] It is a fair summing-up, though he should have added that *An Evening Walk* is much better in all these respects than *Descriptive Sketches*. Unfortunately in the London of 1793 the inflated obscurities were more apparent than the poems' novelty and vigour. As advertisements of the writer's literary talents they were a complete and absolute failure.

By the end of February it must have been clear that literature could not provide an income on which he could marry. With the greatest reluctance—it may be suspected that Wordsworth was already the semi-atheist Coleridge described him as being in 1796— he reverted to the original project of going into the Church. But a young clergyman needs a 'Title', that is, a guarantee to the Bishop, and for his 'Title' Wordsworth was dependent on his Uncle William, now Canon Cookson. And Uncle William's attitude to the nephew with revolutionary views and an illegitimate daughter was a great deal less genial than it had been. Dorothy did her best to plead William's cause with him, but she was unsuccessful. Uncle William was implacable. William was apparently forbidden the Vicarage, and the unhappy Dorothy, who was still living with this uncle and aunt, was told not to contaminate herself by associating with her immoral brother.

In complete despair, Wordsworth had to fall back on the travelling tutorship, if one could be found, which had been the pretext for his visit to France. It meant, of course, giving up any immediate hope of marrying Annette, but the little capital that he had inherited from his parents was now practically exhausted— apart, that is, from his share of the £5,000 withheld by Lord Lonsdale—and there seemed no alternative. In any case a reunion with Annette and Caroline would have been extremely difficult and dangerous as long as England and France were at war. The official declaration had been made on 1 February 1793, and one by

---

[1] Wordsworth to Miss Taylor, 9 Apr. 1801.

one the various peace-time links between the two countries were in process of being severed. Thus a letter from Wordsworth to Annette—it included a long and loving one to her from Dorothy —that was posted in London on 8 March, reached Blois safely on 14 March. But Annette's reply, which was posted on 20 March, was intercepted by the French authorities and never reached England at all.[1]

The French war had further, profounder consequences for Wordsworth. In *The Prelude* he has described the effect of the declaration of war as the first shock his moral nature received:

> No shock
> Given to my moral nature had I known
> Down to that very moment. . . .[2]

To begin with he was wholly pro-French and rejoiced in the English defeats. On the rare occasions when he found himself in Church and the congregation's prayers were requested for the success of the English armies, he writes,

> I only, like an uninvited Guest
> Whom no one own'd sate silent, shall I add,
> Fed on the day of vengeance yet to come?[3]

A literary expression of this anti-English mood was the prose pamphlet *A Letter to the Bishop of Landaff on the extraordinary avowal of his Political Principles contained in the Appendix to his late Sermon: by a Republican.* The pamphlet, which was undoubtedly written for publication, though it was not in fact published until after Wordsworth's death, is a most eloquent and intelligent defence of the French Revolution. Presumably it was too outspoken even for Johnson to publish. *The Analytical Review* in its notice of the Bishop's sermon in March 1793, contented itself with wondering if he did not 'carry his commendation of our laws and government too far'. The fact is that the spring of 1793 found the Whigs and their Radical allies very much on the defensive. The news of the execution of Louis XVI in January had been received in England with a shock of horror, and a number of

---

[1] Legouis, pp. 29, 124.   [2] *Prelude*, X, ll. 234–6.

[3] *Ibid.*, X, ll. 273–5.

earlier eulogists of the Revolution took the first opportunity to make public recantations. Richard Watson, Bishop of Llandaff, was the most eminent of these turncoats. His previous public support of the Revolution had earned him the nickname of 'the Levelling Prelate', and his defection was a serious blow to the Radical cause. It is very much to Wordsworth's credit that he was apparently prepared to say publicly and in print what most of the reformers must have felt.

Watson's sermon was on 'The wisdom and goodness of God in having made both Rich and Poor'. To this somewhat common-place attack on egalitarianism, he added, when the sermon was printed, a long appendix which was the main object of Words-worth's attack. According to Watson, eighteenth-century England was already a sort of Earthly Paradise: 'Were not the poor admirably provided for? Was not the tax collected for them enormous? Had they not hospitals, dispensaries and assistance of every sort?'[1]

Wordsworth's pamphlet is not a startlingly original document. In a sense it had all been said before. Most of the arguments derive from Rousseau and Tom Paine, and there are one or two phrases which suggest that Wordsworth had been dipping into William Godwin's *Enquiry concerning Political Justice and its influence on Morals and Happiness*, which was still red-hot from the press. What is impressive about the letter is its burning sincerity. The rhetorical personifications and the balanced anti-theses that disfigure *Descriptive Sketches* are conspicuous by their absence. Wordsworth is writing here to convince his readers rather than to impress them. Perhaps the most effective para-graphs are those on the social abuses of the period. A monarchy, he argues, implies a nobility and the existence of this class that is by definition exempt from labour, tends to make all work dis-honourable and to encourage racing, gambling, and prostitution. The rich become too rich, and the poor too poor. The remedy is equality—the abolition of the monarchy and of all titles, 'garters

---

[1] Legouis (*The Early Life of William Wordsworth*, translated by J. W. Matthews, 1897, pp. 228–31) gives a useful summary of Watson's appendix and Words-worth's reply.

and other badges of fictitious superiority', and the institution of universal suffrage. In view of his later Toryism it is interesting to find him so contemptuous of Burke's hierarchical society, because of 'the natural tendency of power to corrupt the heart of man'.[1]

A Letter to the Bishop of Landaff is not dated, but the period of its composition can be deduced fairly easily. Watson's sermon had been published on 15 January 1793, and to have been topical Wordsworth's retort would have had to be prepared straight away. It cannot therefore have been written later than February 1793. Presumably its composition was intended to be the first step in that career of author-journalist he had planned for himself. In that case, the failure to find a publisher—or perhaps the realisation that publication might easily involve prosecution by the Government—would have been the last nail in the coffin of that particular daydream.

As long as he was in London, Wordsworth did not write any poetry. But in July a wealthy school-fellow invited him to be his companion on a tour of southern England. The school-fellow, William Calvert, the eldest son of the Duke of Norfolk's agent in Westmorland, promised to pay all the expenses and *faute de mieux* (a travelling tutorship had not in fact materialised) Wordsworth accepted. The tour began with a stay of a month in the Isle of Wight, 'in view of the fleet,' as Wordsworth never forgot, 'which was then preparing for sea off Portsmouth at the commencement of the war'.[2] One of their excursions, apparently, was to the convict prison at Portland, and Wordsworth's feelings of indignation at what he saw there seems to have been the occasion of his return to the writing of poetry. It must be admitted that "The Convict" is not a good poem. Its interest derives partly from its extreme republicanism (the convict is 'less guilty' than the monarch, *i.e.* than *any* monarch) and its strongly anti-clerical bias (the work of the 'mighty destroyers . . . by religion is blest'), and partly from the change that it marks in Wordsworth's poetic allegiances. The poem is not imitation-Gray or imitation-Goldsmith, like *Descriptive Sketches*, but is written in simple and sentimental

---

[1] *Prose Works*, ed. A. B. Grosart, I, 10.
[2] 'Advertisement' to *Guilt and Sorrow* (1842).

anapaests after the manner of the Della Cruscans.[1] Crude though
it is, its composition gave Wordsworth a lot of trouble. The old
leather-bound notebook of his schooldays, which he may have
taken with him on this tour, records a large number of false starts
to the poem, and it was re-written more than once before the
final form was attained which it assumed in *Lyrical Ballads.*

From the Isle of Wight, Wordsworth and Calvert proceeded
on their tour in Calvert's 'whiskey', a kind of light two-wheeled
one-horse carriage. But Calvert's horse was not used to drawing
whiskeys, and, as Dorothy reported to Jane Pollard, 'he began to
caper one day in a most terrible manner, dragged them and their
vehicle into a ditch and broke it to shivers'.[2] Wordsworth and
Calvert both escaped unhurt, 'but they were sufficiently cautious
not to venture again in the same way', and they decided to call
the tour off. Calvert mounted the horse and rode off to the North
of England, and Wordsworth proceeded on foot by gradual stages
to North Wales, where the faithful Jones entertained him 'in the
most delicious of all vales, the Vale of Clwyd'.

Wordsworth may well have been secretly delighted when the
whiskey came to its untimely end. It is always uncomfortable
being dependent on a companion of one's own age, especially
if that companion is a school-fellow. Gray finally quarrelled with
Horace Walpole in the course of their tour. And Calvert, though
good-natured enough, cannot have been a very congenial travelling companion. Years later Wordsworth sent him a complimentary copy of the second edition of *Lyrical Ballads,* 'though
he is fully aware of his friend's indifference to poetry'.[3] *A miso-
mousos* was not exactly the man for Wordsworth. According to
De Quincey Calvert's favourite conversational topic was *oxen,*
though he too pays his tribute to Calvert's kindliness.[4] It was the
younger brother, Raisley Calvert, a much less prosaic person,
who was to leave Wordsworth the all-important legacy in 1795.

---

[1] *e.g.* Charlotte Smith's popular "The Female Exile (1792)" in her *Elegiac Sonnets and Other Poems*, vol. II, 1797.

[2] Dorothy Wordsworth to Jane Pollard, 30 Aug. 1793.

[3] The letter is summarised by de Selincourt in his edition of the *Early Letters,* p. 265.

[4] *Recollections of the Lake Poets,* p. 171.

When Calvert rode off, Wordsworth found himself alone in the middle of Salisbury Plain. In spite of the changes Salisbury Plain has undergone since 1793 it is not difficult to visualise him there. In whatever direction he looked, there was not a sign of human habitation. It must have been an intoxicating experience. For weeks, months, years even, he had never been really alone. Society with its obligations and its restrictions had been exerting its pressures from every side. There was his duty to Annette, his responsibility for Caroline, the respect due to his relations, his obligations as a republican and a reformer. (So we can imagine the internal dialogue proceeding.) He had tried to do the right thing by society, but society had refused to co-operate with him. Nothing had come right; first of all the unwanted baby, then the unobtainable job, then Uncle William's self-righteousness, then the French War, and the poems that no one would read, and the pamphlet that no one would print. But now, at last, he was alone, as he had been long ago after school hours at Hawkshead, with wild nature at its wildest and grandest!

With thoughts like these racing through his head, Wordsworth wandered aimlessly over the Plain for two or three days. 'My ramble', Wordsworth said, when describing his sensations fifty years later, 'left on my mind imaginative impressions the force of which I have felt to this day.'[1] He was particularly impressed, he recalled, by the 'monuments and traces of antiquity, scattered in abundance over that region', and one of the places his wanderings took him to was Stonehenge, already something of a showplace, though not the vulgar showplace it has now become. The mood of exaltation that the Plain inspired terminated in a peculiar mystical experience which is described in Book XII of *The Prelude*:

> I had a reverie and saw the past,
> Saw multitudes of men, and here and there,
> A single Briton in his wolf-skin vest
> With shield and stone-axe, stride across the Wold;
> The voice of spears was heard, the rattling spear
> Shaken by arms of mighty bone, in strength
> Long moulder'd of barbaric majesty.[2]

---

[1] 'Advertisement' to *Guilt and Sorrow* (1842). [2] *Prelude*, XII, ll. 320–6.

A curious phrase follows: 'I called upon the darkness'. His call, whatever it was and to whomsoever addressed, was answered and 'A midnight darkness seem'd to come, and take All objects from my sight'. And then the pitch black was broken by flames. Wordsworth was convinced that he saw a human sacrifice being offered up in the flames of the altar. And dead kings from the tumuli joined the congregation of living worshippers.

Nor was this his only supernatural adventure, as he roamed over Salisbury Plain. He also saw—but this was 'dream', not 'reverie' or 'vision'—some old Druids:

> I saw the bearded Teachers, with white wands
> Uplifted, pointing to the starry sky
> Alternately, and Plain below, while breath
> Of music seem'd to guide them, and the Waste
> Was chear'd with stillness and a pleasant sound.[1]

These experiences of Wordsworth's in August 1793 may or may not impress us today—I, for one, do not find them particularly interesting—but they certainly impressed Wordsworth. Oddly enough he seems to have associated the Ancient Britons of his 'reverie' in some way with the poor of his own time. The earthworks, he says, 'led me unavoidably to compare what we know or guess of these remote times with certain aspects of modern society, and with calamities, principally those consequent upon war, to which, more than other classes of men, the poor are subject'.[2] The inevitability of the comparison may not seem so obvious. The connection, however, was a subjective one. Wordsworth himself was now a poor man, socially rejected, and the war by separating him from Annette was proving calamitous to him personally. It was perhaps natural that in this process of self-identification with Salisbury Plain he should attribute his own troubles to its prehistoric inhabitants.

Wordsworth's self-projection in August 1793 was not limited to Ancient Britons. As he made his way to the Vale of Clwyd by Bath, Bristol, and the valley of the Wye, he found himself taking

---

[1] *Prelude*, XII, ll. 349–53.
[2] 'Advertisement' to *Guilt and Sorrow* (1842).

a new and unsentimental interest in the tramps and beggars who were walking the roads with him. And the theoretical egalitarianism he had learned from Beaupuy now took on a new meaning. He has described the new attitude he found himself adopting to the poor in another passage of Book XII of *The Prelude*:

> When I began to inquire,
> To watch and question those I met, and held
> Familiar talk with them, the lonely roads
> Were schools to me in which I daily read
> With most delight the passions of mankind,
> There saw into the depth of human souls,
> Souls that appear to have no depth at all
> To vulgar eyes.[1]

One of the 'lowly men' whose acquaintance he made when he had left Salisbury Plain behind him was the prototype of Peter Bell, a 'wild rover' with whom Wordsworth walked for some twenty miles in Central Wales, and who told him 'strange stories'. Another humble friend Wordsworth made on this tour was the small heroine of "We are Seven", whom he met among the ruins of Goodrich Castle, on the Wye. Their reappearance in poems written five years later shows how impressionable Wordsworth's mind must have been at this time.

The mood of visionary exaltation which had been inspired by the solitudes of Salisbury Plain coloured Wordsworth's attitude to Nature as well as to Man. The day before he reached Goodrich Castle, he had stopped at Tintern Abbey, and the beauty of the scenery a few miles higher up the Wye revived the ecstasies of his teens. There is an analysis of the changing moods of 1793 in the fifth paragraph of Book XII of *The Prelude*. Translated into prosaic terms, it could be summarised as follows. The year had begun with Wordsworth being more interested in the general problems of political and social reform. But the balance swung from the general to the particular, an interest not in 'social problems' but in the specific cases of this man and that woman.

---

[1] *Prelude*, XII, ll. 161–8.

And this kind of first-hand information was difficult to get hold of
in London:

> therefore did I turn
> To you, ye Pathways, and ye lonely Roads
> Sought you enrich'd with everything I prized,
> With human kindness and with Nature's joy.[1]

There follows an eloquent apostrophe to the 'public road'.
A walking tour is admittedly a second best. The most intoxicating
experience of all is:

> The bliss of walking daily in Life's prime
> Through field or forest with the Maid we love.

But second only to a happy love-affair

> Was that of wandering on from day to day
> Where I could meditate in peace . . .
> Converse with men, where if we meet a face
> We almost meet a friend, on naked Moors
> With long, long ways before, by Cottage Bench
> Or Well-spring where the weary Traveller rests.[2]

The context in which these lines occur makes it clear that they
describe the long solitary walk of August 1793. It was the first
really long walk that Wordsworth had ever taken by himself.
When he went to Italy and the Alps he had had Jones with him all
the time. And when he explored North Wales and climbed up
Snowdon the following year, Jones was with him again.

There were two important differences in the eighteenth century
between long walks on one's own and a walking tour with a
companion. One was that a more serious social stigma attached
to the solitary pedestrian. When Moritz, the German writer,
walked from London to Oxford in 1782 he found that 'A traveller
on foot in this country seems to be considered as a sort of wild
man, or an out-of-the-way being, who is stared at, pitied,
suspected, and shunned by everybody that meets him.'[3] It was less

---

[1] *Prelude*, XII, ll. 123–6.

[2] *Ibid.*, XII, ll. 129–44.

[3] Charles P. Moritz, *Travels, chiefly on foot in 1782* (English translation, 1795),
p. 122.

disreputable if there were two of you. When Coleridge and his Cambridge friend Hucks explored Wales in 1794, though they abandoned, as Hucks says in the book he made out of their adventures, 'all ideas of appearance and gentility', carrying their belongings in 'a wallet or knapsack', they never experienced 'the slightest inconvenience'.[1] The descent, therefore, from Calvert's whiskey to his own two legs was more than a change in Wordsworth's mode of locomotion. It was also a social gesture, a slap in the face of respectability, an identifying of himself with rogues and vagabonds. Equality ceased to be a theoretical doctrine and became a way of life. In all that mattered now the 'wild rover' whom he met in the Wye Valley, and the Little Maid of Goodrich Castle had come to seem as important in the scheme of things as William Pitt—or William Wordsworth.

Another consequence of walking alone was the opportunities it gave for ambulatory composition. The hundred-and-fifty miles that divide Salisbury Plain from the Vale of Clwyd enabled Wordsworth once more to

> teach the sound
> Of Poet's music to strange fields and groves. . . .[2]

But it was a different music from that of *An Evening Walk* and *Descriptive Sketches*. From now on, Wordsworth determined, he would be the poet of humble life:

> Of these, said I, shall be my Song; of these,
> If future years mature me for the task,
> Will I record the praises, making Verse
> Deal boldly with substantial things, in truth . . .
> That justice may be done.[3]

The first product of this determination was the narrative poem in Spenserian stanzas which was finally published in 1842, drastically revised, as *Guilt and Sorrow*. The poem's original title was *Salisbury Plain*. In this its earliest form it records the tragic life-story of a Cumberland woman, now reduced to destitution,

---

[1] J. Hucks, *A Pedestrian Tour through North Wales* (1795), p. 4.
[2] *Prelude*, XII, ll. 139–40.
[3] *Ibid.*, XII, ll. 231–6.

which is told during a night storm to a traveller who had lost
his way on Salisbury Plain.[1] Wordsworth made a start with the
poem during his own wanderings on the Plain, and its composition occupied him on his journey to Jones's cottage in Denbighshire and during the subsequent months. The traveller to whom
the tale is told in this first version is clearly Wordsworth himself,
and his own supernatural experiences on the Plain are assiduously
worked in—the Britons 'with shield and stone-axe', the sacrificial
altar 'fed with living man':

> How deep it groans—the dead,
> Thrilled in their yawning tombs, their helms uprear;
> The sword that slept beneath the warriours head
> Thunders in fiery air: red arms appear
> Uplifted in the gloom and shake the rattling spear.

and the Druidic astronomers, with their long beards and 'wands
uplifted'. It is perhaps significant that the order in which the
ghostly manifestations are catalogued is identical with that in
the autobiographical account already quoted from *The Prelude*.
Wordsworth's 'reveries', it is clear, were a good deal more
substantial than their rather literary character might have suggested. It was a case not of melodrama but of hallucination.
Druids, it will be remembered, were also prominent in the
nightmarish episodes of *The Vale of Esthwaite*.

Salisbury Plain resembles *The Vale of Esthwaite* in another way.
There is precisely the same unco-ordinated collocation of supernatural horror and sober eye-on-the-object realism as in the
earlier poem. The Female Vagrant—as Wordsworth christened
his heroine when excerpting her story to pad out *Lyrical Ballads*—
describes her early life on Derwentwater in charming but meticulous detail:

> Can I forget my seat beneath the thorn,
> My garden stored with peas and mint and thyme,
> And rose and lilly for the sabbath morn,
> The church-inviting bells' delightful chime,

---

[1] This first version has not been printed separately. It can, however, be reconstructed from the variant readings to *Guilt and Sorrow* recorded by de Selincourt
in his edition of *The Poetical Works*, I, 96–118, 334–41.

The merriment and song at shearing time,
My hen's rich nest with long grass overgrown,
The cowslip gathering at the morning prime,
The hazel copse with teeming clusters brown
[Line missing in MS.].

Can I forget the casement where I fed
The red-breast when the fields were whitened o'er,
My snowy kerchiefs on the hawthorn spread,
My humming wheel and glittering table store;
The well-known knocking at the evening door,
The hunted slipper and the blinded game,
That dance that loudly beat the merry floor
The ballad chaunted round the brightening flame,
While down the ravaged hills the storm unheeded came.

But between this pastoral realism and the eerie pictures of Salisbury Plain at night that precede it no connection whatever is established. Like oil and water, the two elements in the poem do not mix. When he revised the poem a year or two later, Wordsworth realised what was wrong and cut out the supernatural stanzas altogether.

The clash between objectivity and subjectivity, between what he saw and what he imagined he saw, was a symptom, in the case of *The Vale of Esthwaite*, of a temporarily disorganised personality. For the moment Wordsworth had become schizophrenic. One side of his personality, the affective, intuitive, inward-looking side of him, had somehow lost touch with the rational, social, outward-looking side. It is possible, as I have suggested, that the earlier split in Wordsworth's nature is to be connected with the break with Mary of Esthwaite Water, and that *The Vale of Esthwaite* should be regarded as in part a kind of private catharsis on his part, an attempt to work the neurosis out of his system. *Salisbury Plain* in its first form is clearly the expression of a similar psychic condition. It fails as poetry, as *The Vale of Esthwaite* did, because the opposite and discordant qualities have neither been balanced nor reconciled. And the literary failure is only explicable, once more, in extra-literary terms. Wordsworth *could not* fuse the warring elements in his poem because he could not control an inner war within himself.

But Wordsworth had discovered something very important about himself in those two or three days on Salisbury Plain. One way of putting it would be to say that he had discovered his subconscious mind. In *The Prelude* he describes his 'mood' on 'the Plain of Sarum' as a conviction

> that in some sort I possess'd
> A privilege, and that a work of mine,
> Proceeding from the depth of untaught things,
> Enduring and creative, might become
> A power like one of Nature's.[1]

The crucial word here is 'privilege'. A poet is different from other people, and superior to them, because he possesses, deep down inside himself, the creative gift. And what that was he had defined in lines immediately preceding this passage:

> a sense
> By which he is enabled to perceive
> Something unseen before . . .[2]

The visions he had had on the Plain proved conclusively that he possessed such a gift. But the discovery that he could see things that nobody had seen before had only been made after he had excluded from his mind all his immediate moral duties and social responsibilities. Annette, Caroline, Dorothy, Uncle William, the importance of republicanism, the wickedness of war—all these ties and convictions had to be forgotten, mentally obliterated, as it were, before the subconscious mind could be brought into play. The accumulated frustrations had made such a period of social irresponsibility inevitable, but a persistence of the mood would have been incompatible with sanity. As he fell into conversation with the casual acquaintances of the public road, the world of social reality flooded back, and Wordsworth was once again the humanitarian and the conscious observer of the external world. It is more than possible that the two moods chased each other back

---

[1] *Prelude*, XII, ll. 308–12.   [2] *Prelude*, XII, ll. 303–5.

and forth. As conscience reasserted itself, the reproachful eyes of Annette must have stared at him out of the darkness. In such circumstances another escape into the world of 'reverie' may well have become an imperious necessity. And in default of the Druids of Salisbury Plain the beauty of natural scenery could still provide such a temporary escape, as the "Lines composed a Few Miles above Tintern Abbey" demonstrate:

> when first
> I came among these hills; when like a roe
> I bounded o'er the mountains, by the sides
> Of the deep rivers, and the lonely streams,
> Wherever nature led me: more like a man
> Flying from something that he dreads than one
> Who sought the thing he loved.

The last part of this quotation was adduced earlier in this book as evidence of Wordsworth's attitude to nature as a youth. In his edition of *The Prelude*, Professor de Selincourt has cited it to define 'his first moral crisis (*i.e.* in August 1793)': 'It is a new thing and typical of his psychological state at this time, that he should come to Nature fleeing from something that he dreads, *i.e.*, in reaction from his moral sufferings. He now finds distraction in purely sensuous pleasure, from which moral feeling and all his deeper "inner faculties" are excluded.'[1] The comment is an admirable one, but it applies, I think, to all of Wordsworth's moral crises. It defines the boy's reaction to the tyranny of the Cooksons, and it defines the adolescent's attitude to an all-too-human Mary, just as it defines the defiance of this young man of twenty-three in the face of the contrariness of human affairs. It remained, indeed, a permanent element I believe, in the attitude of the adult Wordsworth to nature. *The Prelude* might almost be called its rationalisation, though *The Prelude* is, of course, many other things as well.

---

[1] p. 592.

Chapter Four

THE HUMAN HEART

IF poetry does indeed commence, as Wordsworth himself was to maintain, in emotion recollected in tranquillity, a poem written in the middle of a moral crisis is not likely to be a good one. *Salisbury Plain* is not, it must be admitted, a good poem. The Spenserian stanza Wordsworth inherited from Beattie's *Minstrel* is not a suitable vehicle for tragic narrative. And the nineteen stanzas (out of a total of sixty-one) in which the Radical moral is pointed in turgid rhetoric, cannot be said to adorn this tale. But, unsatisfactory though the poem is in its first form, there are some brilliant things in it, and one passage in the Female Vagrant's autobiography is particularly worth attention, since it points the way to some of Wordsworth's greatest triumphs.

Her father had been a 'statesman', that is, a smallholder own- ing the land he farmed, on the side of Derwentwater, who was dependent for his livelihood on a flock of sheep and the fish he caught in the lake. But when she was twenty years old her father got into debt, and 'His little range of water was denied'. Harsh creditors took possession of the property, and the girl and her father had to go:

> Can I forget that miserable hour
> When, from the last hill-top, my sire surveyed,
> Peering above the trees, the steeple tower
> That on his marriage day sweet music made!
> There at my birth my mother's bones were laid
> And there, till then, he hoped his own might rest:
> Bidding me trust in God, he stood and prayed;—
> I could not pray:—by human grief oppressed
> Viewing our glimmering cot through tears that never ceased.[1]

I could not pray. Except for those four words, it is a common- place enough stanza, a superior specimen only of Della Cruscan

---

[1] *The Poetical Works*, ed. E. de Selincourt, I, 108.

sentimentality. But the girl's inability to pray, the conventional words sticking almost involuntarily in her throat, as it were, is an insight of a higher order altogether. In this one touch Wordsworth shows that he had got inside the girl and was feeling with her feelings. For the moment, if only a moment, the dualism of imagination and observation had been transcended.

In his later poems, as the analysis of "She dwelt among the untrodden ways" in Chapter One of this book has exemplified Wordsworth was to exploit this negative form of emotion more fully. But when Matthew, returning from his daughter's grave, meets the beautiful unknown child and

> looked at her, and looked again:
> And did not wish her mine![1]

and when Michael continues, after Luke's defection, to go up to the uncompleted sheepfold,

> And never lifted up a single stone,[2]

Wordsworth was only refining a feeling that is adumbrated in the four words of *Salisbury Plain*. Its essence is the refusal, or inability, to conform to a pattern of behaviour that social convention would prescribe through an instinctive, unformulated loyalty to a different emotional code. The girl ought to have prayed. Not to pray was to disobey her father and to flout the teachings of orthodox Christianity. But the prayer would have been insincere. Only a shallow and selfish girl could have prayed under those special circumstances. She wins our pity and sympathy not only in spite of her disregard of her father's bidding and the consolations of religion, but actually because of this disregard. There are occasions—Cordelia's is the classic case—when it is *right* to disappoint one's father and to deny the obligations of conventional goodness. The one compensatory condition is that the convention-flouter must suffer acutely, as Wordsworth's heroine does, when making the refusal.

The intuition was an isolated one. The importance of the passage is that it represents the complete fusion, for the first time

---

[1] "The Two April Mornings", ll. 55-6.   [2] "Michael", l. 466.

in Wordsworth's poetry, of objective and subjective elements. The best passages in *An Evening Walk* had been strictly objective, though they undoubtedly owe the precision and delicacy with which they are drawn to the subjective associations that Esthwaite Water possessed for him. But in the heroine of *Salisbury Plain* Wordsworth has momentarily combined outward-looking and inward-looking. The pathos of the passage derives from the clash it describes in her between the claims of society and the claims of the individual. Unfortunately, except in this one passage, the claims and obligations of society are so distorted and caricatured in the poem that a genuinely tragic tension is not maintained. For the consolidation of this new kind of poetry—essentially narrative and dramatic as against the descriptive and reflective mode of the earlier poems—the personal crisis had first to be resolved. And the later months of 1793 contributed little or nothing to its resolution. After some weeks with Jones in the Vale of Clwyd Wordsworth proceeded to the Lake District, which he had not seen for four years, and stayed with relatives and friends there, including the Calverts, who owned a farmhouse called Windy Brow, near Keswick, where he was always welcome. This is a period in his life about which we know little or nothing.[1] He never

---

[1] The intriguing suggestion has been made that Wordsworth may have been in France at this time, either with Annette or (more probably) in an abortive attempt to see her. According to Carlyle, who is hardly likely to have misunderstood him over a matter that he was himself so interested in, Wordsworth claimed in 1840 in a private conversation with Carlyle to have been an eyewitness of the execution of Antoine Joseph Gorsas, the Girondist deputy and publicist. Gorsas was executed on 7 Oct. 1793, and it would have been perfectly possible for an Englishman with Girondist connections like Wordsworth to land near Caen, which was in Girondist hands in the late summer of 1793, and then make his way to Paris. The details of the hypothesis have been worked out by G. M. Harper (*William Wordsworth*, 2nd edition, 1929, pp. 151–2), and some further confirmation has since been provided by J. R. MacGillivray, *Times Literary Supplement*, 12 June 1930. It may also be worth pointing out that Wordsworth told W. F. Hook (*The Life and Letters of Walter Farquhar Hook*, 6th edition, 1881, p. 304), in a letter dated 5 Feb. 1840, that he had lived 'nearly four years' of his life 'in countries where Popery was the established or prevailing religion'. In fact, so far as is known, he had only spent 37 months in such countries by 1840. If he had also been in France during the late summer and autumn of 1793 'nearly four years' would have been a round figure not far from the truth. Nevertheless the hypothesis cannot, I fear, be accepted. Its initial premise is that Wordsworth

referred to it specifically in any of his later poems or letters, and the silence suggests a condition of numbed unhappiness. It was only in February 1794 that he and Dorothy were at last reunited. They had not seen each other for three and a half years, but the time that they spent together alone at Windy Brow in March and April proved how indispensable they still were to each other. The partial revision of *An Evening Walk*, which dates from this period, suggests that it was also a further turning-point in his poetic evolution. Raisley Calvert now offered Wordsworth a share of his income. The French war showed no sign of ending and the question of the maintenance of Annette and Caroline did not arise, and thus the immediate problem of bread and butter became less acute. He had already decided that he could not 'bow down' his mind to take orders—'and as for the law', he told Mathews, 'I have neither strength of mind, purse, or constitution, to engage in that pursuit'.[1] Literary journalism, however, still seemed a possibility, and in the summer of 1794 he and Mathews were seriously discussing the starting of a Radical monthly that was to be called "The Philanthropist". Raisley Calvert, who was a consumptive, died in January 1795, leaving Wordsworth a legacy of £900, and there then followed some unproductive months in London. August was spent with some new Bristol friends called Pinney—he had no difficulty apparently at this time of his life in turning the merest acquaintances into devoted friends—and the Pinneys immediately provided a handsome furnished house, rent-free, in the north-west corner of Dorset, in which he and Dorothy were at last able to set up house together. The six-year old dream had come true.

The house was called Racedown Lodge. It had been built in the 1760s by one of the Pinneys, a local nabob, as 'a lee port in

was not able to mention the episode later, except in the unguarded moment with Carlyle, because it involved a disclosure of his liaison with Annette. But the Annette affair was an open secret among Wordsworth's intimates, and it seems extraordinary that one of them, *e.g.* Crabb Robinson, should never have referred in a private letter or journal to so exciting an episode as the 1793 expedition—if it did ever take place. The easier alternative is either that Carlyle misunderstood Wordsworth or that Wordsworth was romancing (a not unknown occurrence).

[1] Wordsworth to William Mathews, 17 Feb. 1794.

a storm' and, though small, was elegant and comfortable. Among other conveniences, it contained a really good collection of books —which had not, however, been added to since the house was built. Wordsworth's feelings, as he set out for Racedown from Bristol for the first time, are described at the beginning of *The Prelude*. Dorothy told a friend that his 'living in the unsettled way in which he has hitherto lived in London is altogether unfavourable to mental exertion'.[1] In the phraseology of *The Prelude* this becomes:

>   it is shaken off,
> As by miraculous gift 'tis shaken off,
> That burthen of my own unnatural self,
> The heavy weight of many a weary day
> Not mine, and such as were not made for me.
> Long months of peace (if such bold word accord
> With any promises of human life),
> Long months of ease and undisturb'd delight
> Are mine in prospect. . . .[2]

But ease and peace are not the only things he is looking forward to; already—he says—he feels a creative urge within him:

>   the hope
> Of active days, of dignity and thought,
> Of prowess in an honourable field,
> Pure passions, virtue, knowledge, and delight,
> The holy life of music and of verse.[3]

The first-fruits of the leisure of Racedown and the stimulating company of Dorothy were a revised and expanded version of *Salisbury Plain*. It was now called *Adventures on Salisbury Plain*, and by eliminating the rhetorical moralisings and the supernatural horrors Wordsworth succeeded in giving the poem a unity of atmosphere it had previously lacked. He had met Coleridge once or twice in Bristol just before moving into Racedown and his recitation of the poem to Coleridge in 1796 was an experience the

---

[1] Dorothy Wordsworth to Jane Marshall, 2 Sept. 1795.
[2] *Prelude*, I, ll. 21–9.   [3] *Ibid.*, I, ll. 50–4.

latter never forgot.[1] What most impressed Coleridge, as we have seen, was the way 'forms, incidents, and situations of which, from the common view, custom had bedimmed all the lustre' were bathed in an atmosphere of 'the ideal world'—the combination, in other words, of observation and intuition. To an enlarged version of the Female Vagrant's[2] story Wordsworth had now added the parallel plot of a benevolent murderer—a sailor whose guilty secret prevented his returning to his beloved wife, and who finally gives himself up to the authorities after an accidental encounter with her as she lies dying. In spite of the crudity of the story, the sailor's sense of guilt is conveyed with considerable power. Wordsworth has to some extent got inside this guilty sailor as he had got inside the Female Vagrant, when she found herself driven with her father from their Derwentwater farm. In both cases he was, no doubt, drawing partly on his own experience. It may not be altogether a coincidence that at the time he was at work on this conscience-stricken sailor, a letter got through from Annette, the first news apparently that he had had of her and of Caroline for over two and a half years.

Wordsworth told Francis Wrangham, a young poet with whom he was collaborating at this time in an abortive Juvenalian satire on the Government, that *Adventures on Salisbury Plain* was written 'to expose the vices of the penal law and the calamities of war as they affect individuals'. The final effect, however, that the poem leaves is of a less limited objective. It is almost the whole social order of eighteenth-century England that is exposed. The revolutionary conclusion is left implicit, but there can be no doubt what the reader's reaction is expected to be to a society that harries the woman and the sailor, both of whom are fundamentally good at heart, in the relentless manner described in the poem. If it makes depressing and often unconvincing reading, it remains unforgettable nevertheless because of the intensity of the

---

[1] See, however, note 1, on p. 15 above.
[2] The woman is not called 'The Female Vagrant' in the text of the poem. It is the title Wordsworth gave to the long extract from the poem (in its revised form) that is printed in *Lyrical Ballads* (1798).

pessimism. Never before in the whole of English literature had the process by which those that have not are deprived of even that which they have, been painted in such sombre colours. Wordsworth's later attempts to mitigate the social criticism in the version that he published in 1842 as *Guilt and Sorrow* are almost comically ineffective.

The next and most ambitious literary product of the Racedown period was the five-act tragedy called *The Borderers*. Between its composition in the autumn and winter of 1796 and the completion of the revised and expanded *Salisbury Plain* nearly a year had elapsed, but the interval is insufficient to explain the striking differences between the two works. There is an unsolved problem here. The change in Wordsworth's outlook has been too often reduced to the books he may or may not have read. Godwin's *Political Justice*, in particular, has been a veritable King Charles's head to Wordsworthian commentators, though it is difficult to find any two of them agreeing as to the nature or extent of its influence on him. The period of his immersion in Godwin has been variously ascribed to 1793, 1795, and 1796. And a variety of dates has also been suggested for the recovery from Godwinism. According to H. W. Garrod, for example, *The Borderers* is to be regarded as a sort of dramatic exposition of Godwin's philosophy.[1] More recently, however, the trend of critical opinion has been to accept de Selincourt's view that *The Borderers* was intended to refute Godwin.[2] Wordsworth certainly possessed a copy of *Political Justice* during the gestatory period preceding the composition of *The Borderers*. In a letter to Mathews, dated 21 March 1796, he says: 'I have received from Montague, Godwyn's second edition. I expect to find the work much improved. I cannot say that I have been encouraged in this hope by the perusal of the second preface, which is all I have yet looked into. Such a piece of barbarous writing I have not often seen. It contains scarce one sentence decently written.' This is not the voice of

---

[1] In the second edition (1927) of his *Wordsworth: Lectures and Essays*, pp. 91–3, Garrod has announced himself a convert to de Selincourt's view.

[2] See his edition of *The Prelude*, pp. 584–7, and his *Oxford Lectures on Poetry* (1934).

a disciple clearly. But is it that of a disillusioned enthusiast either? The mis-spelling of Godwin's name—which is repeated in later letters as well as in an unpublished prose fragment of 1799 which denounces 'such books as Mr. Godwyn's Mr. Paley's and those of the whole tribe of authors of that class'[1]—does not suggest a close acquaintance with Godwin's writings.[2] Indeed, the most recent editor of *Political Justice* finds it 'hard to believe that the influence of Godwin on Wordsworth was at all significant'. He adds that if Oswald, the villain of *The Borderers*, is really intended to be a mouthpiece of Godwinism, this only shows Wordsworth's 'profound ignorance of most of Godwin's teaching'.[3] It must be added that it also shows—the exaltation of David Hartley's *Observations on Man* as a major influence on Wordsworth's thought is another example of the same fallacy— a profound ignorance on the part of the commentators of the way Wordsworth's mind worked. Unlike Shelley, in whom *Political Justice* effected an intellectual revolution, the young Wordsworth did not generally absorb ideas directly from books, but at second-hand through the conversation of his friends. His intellectual mentors, such as Taylor, Beaupuy and Coleridge, took the place of books. What Wordsworth went to books for were for facts and for poetry. It is significant that his library, at the time of his death, contained none of the philosophical classics, and very few books that could be called philosophical in any sense.

If *The Borderers* is not an exposition or refutation of Godwinism, what is it? The difference from *Salisbury Plain* is certainly a striking one. That poem had been concerned with the fate of individuals crushed under the Juggernaut of modern society; its villain was the whole contemporary social order. In *The Borderers*, on the other hand, the action takes place in the thirteenth century, just after the Battle of Evesham apparently, and the social order— so far as there can be said to be one at all in the play, it can only be described as one of benevolent anarchy—is essentially incidental.

---

[1] See de Selincourt's *Prelude* (1932 re-issue), p. 608A.

[2] Unlike that of many poets Wordsworth's spelling is normally impeccably accurate. It is most unusual to find him mis-spelling a proper name.

[3] *Enquiry concerning Political Justice*, ed. F. E. L. Priestley (1946), III, 102–3.

All the emphasis is on the individual *dramatis personæ*, especially Marmaduke, the noble and virtuous leader of this robber band operating on the Scotch border, and his lieutenant Oswald, whose motiveless malignity is the real subject of the play. 'Let us suppose', Wordsworth writes in the remarkable prefatory essay that he eventually discarded, 'a young man of great intellectual power yet without any solid principles of genuine benevolence. His master passions are pride and the love of distinction. He has deeply imbibed a spirit of enterprise in a tumultuous age. He goes into the world and is betrayed into a great crime.'[1] Oswald is the incarnation of this supposition. The idiom of the play is imitation-Shakespeare and unfortunately Oswald often has to out-Iago Iago. Some of the results are decidedly unhappy. As drama and dramatic poetry, it must be admitted, *The Borderers* possesses little or no interest, but it should not really be read as drama but as concealed autobiography. Why did Wordsworth find it necessary to suppose this strange young man, who is 'betrayed into a great crime'? This is the question the modern reader cannot help asking. One answer that naturally suggests itself to us now is that Wordsworth is himself the young man, that his abandonment of Annette is the great crime, and that the play is one more expression of the sense of guilt with which Wordsworth was haunted at this time. It is difficult to avoid some such interpretation of the play, though Oswald's crime—he had marooned his captain on an uninhabited islet in the Mediterranean—was very different from Wordsworth's.

The discarded preface is interesting in this connection. Parts of it read almost like a retraction of *Salisbury Plain*. Wordsworth's hypothetical young man has 'strong misanthropic feelings'. 'He has rebelled against the world and the laws of the world, and he regards them as tyrannical masters; convinced that he is right in some of his conclusions, he nourishes a contempt for mankind, the more dangerous because he has been led to it by reflection.' Finally, to make up for the traditional religion and morality he has

---

[1] The discarded preface has been printed by de Selincourt in his edition of *The Poetical Works*, I, 345–9.

discarded, he has become superstitious and is now a believer in 'invisible agents'. No doubt this unpleasant young man is not an exact or exclusive portrait of Wordsworth in his revolutionary phase. Robespierre's features can be detected, and there were probably other English and French contemporaries who also contributed to it.[1] The sin of which they are all guilty—the net is wide enough to include even Godwin's philosophy—is pride. Pride is the root of all this evil, pride in their intelligence, pride in their freedom from vulgar illusions, pride in their hardihood in following an argument to its paradoxical conclusion. Wordsworth does not draw the political corollary—a distrust of ready-made systems and constitutional blue-prints—but the implications of *The Borderers* are clear enough. He is no longer, in the political sense of the word, a revolutionary, and he has disavowed once and for all the systematising rationalism of the eighteenth century of which the French Revolution was the political manifestation.

By writing *The Borderers* Wordsworth was able to clear his mind of cant. But the catharsis was a private one and the play has little or no literary interest. As poetry it is decidedly inferior to *Adventures on Salisbury Plain*. No such apology, however, is required for its successor *The Ruined Cottage*, which Wordsworth finished in the spring of 1797. Here at last we meet poetry of the very highest quality.

The Ruined Cottage was eventually worked into Book I of *The Excursion*, and this is the form in which the poem is generally read today.[2] But the philosophical Scotchman, the Wanderer of *The Excursion*, whose comments and biography now make up nearly half of Book I, was a later accretion, and in the poem's original form the story of Margaret and her husband is related by

---

[1] The lineaments of Falkland, the villain-hero of Godwin's novel *Things as They Are: or, The Adventures of Caleb Williams* (1794), can certainly be detected in it. Godwin the novelist was perhaps a more important influence on Wordsworth than Godwin the philosopher.

[2] A text that is considerably closer to the poem that Wordsworth wrote in 1797 will be found in Helen Darbishire's edition of *The Excursion* (1949), pp. 379–399. My quotations are all based on this version, which Miss Darbishire dates Jan.–Feb. 1798.

a colourless pedlar who lets the tragic facts speak for themselves.
The story is a simple one, as the narrator admits:

> 'Tis a common tale
> By moving accidents uncharactered,
> A tale of silent suffering, hardly clothed
> In bodily form, and to the grosser sense
> But ill adapted, scarcely palpable
> To him who does not think.[1]

The cottage that has become a ruin had been recently inhabited
by a weaver and his wife and their two children. But Robert
fell ill, and when he recovered, he could find no one to employ
him or his loom. Their savings had gone, and after a miserable
interval of unemployment Robert disappeared one morning to
join the army. He never came back, though Margaret, gradually
becoming weaker and more slovenly, kept on hoping against
hope for his return. The baby died, the cottage began to collapse
and to let in the rain, and Margaret finally caught a chill:

> Stranger, here
> In sickness she remained, and here she died,
> Last human tenant of these ruined walls.[2]

This was the first poem of Wordsworth's that Coleridge read
when he paid the short visit to Racedown in June 1797 which
was the beginning of their intimacy. Coleridge was enormously
impressed with it. The poem, he wrote at the time, is 'superior,
I hesitate not to aver, to anything in our language which in any
way resembles it',[3] and this verdict was repeated as late as 1815, in
a letter to Lady Beaumont: '*The Ruined Cottage*, which I have ever
thought the finest poem in our language, comparing it with any
of the same or similar *length*'.[4] More recently it has been described
by Mr. F. R. Leavis, in an acute essay, as 'the finest thing that
Wordsworth wrote'.[5]

---

[1] ll. 486–91 (=*Excursion*, I, ll. 636–9).
[2] ll. 740–2 (=*Excursion*, I, ll. 914–16). Text partly from Coleridge's letter to
J. P. Estlin, written from Racedown, June 1797.
[3] Coleridge to J. P. Estlin, June 1797.
[4] Coleridge to Lady Beaumont, 3 Apr. 1815.
[5] *Revaluation* (1936), p. 179.

Technically, there are two points of special interest about *The Ruined Cottage*. One is that it is in blank verse. Apart from *The Borderers* and a fine fragmentary address to Milton probably written at Cambridge, it was Wordsworth's first serious exercise in the metre in which most of his greatest poetry was to be written. The original conclusion—the first part of the poem to be composed, according to Wordsworth's own account—betrays from time to time the influence of Augustan tragedy:

> Five tedious years
> She lingered in unquiet widowhood
> A wife and widow. Needs must it have been
> A sore heart-wasting. Master, I have heard
> That in that broken arbour she would sit
> The idle length of half a sabbath day
> There—where you see the toadstool's lazy head,
> And when a dog passed by she still would quit
> The shade and look abroad. On this old Bench
> For hours she sate, and evermore, her eye
> Was busy in the distance, shaping things
> Which made her heart beat quick. Seest thou that path?
> The greensward now has broken its grey line;
> There to and fro she paced through many a day
> Of the warm summer, from a belt of flax
> That girt her waist spinning the long-drawn thread
> With backward steps. . . .[1]

But, although there are echoes here of such things as Home's *Douglas* (one of the sources, incidentally, of the blank verse of *The Borderers*), the dominant influence is that of William Crowe's *Lewesdon Hill* (1788). In later life Wordsworth praised Crowe's 'excellent loco-descriptive Poem' more than once, but it has not hitherto been known that he first got to know the poem at Racedown. An unpublished letter from Azariah Pinney, written on 26 November 1795, now makes this certain. 'I shall send you by this opportunity,' Pinney wrote, 'Luesdon Hill, and Louvet, but will keep Madame Roland till I have the pleasure of seeing

---

[1] ll. 696–712 (=*Excursion*, I, ll. 871–87). Text from Coleridge's letter to Estlin.

you.'[1] The hill that was the subject of Crowe's poem is only a mile or two from Racedown Lodge, so that the present was eminently suitable. That Wordsworth read the poem—which has considerable merit, apart from the really admirable blank verse in which it is written—with care and attention is proved by the presence in it of one of the most famous of all the phrases in *The Prelude*, 'a dedicated Spirit'. Other echoes of Crowe in *The Prelude* make it almost certain that the verbal identity is not, as it might otherwise have been thought, a coincidence.

A more important technical point is the use of significant detail. The passage just quoted owes most of its reality to the toadstool, the dog, the overgrown path and the belt of flax. Without these concrete particulars, it would not differ much from the run of Della Cruscan descriptions, vague and generalised, such as Southey's poem on the same subject or 'Perdita' Robinson's "The Widow's Home".[2] Wordsworth's detail is significant in the sense that it illustrates or symbolises the central meaning of the poem. His detail has here become functional, whereas it was only decorative in *An Evening Walk*. The grey line of the path that has been broken by the invading green of the long grass is not only a careful piece of observation but in a sense typifies the process of ruin which has overtaken everything human and man-made in the poem. And the toadstool is not simply a picturesque natural object that adds colour to the description. Its primary function is to remind the reader that nature's invasion of the cottage must not be considered beneficent. The toadstool, in this context, is the symbol of a moral defeat.

Wordsworth's discovery of the potentialities of symbolic detail marks one further stage in the fusion of the objective and the sub-

---

[1] I am indebted to Lady Pinney for permission to use this letter. 'Louvet' is no doubt *Quelques notices pour l'histoire, et le récit de mes perils depuis le 31 Mai 1793* (1795)—or possibly one of the two English translations of the book that appeared in 1795. 'Madame Roland' is presumably *Appel à l'impartiale posterité* (1795).

[2] Southey's "The Ruined Cottage", one of his 'English Eclogues', was not written until 1799 and may owe something to Wordsworth's poem. "The Widow's Home" will be found in Mary Robinson's *Lyrical Tales* (1800), a collection, as its title indicates, of facile imitations of *Lyrical Ballads*.

jective that began in *Salisbury Plain*. But the use of physical objects like the grass and the toadstool, brilliant though it is, is not the most important achievement in *The Ruined Cottage*. The poem's greatness derives from the attitude that Wordsworth and his narrator adopt to Robert and Margaret. In a sense, it is a completely detached attitude. There is no condescension, no criticism, no sentimentality or exaggeration. Wordsworth does not smile, simper, deplore, or applaud, he simply states. There can be no question here of either the guilty conscience or the grudge against society that was certainly present in *Salisbury Plain*. The pride that he had been wrestling with in *The Borderers* has been replaced by a healthy humility. Wordsworth, up to a point, is simply a recorder of events. As his own note makes clear, the basis of the poem is observation: 'the state in which I represent Robert's mind to be I had frequent opportunities of *observing* at the commencement of our rupture with France in '93'. 'All that relates to Margaret and the ruined cottage etc., was taken from *observations* made in the South-West of England.'[1] But though a good observer may make a good reporter, a good poet must also be emotionally involved. A strong subjective element is also present in the poem, if it is not easily defined.

Some of Wordsworth's biographers have tried to give the poem a personal interpretation. Margaret's survival for exactly five years after Robert's departure is certainly curious. In 1797 when the first draft of *The Ruined Cottage* was completed five years had elapsed since Wordsworth had left Annette 'A wife and widow'. And the fact that the five years was later changed to nine might suggest that Wordsworth was anxious to cover up an indiscretion. I suspect, however, that it is a mere coincidence. There is a pathetic soldier's widow with two children in *An Evening Walk*, and as the passage describing them is to be found in the first draft of that poem (1788?) one widow at least can have no connection with Annette. I doubt whether any of the other widows and deserted mothers have either. Margaret, the Female Vagrant, Martha Ray, Ruth and the others are primarily social outcasts, the pathetic flotsam and jetsam of an imperfect social system like

---

[1] I.F. note to *The Excursion*. My italics.

Simon Lee, the Idiot Boy, the Leechgatherer and the Cumberland Beggar. Their sex and motherhood is not the real point about them. The real point about them as about all Wordsworth's most convincing heroes and heroines is their unhappiness. He was profoundly sorry for the world's failures, the unwanted, the unloved, not because Annette was unwanted or unloved (that heroic soul could always find for herself a social function), but because during at least three periods of his life he had known the bitter humiliation of social failure himself. In the draper's shop at Penrith, in the miserable period after the quarrel with Mary of Esthwaite Water, and in the crisis of 1793, Wordsworth had experienced most of Margaret's miseries. In a sense he *was* Margaret. But the shame, the rancour and the frustration had to be outgrown and lived down before he could look back on his own past calmly and dispassionately. The writing of *The Ruined Cottage* is evidence that at last, four years after the last of the crises, he had acquired the necessary emotional readjustment and a healthy balance of social detachment and commitment.

The reconciliation was accelerated by Dorothy Wordsworth. Her role in this phase of her brother's recovery can be compared with Taylor's and Fleming's at Hawkshead. And the place co-operated with her. In retrospect Racedown seemed to Dorothy 'the place dearest to my recollections upon the whole surface of this island'.[1] It was, she said, 'the first home I had', and it was precisely the creation of a home, with the emotional security that the word implies, that was the essential service she performed for Wordsworth. There was even a child in the home. Living with them, and theoretically helping to pay their bills, was little Basil Montagu, the motherless son of Wordsworth's Godwinian friend. He is the Edward of the "Anecdote for Fathers, shewing how the Art of Lying may be taught". And Wordsworth's progress in human understanding at Racedown may be gauged by comparing this poem, and its smiling acknowledgment of the validity of the boy's irrational logic, with the postscript to a letter written soon after they settled there. 'Basil is quite well', Wordsworth writes in this postscript, '*quant au physique, mais pour le moral il-y-a*

---

[1] *Memoirs of William Wordsworth* (1851), I, 94.

bien à craindre. Among other things he lies like a little devil.'[1] The little devil was three years old, when this uncharitable comment was made! "Anecdote for Fathers" was written only two years later, but in those two years Wordsworth had acquired a new humility. It was perhaps the most important lesson that his wise and affectionate sister taught him. In Dorothy's ethical system the importance of the other person's point of view even extended to birds and insects. A little-known poem in the Lucy series ("Among all lovely things my Love had been") records an affecting incident of their first autumn at Racedown which centred round a glow-worm. Dorothy had never seen one, and when Wordsworth, riding back late one night, found a glow-worm, he carefully conveyed it on a leaf to their garden:

> The whole next day, I hoped, and hoped with fear;
> At night the Glow-worm shone beneath the Tree:
> I led my Lucy to the spot, 'Look here!'
> Oh! joy it was for her and joy for me!

Wordsworth remained a philosophical pessimist throughout the Racedown period, but episodes such as this must have helped to take the bitterness out of his pessimism.

In July 1797 the Wordsworths, little Basil and their admirable maid Peggy transferred themselves to Alfoxden, a small manor house in the Quantocks that was only a few miles from the Coleridges' cottage at Nether Stowey. They had been economical at Racedown, living only on vegetables at one time and were not in the least alarmed apparently by the rent of £23 which the new house was to cost them. It must have been a most attractive place then. Hazlitt spent a night at Alfoxden the following June, 'in an old room', as he described it twenty-five years later, 'with blue hangings, and covered with the round-faced family portraits of the age of George I and II and from the wooded declivity of the adjoining park that overlooked my window, at the dawn of day, could—

"hear the loud stag speak".'[2]

---

[1] Wordsworth to Francis Wrangham, 7 Mar. 1796.
[2] "My First Acquaintance with Poets."

The lease had been negotiated by Coleridge's friend Thomas Poole, a local squire with Radical views, who soon became one of Wordsworth's best friends too (he is the original of Michael). And the first poem that Wordsworth wrote at Alfoxden, the lost *Somersetshire Tragedy*, was the result of an early walk that Poole took with the two poets to the scene of a recent murder, 'Walford's Gibbet', as the place is still called, about half-way between Nether Stowey and Alfoxden. Poole had known this murderer well—he was a charcoal-burner, good-tempered, generous, popular, and enormously strong—and the story he told them impressed Wordsworth so much that he decided to base a poem on it. At the request of the two poets Poole also wrote a detailed account of the murder in prose.

With the exception of "The Old Cumberland Beggar", which was begun at Racedown and finished at Alfoxden, the *Somersetshire Tragedy* was the only poem of any length that Wordsworth wrote between the first draft of *The Ruined Cottage* and *Lyrical Ballads*. It is a minor disaster that Gordon Wordsworth, the poet's grandson, destroyed the only MS. of the poem on the ground that 'It was in no way calculated to add to his reputation, and had even less poetical merit than "The Convict", the only one of his published poems to which it bears resemblance'.[1] A somewhat less unkind verdict had been pronounced by J. Dykes Campbell, the Coleridge expert, who thought the poem 'one of the great poet's failures—not more of a failure, perhaps, than some which he did not himself recognize as such, but no better'.[2] Failure or not as poetry it can hardly have failed to be a document of the greatest psychological interest. The poem consisted of some 400 lines of realistic narrative, and it is difficult to resist the suspicion that its real offence was a contravention of Victorian notions of propriety. The Wordsworths, it will be remembered, took similar precautions to prevent the liaison with Annette Vallon being discovered. The fullest account of the *Somersetshire Tragedy* is to be found in the second edition of *The Quantocks and their Associations* (1891) by William Luke Nichols. In 1800 Wordsworth had given Poole

---

[1] Note dated May 1931 in MS. D.C.I, 37A (Wordsworth Museum, Grasmere).
[2] *Athenæum*, 6 Sept. 1890.

copies of a number of his shorter poems, including the only MS. of the *Somersetshire Tragedy*, and these MSS. were eventually bought by Nichols, a Somersetshire clergyman living near Alfoxden, from Poole's heir. Nichols had intended to publish the poem, but on his death his brother decided against publication and the notebook was bought by Gordon Wordsworth, who cut out the seven leaves containing the *Somersetshire Tragedy*. The mutilated notebook, complete with Gordon Wordsworth's apologia, is now in the Wordsworth Museum at Grasmere.

The poem cannot have been a very hair-raising performance if a Victorian clergyman contemplated publishing it. Nichols himself only described it as 'more suited to the sombre muse of nature's sternest painter, Crabbe, than the cheerful poet of Rydal Mount'.[1] The story that the poem recounts, as summarised by Nichols—unfortunately he does not quote a single line of it—suggests a persistence and intensification of the objective realism of *The Ruined Cottage*. John Walford—'poor Jack Walford', as the village still called him—had fallen in love with Ann Rice ('the Agnes of Wordsworth's poem'), but the match was opposed by his stepmother. While in the woods he was pursued soon after this and solicited by 'a poor stupid creature, almost an idiot', called Jenny, by whom he had a child. The parish officers then gave Walford the alternatives of marrying the girl or giving security for the infant's maintenance, and from pique at his stepmother's unrelenting opposition to Ann he decided to marry Jenny. The marriage was a failure from the start and instead of going home at night he used 'to linger about the homes of the neighbours in the manner graphically described in the poem of Wordsworth'. A fortnight after the marriage, Walford gave Jenny a shilling to spend on cider in the next village, but as it was dark she insisted on his coming with her and on the way there they quarrelled, and in a sudden fit of temper he killed her with a blow of the fist. He was hanged on the spot where the murder was committed. A few minutes before the end, he asked if Ann Rice was there and they had a short, whispered colloquy in the cart. Walford's last words were: 'I am guilty of the crime that I am

---

[1] *Op. cit.*, p. 41.

going to die for, but I did it without foreintending it, and I hope God and the world have forgiven me.'

> All were amazed, afraid to breathe. It was a silence to be felt. The hum of that vast multitude was so hushed that *even the twittering of the birds in the neighbouring woods was distinctly audible.* He opened his hand, the handkerchief fell; and he died instantaneously and without a struggle; a shivering sound arose, produced by the spectators drawing their breath forcibly through their teeth at the moment. A dead silence succeeded for some ten minutes, when the people began slowly to disperse, discussing in whispered tones the sad fate of him, for whom probably not a single human being present went away without a feeling of pity.[1]

The poetic possibilities of Walford's crime are obvious enough. Why then did Wordsworth not complete the poem? According to Nichols 'it bears neither title nor epigraph, some of the lines are unfinished, and the whole poem shows signs of perfunctory labour and haste'.[2] One reason may have been that Wordsworth was interrupted. Poole's influence had succeeded in interesting Covent Garden Theatre in *The Borderers*, and this involved first of all the preparation of an abbreviated text of the play and then an expedition to London to discuss further alterations. In the end 'the piece was *judiciously* returned as not calculated for the Stage',[3] but by the time Wordsworth was back at Alfoxden it

---

[1] *Op. cit.*, p. 47. In this passage Nichols is merely summarising Poole's account of the execution. Poole's "John Walford", a most impressive piece of writing, which Coleridge had contemplated printing in *The Friend*, eventually appeared in *The Bath and Bristol Magazine ; or, Western Miscellany*, II (1833), 168–79. Poole was 68 in 1833 and his statement, in a prefatory note signed 'Quantockius', that he had been asked 'to draw up the story in writing' by Wordsworth and Southey during a walk near the site of the execution must have been due to a failure of memory. Nichols makes it clear that it was Coleridge, not Southey, who accompanied Wordsworth and Poole. Poole dates the narrative Mar. 1797, but this too is almost certainly wrong, as the Wordsworths were then still at Racedown. It appears from Nichols's summary of it that Wordsworth's poem, though based on Poole's narrative, did not stick slavishly to the facts recorded there. Thus the description of Walford lingering round the homes of his neighbours after the marriage, which Nichols praises for its vividness, has no counterpart in Poole's version.

[2] *Op. cit.*, p. 40.

[3] I.F. note.

was January. In the two or three months that had elapsed, he may well have found that the tragic mood of the poem's first draft had melted away. By the beginning of 1798 the pessimism of Racedown had melted into a temperate optimism. There was some good in almost everybody and in almost every situation—a creditable conclusion but one that can hardly have been compatible with the Crabbe-like realism with which he had drawn the sordid amours of Jenny and Walford.

In any case, Wordsworth had temporarily lost interest in narrative poems written in blank verse. He was now busy with those experiments 'to ascertain how far the language of conversation in the middle and lower classes of society is adapted to the purposes of poetic pleasure', which were published later in the year as *Lyrical Ballads*. The first experiment in this mode, a collaboration with Coleridge in the ballad that eventually became *The Ancient Mariner*, had ended in an agreement to divide the labour. Coleridge's ballads were to be on supernatural, 'or at least romantic', themes; Wordsworth's were 'to give the charm of novelty to things of everyday, and to excite a feeling analogous to the supernatural, by awakening the mind's attention to the lethargy of custom, and directing it to the loveliness and the wonders of the world before us'. That at any rate is Coleridge's account of it in Chapter XIV of his *Biographia Literaria* (1817). But it is probably not the whole story as regards Wordsworth's ballads. While kicking his heels in London during the negotiations with Covent Garden Theatre Wordsworth had seen a good deal of Southey, who was also experimenting with ballads on modern themes at this time. It is possible that Southey may have drawn his attention to another contemporary balladist—William Blake. Wordsworth was certainly one of the earliest of Blake's admirers. We now know that in or about 1804 four of Blake's poems were entered into his Commonplace Book. They were "Holy Thursday" and "Laughing Song" from *Songs of Innocence*, "The Tiger" from *Songs of Experience*, and "I love the jocund dance" from *Poetical Sketches*. How much earlier he knew Blake's poems it is impossible to say, but the one poem that he wrote on this visit to London in 1797 is curiously Blake-like. Susan is one of the country girls in "Laughing Song" and it may not be simply a coincidence that Wordsworth's poem is "The Reverie of Poor Susan":[1]

> At the corner of Wood Street, when daylight appears,
> Hangs a Thrush that sings loud, it has sung for three years:
> Poor Susan has passed by the spot, and has heard
> In the silence of morning the song of the Bird.
>
> 'Tis a note of enchantment; what ails her? She sees
> A mountain ascending, a vision of trees;
> Bright volumes of vapour through Lothbury glide,
> And a river flows on through the vale of Cheapside.
>
> Green pastures she views in the midst of the dale,
> Down which she so often has tripped with her pail;
> And a single small cottage, a nest like a dove's,
> The one only dwelling on earth that she loves.
>
> She looks, and her heart is in heaven: but they fade,
> The mist and the river, the hill and the shade:
> The stream will not flow, and the hill will not rise,
> And the colours have all passed away from her eyes!

Wordsworth also took some actual street ballads back with him to Alfoxden. There is at least a strong presumption that he did so. It has usually been assumed that his knowledge of "The Babes in the Wood" and the similar broadside ballads which were his models for "Goody Blake and Harry Gill" and some of the other *Lyrical Ballads*, derived from Percy's *Reliques of Ancient Poetry*. Wordsworth was, of course, an admirer of Percy's collection. In the "Essay, Supplementary to the Preface" of 1815, he said publicly that English poetry had been 'absolutely redeemed by

---

[1] This is not as improbable as it may seem. Helen Darbishire has called attention to Wordsworth's 'remarkable lack of invention when it came to providing names for his poetical characters' (*The Poet Wordsworth*, 1950, p. 33). It is interesting, for example, to find that when *Salisbury Plain* was being revised in 1799 the only name he could think of for his murderer-hero was Walford. The case of Martha Ray, the heroine of "The Thorn", is even more curious. There was a historical Martha Ray, the mistress of Lord Sandwich, whose murder in 1779 had created a sensation in London. And their illegitimate son, as Wordsworth *must* have known, was his intimate friend Basil Montagu, the father of little Basil!

it', and that he and his friends all had great obligations to the *Reliques*. But he did not acquire a copy of Percy until he was in Hamburg in September 1798, and when he quotes 'one of the most justly-admired stanzas of the *Babes in the Wood*' in the Preface to the second edition of *Lyrical Ballads* it is from a different version than that of Percy, who incidentally knew the poem as "The Children in the Wood". The only edition of the poem which combines the title "Babes in the Wood" with the readings used by Wordsworth is a London broadside dated by the British Museum *c.* 1800, and it is a moral certainty, I think, that Wordsworth possessed a copy of this broadside. The fact is worth labouring because of its implications. Instead of taking the beautiful but more or less "literary" ballads collected by Percy as his models, Wordsworth had deliberately preferred the crude sub-literary street-ballads of his own time. His object, it is clear, was to reach the middle and lower classes of society by writing the kind of poetry that they normally read. A letter that he wrote to Wrangham in 1808 seems to confirm the supposition. Some of his poems, he told Wrangham, had been written with a view to their eventual circulation as broadsides—and so, perhaps, to their supplanting the halfpenny ballads of the time, 'flowers and useful herbs to take the place of weeds'.[1] He does not specify the poems to Wrangham, but he was presumably referring to "Goody Blake and Harry Gill", "Simon Lee", "We are Seven" (which did eventually achieve several broadside editions), "The Last of the Flock", "The Idiot Boy", and the other poems of this kind in *Lyrical Ballads* and the later collections.

The immediate stimulus may have been the rejection of *The Borderers* by the Patentee of Covent Garden Theatre. If the upper classes did not want his poetry, he may well have said to himself, he would take it to the lower classes! The significant thing, however, is Wordsworth's return to action. Since the disastrous failures of 1793 he had managed to remain outside and detached from the world of social reality. Partly through the kindness of friends and relations and partly through Raisley Calvert's legacy Wordsworth had succeeded in deferring for over five

---

[1] Wordsworth to Francis Wrangham, 5 June 1808.

years the necessity to commit himself to a profession. The
various careers that seemed at one time or another to be hanging
over his head—in the Church, at the Bar, as a tutor and as
a journalist—had all somehow been evaded. Wordsworth does
not even seem at this time to have taken any positive steps to
get his poems published. As far as can be discovered, with the
exception of "The Birth of Love", a frigid translation of a French
anacreontic that was included in Francis Wrangham's privately
printed *Poems* (1795), he did not publish one line of poetry after
An Evening Walk and *Descriptive Sketches* until "The Convict"
appeared in the *Morning Post*, 14 December 1797.[1] Various efforts,

---

[1] A discovery announced by J. R. MacGillivray, *Review of English Studies*, Jan.
1954, pp. 61–6, makes it necessary to qualify this statement. As he has pointed out,
The Weekly Entertainer of Sherborne includes in its issue of 21 Nov. 1796, a poem
of 32 lines entitled "Address to the Ocean" which is signed W. W. Unfortunately
there can be no doubt that the poem, an appalling specimen of Della Cruscan
sentimentality, is Wordsworth's work, as parts of it survive in Wordsworth's own
hand among the MSS. at Dove Cottage. A short letter from Wordsworth, signed
in full and written from Racedown Lodge, had also been printed in *The Weekly
Entertainer* of 7 Nov. 1796. I cannot, however, accept Helen Darbishire's attribution (*English Studies Today*, ed. C. L. Wrenn and G. Bullough, 1951, pp. 150 ff.)
of a blank verse "Address to Silence" which appeared in the issue of 6 Mar.
1797 above the initials W. C. The case for Wordsworth's authorship of this com-
petent exercise *à la* James Thomson (it is stylistically at the opposite pole from
"Address to the Ocean" in spite of the similarity of titles) is (i) that Dorothy
Wordsworth transcribed most of it into a notebook, now at Dove Cottage, which
contains other poems by Wordsworth (as well as extracts from Donne and
Massinger) and that this transcription is signed 'WW', (ii) that Joseph Gill, the
Pinneys' factotum at Racedown, entered in his diary on 1 Jan. 1797, 'Mr. P[inney]
of Blackdown to send Mr. Wordsworth's poem to "The Entertainer"'. But (i) it
is far from certain that Dorothy Wordsworth did sign the transcription 'WW'—
there is a final scrawl that *might* be 'UW' (though neither the U nor the W
resemble the capital letters she uses elsewhere) but is more likely to be a mere
flourish of the pen, and (ii) the poem in *The Weekly Entertainer* is said to have
been 'Read at a Literary Club'. Poems similar in style to the "Address to Silence"
appeared in *The Weekly Entertainer* on 23 Jan., 2 Mar., 17 Apr. and 2 Oct. 1797,
all of which had originally been contributed to a Literary Club at Tavistock.
The Club's Correspondent-Secretary was a certain John Commins, who describes
the Club's programme (members' contributions were to be 'for the most part, of
the moral kind') in the issue of 15 Dec. 1796, and I have no doubt that W. C.
was one of his team, a relative possibly. Miss Darbyshire has also missed the implications of the entry in Gill's diary. The fact that he does not specify which poem
was to go to *The Entertainer* must mean that it was the poem they were all talking
about, and in Jan. 1797 only one of Wordsworth's poems fell into such a category.

it is true, were made by Coleridge and the Pinneys to get *Salisbury Plain* printed in 1796 and 1797, but Wordsworth's part in these negotiations seems to have been a passive one. It is impossible not to be reminded of the state of mind in which he went to France in 1791—'doomed to be an idler through my whole life'. But in the spring of 1798—almost exactly six years since Caroline had been conceived and Wordsworth had become the prophet of resolution—he re-enters the market-place once again. If anything the sudden self-confidence is perhaps even more marked, though it was now more justified.

The title *Lyrical Ballads* was itself a challenge. To eighteenth-century neo-classicism the ballad was one *genre* and the lyric another very different one, and so a lyrical ballad was *ipso facto* an irregular hybrid like tragi-comedy. Wordsworth's intention no doubt—if, as seems likely, he rather than Coleridge was responsible for the collection's title—was to make it clear that these were ballads with a difference. The essence of a ballad, whether it was traditional or contemporary, was the tragic story it narrated. But in Wordsworth's ballads the emphasis is not on the story, the series of dramatic events, but on the emotions embodied in the story. In a well-known note on "The Thorn" in the second edition of *Lyrical Ballads* he has specifically identified 'Poetry' and 'passion'. Poetry 'is the history or science of feelings'. As the lyric was the poetic form traditionally consecrated to the out-pouring of feelings, it was natural to differentiate these ballads from the ordinary broadside ballads by calling them lyrical ballads. The implication is that the stories they recount are not particularly interesting in themselves, until they are reduced, as Wordsworth reduces them, to their pathetic human essentials. But in Wordsworth's ballads—as in much of the crude folk-poetry on which they are modelled—emotionality is not the whole story. The heart-rending situation must be actualised. We must be able

---

This was the revised *Salisbury Plain*, whose publication the young Pinneys and Coleridge had been trying to arrange in 1796 (see note 1, p. 15 above). *Salisbury Plain* may have been submitted to *The Weekly Entertainer*, but the space available for poetry in that journal was strictly limited and if *Salisbury Plain* had been accepted there it could only have been published in some ten or twenty instalments. No doubt the project was dropped at an early stage.

to see and hear the heroes and heroines enacting their tragic stories. It is the life-giving quality that is the *desideratum*, and at his best Wordsworth had it in as supreme a measure as any of the traditional balladists. Who that has once read "We are Seven" or "The Idiot Boy"can possibly forget them? Grotesque though the stories may be they remain indelibly fixed in the memory—a fact that is an unconscious tribute to Wordsworth's intuitive artistry. Somehow or other he hit upon themes that satisfy a profound psychological hunger in the modern mind. We remember these poems because we cannot help remembering them. In spite of their unpretentiousness and their inelegance they show a remarkable insight into that 'one human heart' which 'we have all of us'.[1]

The more elaborate poems written in this period, such as *Peter Bell* and the account of the old soldier met by moonlight which was later worked into Book IV of *The Prelude*, show many of the same qualities, and it is not surprising that Wordsworth, under Coleridge's promptings, now began to plan a philosophical poem which would expound systematically the basis of his ethical insights. A title was selected, "The Recluse", and a fragmentary prologue—a hundred lines of magnificent Miltonic verse—was actually written.

The Recluse was a ghost that haunted Wordsworth for the rest of his life. This was to be his *magnum opus*, the proof that he did really possess, as Coleridge was never tired of repeating, 'more of the genius of a great philosophic poet than any man I ever knew, or, as I believe, has existed in England since Milton'. But, somehow, although Wordsworth was always about to get to work on *The Recluse*, the poem never got written. The scheme—a new system of psychology, followed by a historical survey of the various kinds of social organisation, terminating (according to Coleridge[2]) in a proof that a redemption process operated both in human nature and in society—was fundamentally uncongenial. In spite of the great prologue, which was finally printed in the Preface to *The Excursion*, there need be no regrets that *The*

---

[1] "The Old Cumberland Beggar", l. 153.
[2] *Table Talk*, 21 July 1832.

Recluse was never written. (The so-called "Part First. Book First" is simply a rather feeble continuation of *The Prelude*, describing, as its title indicates, the Wordsworths' 'Home at Grasmere'.) The point of interest is that it was ever projected. The actual impingement on contemporary society that was implied in the scheme of the *Lyrical Ballads* is equally evident in the prologue to *The Recluse*:

> Paradise, and groves
> Elysian, Fortunate Fields—like those of old
> Sought in the Atlantic Main—why should they be
> A history only of departed things,
> Or a mere fiction of what never was?

Wordsworth's poem, it will be seen, was to be a guide to Utopia, or at least, as he put it more modestly himself in a letter written soon after these lines, 'a work of considerable utility'.[1] The title that he projected was "The Recluse; or views of Nature, Men, and Society".

But the missionary spirit that is so evident in *Lyrical Ballads* and *The Recluse* receded in the early summer of 1798. Instead of active intervention in contemporary society, Wordsworth began to preach 'a wise passiveness'. The concept was originally applied to the narrator of *The Ruined Cottage*, who was metamorphosed about this time into the philosophical pedlar we meet in *The Excursion*. The pedlar, who was largely just a mouthpiece for Wordsworth himself, was characterised by:

> a holy indolence
> Compared to which our best activity
> Is ofttimes deadly bane.

The only activity compatible with wise passiveness and holy indolence was the absorption of natural scenery. The pedlar used to 'feed his spirit' by contemplating mountains, and when in "Expostulation and Reply" Matthew (who was really Hazlitt) protests against William's day-dreaming, he is told that:

> we can feed this mind of ours,
> In a wise passiveness.

---

[1] Wordsworth to James Losh, 11 Mar. 1798.

The gap between this quietism and the propagandist note that is sounded so clearly in some of the earlier *Lyrical Ballads* does not need to be emphasised. They are two completely different kinds of didacticism. One is the nature-mysticism of "The Tables Turned":

> One impulse from a vernal wood
> May teach you more of man;
> Of moral evil and of good,
> Than all the sages can.

The other is the social propaganda of

> Now think, ye farmers all, I pray,
> Of Goody Blake and Harry Gill.

And the contradiction between the tone of these two Voices is as complete as the discrepancy of doctrine. The curious thing is that they are almost contemporary. "Goody Blake and Harry Gill" can probably be dated January-February 1798. And the passage describing the pedlar's "holy indolence" is to be found in a note-book that Wordsworth was using between 20 January and 5 March 1798. Its probable date is also February 1798.

What was going on in the emotional recesses of Wordsworth's mind in the spring of 1798? A summary of the change would be to say that the trend to a greater and purer objectivity that is traceable in the sequence of his poems from *Salisbury Plain* and *The Borderers* to "The Old Cumberland Beggar" and "The Reverie of Poor Susan" was suddenly reversed. His eye turned more and more from the external object to the internal mental process. Other people became less important, and he began to be more absorbed in himself. In Wordsworth's own terminology, Imagination and Memory began to displace Observation and Description.

The poem in which this new subjectivity becomes most conspicuous is the famous "Lines composed a Few Miles above Tintern Abbey", which occupies the last ten pages of *Lyrical Ballads*, and was written at least a month later than any other poem in the volume. When Wordsworth came to classify his poems in the collected edition of 1815 under the predominant faculty each displayed, "Tintern Abbey" was appropriately included among the 'Poems of Imagination'. The one other poem from *Lyrical*

Ballads grouped under this heading was "The Thorn", which was the only one of the ballads proper not to be based upon fact. Most of the other ballads were classified as 'Poems founded on the Affections' and it is significant that they all have a factual basis. The essential difference between Wordsworth's objective and subjective moods is precisely the proportion maintained between fact and fancy.

In terms of Wordsworth's mental evolution the importance of "Tintern Abbey" is that it records his discovery that 'the mighty world Of eye and ear' is half created in the process of perception. The discovery had implications that have not always been realised. Whereas in revising *Salisbury Plain* as well as in writing *The Ruined Cottage* and the *Somersetshire Tragedy* Wordsworth was careful to exclude all that was unrealistic or improbable, "Tintern Abbey" embodies what can only be called a series of concessions to irrationality. A certain defiance of everyday probability was a necessary preparation for the poem's mystical conclusion. The first warning comes when the description of the view a few miles above the Abbey ends with some speculations by the poet as to the source of the smoke rising among the trees. Is it gipsies ('vagrant dwellers in the houseless woods')? Or is it the fire outside a hermit's cave ('where by his fire The Hermit sits alone')? The transition from the realities of 1798 to the Middle Ages of a Gothic romance is extraordinarily abrupt. The hermit recalls the curfew of *An Evening Walk*, but his function is not like the curfew's to re-establish a connection with the pastoral tradition so much as to emphasise the picturesqueness of the view. Hermits were one of the conventional properties of a late eighteenth-century landscape, and their presence guaranteed the æsthetic, non-documentary qualities of the picture. The effect of this hermit is to exclude from Wordsworth's initial premises in the poem's argument any question of who actually lived in 'these pastoral farms' or who really cultivated

> These plots of cottage-ground, these orchard-tufts . . .

In other words, the basis of the nature-mysticism is strictly non-human. It is perhaps significant that the best that Wordsworth can

find to say for the gardens and orchards is that, being mainly
green in July, they do not 'disturb The wild green landscape'.

The gap between this concept of a nature which is always in
danger of being 'disturbed' by man, and the nature of the poem's
climax, in which Wordsworth is often able to hear

The still, sad music of humanity,

is a wide one. It looks as though he was consoling himself here,
as in the later "Intimations of Immortality", for the loss of youth's
'dizzy raptures' in the contemplation of picturesque scenery, by
making as much as possible of his newly-acquired philanthropy.
What is asserted, however, is that nothing essential has been lost,
while much has been added. The validity of the assertion is not
self-evident. And another and equally illogical form of self-
consolation can also be discerned. Wordsworth is also consoling
himself for the failure of his human contacts. If he had failed, as
he was perhaps beginning to suspect he had, in his role of the
people's poet, the man who would transmute the sub-literary
broadside ballads of the eighteenth century as Shakespeare had
transmuted the crude popular dramas of the sixteenth century,
at least his appreciation of nature was still profound and intense.

The logical contradiction which is at the heart of "Tintern
Abbey" conceals a confession of failure. But the poem does not
read like a confession of failure. Rhetorically it is superbly assured
and persuasive. With the exception of the fragmentary prologue
to *The Recluse* Wordsworth had written nothing possessing a
similar declamatory fervour since the address to Liberty at the
end of *Descriptive Sketches*. That had been intended as the introduction to a career that never eventuated—that of the revolutionary
publicist. And its ultimate inspiration had been Annette's love and
belief in him and the talks and walks with Beaupuy. "Tintern
Abbey" was also an introduction, but this time to his career as
the prophet of nature. Here, for the first time practically, Wordsworth speaks the language that he was afterwards to speak in
prose and in verse, in the tract on the Convention of Cintra as
well as in *The Prelude* and *The Excursion*, in private letters and even
in domestic conversation. With its long sentences, its involved

grammar and its polysyllabic vocabulary it was a form of discourse that abandoned all pretence to being the poetry of the people. But it was a style that came much more easily to Wordsworth, sometimes indeed too easily, and it clearly expressed something fundamental in him that had hitherto been denied an outlet. Formally these elaborate monologues seem to derive from Coleridge, who practised a similar art both in verse and in conversation. Coleridge had now taken the place of Beaupuy. And the place of Annette as ultimate inspirer was taken by a brunette of twenty-six, whose 'wild eyes'[1] now drove Annette's out of Wordsworth's head as effectually as Annette had displaced Mary of Esthwaite some six years ago. The new love—it is the only word that can be used—was his sister Dorothy.[2]

It is no accident that "Tintern Abbey" ends with the famous tribute to Dorothy Wordsworth. In this 'dear, dear Sister' Wordsworth seemed to have found the resolution of his psychological contradictions. She was his link with humanity, the one human being from whom he had no secrets or reservations, and she was also at this time at just the same stage of ecstatic connoisseurship of natural beauty that he looked back to so regretfully in his own adolescence:

> in thy voice I catch
> The language of my former heart . . .

---

[1] Thelwall's "Lines written at Bridgewater"—composed 29 July 1797, though only printed in *The Fairy of the Lake* (1802), p. 130—also contain a reference to Dorothy's bright eyes. Thelwall wished, he says, to settle down near 'My Samuel' and

> Alfoxden's musing tenant, and the maid
> Of ardent eye, who with fraternal love
> Sweetens his solitude.

[2] The suggestion is not a new one. L. A. Willoughby (*German Studies presented to Professor H. G. Fiedler*, 1938, p. 434) has already called attention to 'the lover-like terms on which she stood with her brother'. He cites similar statements that have been made by Herbert Read and I. A. Faussett. Dorothy's Grasmere journals—which de Selincourt was the first to print in full (1941), the earlier editions by William Knight being more or less expurgated—seem to me to clinch the matter. Unfortunately the MS. of the Alfoxden journal has disappeared, except the entry for 20 Jan. 1798, and we have to make do with Knight's text.

If anything Dorothy's sense of the picturesque was even finer than William's had been. The first entry in the Alfoxden Journal, for 20 January 1798, is curiously similar in its conscious precision to *An Evening Walk*, though the visual details are even more brilliant:

> The green paths down the hill-sides are channels for streams. The young wheat is streaked by silver lines of water running between the ridges, the sheep are gathered together on the slopes. After the wet dark days, the country seems more populous. It peoples itself in the sunbeams. . . . The slanting woods of an unvarying brown, showing the light through the thin net-work of their upper boughs. Upon the highest ridge of that round hill covered with planted oaks, the shafts of the trees show in the light like the columns of a ruin.

It is all perhaps a little too sophisticated, but in its own way it could hardly be better done. The Alfoxden Journal ends on 22 May—seven weeks before the walking tour in South Wales which took the Wordsworths to Tintern; and it retains to the end a much greater interest in the landscape than in William. There is no hint of unsisterly feelings. On William's side too there is nothing for the most determined scandalmonger to get hold of before "Tintern Abbey". No doubt the progress to mutual infatuation was gradual and unconscious. But it had certainly begun, for Wordsworth at any rate, by July 1798, and directly or indirectly most of Wordsworth's poems written in the years immediately following seem to be coloured by it.

To Keats "Tintern Abbey" seemed a poem full of dark passages. Wordsworth had not attained in it, he felt, a balance of good and evil. At the time when he wrote it he was in a moral mist, Keats thought, and was only conscious of the 'burden of the Mystery'. 'To this Point was Wordsworth come, as far as I can conceive when he wrote "Tintern Abbey" and it seems to me that his Genius is explorative of those dark Passages.'[1] The comment was a perceptive one. "Tintern Abbey" is a difficult poem to understand even with all the information that we possess about what may have been going on in Wordsworth's mind on 13 July 1798.

---

[1] Keats to John Hamilton Reynolds, 3 May 1818.

Keats thought its composition might perhaps mark Wordsworth's transition from the Chamber of Maiden Thought to a maturer, more socially conscious poetry. There can be no doubt certainly about the poem's transitional character, and the best of the poems that succeed it, if not necessarily more mature, are decidedly more complex and more 'interesting' than most of the contents of *Lyrical Ballads*. But the biographical evidence suggests that Wordsworth's development after "Tintern Abbey" was in the opposite direction from that proposed by Keats—not to a more public poetry but to a more private poetry, one that may perhaps be characterised as an adult reversion to pre-adolescent modes of feeling.

Chapter Five

EGOTISTICAL SUBLIME

I

THE relapse into subjectivity in the spring and summer of 1798 is a central fact in Wordsworth's inner biography, but to look round exclusively for external causes for it would be uncritical. Certainly his sister cannot be blamed for the form their relationship now began to assume. Wordsworth was the victim of psychical forces within himself, the product of his unhappy childhood, which it would have been impossible for him to resist, even if he had been aware of them, and on which external circumstances had little influence. The rhythm of his neurosis seems to have demanded at a certain stage in its sexennial progress a withdrawal from promiscuous social intercourse and a period of intense attachment, emotional, and intellectual, to two or three intimates. John Fleming, William Taylor, and Mary of Esthwaite Water formed one such group (1785–6). Annette and Beaupuy made up a second group (1791–2). A third group (1797–8) was composed of Coleridge and Dorothy, who with Wordsworth himself made up at this time, as Coleridge put it, 'Three persons and one soul'.

The positive impulsions deep down in Wordsworth's being were complemented by equally profound negative revulsions. The corollary of Love was Hate. Over against the inner circle of his intimates were ranged the enemies and the persecutors. Their presence in the background, vaguely sinister figures, is an element in Wordsworth's psychological evolution that must not be overlooked. In his adolescence, no doubt, the Cooksons were the principal enemy, though some of the uncouth schoolboys at Hawkshead, the rough sons of rough Lancashire farmers, may often have provided a secondary menace. In the period in France, the monarchy and the aristocratic system—with the avaricious

and despotic Lord Lonsdale providing an English counterpart—
must have been the overt enemies, even if Wordsworth may not
have regarded them as such in a very personal sense. And in the
Alfoxden phase their place was taken by the English ruling class
and its local representatives. 'The aristocrats seem to persecute
even Wordsworth', Coleridge wrote at the time.[1]

Coleridge has told the story of the Government spy in his
Biographia Literaria, and the official point of view has recently been
reconstructed from the files of the Home Office.[2] It must be
remembered that 1797 represented from the English point of view
the lowest ebb in the war against France. Buonaparte had con-
quered Italy, Austria had crept out of the war, and England, without a victory to its credit and with a naval mutiny at Spithead and
the Nore on its hands, was now facing France single-handed. In the
general atmosphere of near-hysteria, the arrival of two eccentric
strangers at Alfoxden Manor naturally aroused local suspicion.
Lord Somerville, of Fitzhead Court, Taunton, decided that something would have to be done about the Wordsworths—a motion
in which he was supported by Sir Philip Hale of Boymore, near
Bridgwater. Finally a Dr. Lysons of Bath wrote to the Duke
of Portland, the Home Secretary, to report the local rumours—
'They have been heard to say they should be rewarded . . .
and were very attentive to the River near them'. A minor Home
Office official called Walsh, who was sent down to look into the
matter, was told that 'some French people had got possession of
the Mansion House and that they were washing and Mending
their cloaths all Sunday'. On arriving at Stowey he found,
however, that this was 'no French affair, but a mischiefuous gang
of disaffected Englishmen'. This 'Sett of violent Democrats'
included, as he reported to his superior, '*Wordsworth* a name I
think known to Mr. Ford'. Walsh's principal informant was
Thomas Jones of Alfoxden Farm, who had been enlisted by the
Wordsworths to wait at table at a dinner party they gave one

---

[1] Coleridge to John Thelwall, [autumn] 1797.
[2] See A. J. Eagleston, "Wordsworth, Coleridge, and the Spy", *Nineteenth
Century and After*, Aug. 1908, E. K. Chambers, *Samuel Taylor Coleridge* (1938),
pp. 82–3, and G. W. Meyer, *American Scholar*, winter 1950–1.

Sunday in August 1797. Peggy, the Wordsworth's one servant, who had come with them from Racedown and who told Jones that 'Her Master was a Phylosopher', had no less than fourteen mouths to feed on this occasion. They included Coleridge's, Poole's and that of 'a little Stout Man with dark cropt Hair and wore a White Hat and Glasses who after Dinner got up and talked so loud and was in such a passion that Jones was frightened'. The little stout man was John Thelwall, the notorious Radical, whose prosecution for sedition by the Government and triumphant acquittal by a London jury had not exactly endeared him to the authorities. Thelwall was staying with Coleridge at this time and after he left the affair died down. But the knowledge that every word and movement of his was liable to be reported to the Home Office must have been an irritant to Wordsworth for the whole of the eleven months at Alfoxden. He was apparently already on some Home Office black book (to be 'known to Mr. Ford' was presumably the eighteenth-century equivalent of the attentions of M.I.5). And it was certainly because of his political reputation that he was refused a renewal of the lease of Alfoxden. In moments of depression he may well have felt that he was being hounded out of Somerset. The political gulf that divided him from the gentry of the Quantocks was perhaps a less serious matter, however, in terms of self-esteem, than his failure to establish a friendly relationship with his humbler neighbours. The prophet of the universal heart had not been liked by the villagers of Stowey, who much preferred the less reserved Coleridge. Unlike Coleridge, Wordsworth was a life-long water-drinker, and he had preferred to the company of the bar-parlour the Alfoxden woods, where, according to his own account, he 'used to take great delight in noticing the habits, tricks, and physiognomy of asses'.[1]

The Wordsworths left Alfoxden on 25 June 1798. There followed a period of nearly a year when, with brief intervals, William and Dorothy were entirely and uninterruptedly alone, as they had never been hitherto. At Racedown and Alfoxden little Basil Montagu had been with them all the time, to say

---

[1] I.F. note to *Peter Bell*.

nothing of the faithful Peggy and the sequence of visitors and callers. Now they were to be really alone, as cut off from the rest of mankind as if they had been on a desert island.

Their first taste of this new freedom was the short walking tour they took in South Wales in July (Thelwall was now established in a farm on the Wye), of which the literary memorial is "Lines composed a Few Miles above Tintern Abbey". But this tour only lasted four or five days. In September, however, they sailed to Germany, ostensibly to equip themselves to translate German books ('the most profitable species of literary labour', as Dorothy assured their relations[1]), and after parting from Coleridge at Hamburg, they settled down for the winter in the little town of Goslar near Hanover. In the spring of 1799, a further two months were spent rambling round Germany, and they were not back in England until May. So for some seven consecutive months they were entirely dependent upon each other's society. They made no German friends at all and they learnt next to no German. During the whole period Wordsworth did not even read more than a handful of books in any language. 'As I have no books', he wrote to Coleridge, 'I have been obliged to write in self-defence.'[2] It was a bitterly cold winter, and, as he took his lonely daily walk on the old ramparts of the town, in a pelisse lined with fur and a dog-skin bonnet, he used to recite the new poems aloud. 'I had no companion but a kingfisher,' he recalled later, 'a beautiful creature, that used to glance by me. I consequently became much attached to it.'[3] It is characteristic of Wordsworth's complete isolation from human society at this time that the one inhabitant of Germany for whom he felt any affection was a bird.

The Goslar poems are probably the finest that Wordsworth ever wrote. They include most of Book I of *The Prelude*, as well as some of the best passages in the later Books, such as "There was a Boy" and the two childhood episodes in Book XI (the wait for

---

[1] Dorothy Wordsworth to Mrs. Rawson, 13 June 1798.

[2] Wordsworth to Coleridge, Dec. 1798 or Jan. 1799.

[3] I.F. note to "Written in Germany on one of the Coldest Days of the Century".

the horses to take the boys home for Christmas from Hawkshead, and the discovery of the place where the murderer had been hanged above Penrith). Another Goslar poem, "Nutting", was originally intended for *The Prelude*. He also wrote four of the Lucy poems there, "Lucy Gray", the poems about Matthew the schoolmaster, "Ruth", and "The Poet's Epitaph", as well as a few less successful pieces like "To a Sexton".

One thing that the Goslar poems have in common is that they are almost all connected, directly or indirectly, with Wordsworth's childhood or boyhood. Between the originating experiences and their translation into poetry some fifteen or twenty years had intervened. This characteristic differentiates them sharply from *Lyrical Ballads*, which were many of them based upon conversations and events that had actually taken place at Alfoxden shortly before they were written. "To my Sister", "Simon Lee", "Anecdote for Fathers", "Lines written in Early Spring", "The Last of the Flock", "Expostulation and Reply", and "The Tables Turned"are all about Alfoxden or derive from experiences at Alfoxden, and though "Tintern Abbey" is partly about the 1793 visit, its real subject is the revisiting of the Wye Valley in 1798. With this one partial exception, the formula 'emotion recollected in tranquillity' (first promulgated in the Preface to the second edition of *Lyrical Ballads*, 1800) does not apply to any of the poems in *Lyrical Ballads*. On the other hand, it provides an excellent definition of the Goslar poems. There is a critical clue here that it will be worth following up.

The Alfoxden poems are emotionally impersonal poems; the Goslar poems are, directly or indirectly, almost all of them intensely personal poems. That is one way of putting it. The difference can also be put in another way. While at Alfoxden Wordsworth derived poetic stimulus from the everyday events of the real world—a conversation with his sister, an argument with Hazlitt, an encounter with a humble neighbour, a misunderstanding with little Basil. At Goslar on the other hand, and indeed all the time he was in Germany, the world of immediate experience needed to be excluded, if poetry was to be written.

"Written in Germany, on one of the Coldest Days of the Century," the poem about the fly trying to warm itself on the stove in their Goslar lodgings, is one of the few failures. The Lucy poems, however, and the reminiscences of childhood cannot be called escapist. If there was a reluctance to come to terms with contemporary life, there was certainly no escape into mere fancy. It is significant that "The Danish Boy", one of Wordsworth's few adult attempts at the supernatural and a poem which he himself described as 'entirely fancy', is one of the poorer Goslar poems. An element of objective reality enters into all the better poems, but it is reality seen through the memories of childhood or even perhaps, as in the Lucy and Matthew series, through the metamorphoses of the subconscious mind.

It is not unreasonable, I think, to connect these changes of poetic method with the change in Wordsworth's feelings towards his sister. If "Tintern Abbey" shows William already half in love with Dorothy, though completely unconscious of it, the Goslar period seems to represent a determined attempt to *refuse* conscious recognition to the new and explosive situation that was developing. Some such interpretation is certainly suggested by the Lucy poems. In terms of literary origins Lucy derives from Robert Anderson's song "Lucy Gray of Allendale". But even in "She dwelt among the untrodden ways", probably the first to be written of the series, non-literary aspects are also clearly discernible. If Lucy is (i) a folk-song heroine, she is also (ii) a nature-spirit and (iii) a real woman beloved by Wordsworth. The identity of the third Lucy, the real woman, is the immediate problem. Although so prodigal of other biographical information in the comments that he dictated to Isabella Fenwick, Wordsworth's I.F. notes on these poems are laconic in the extreme: 'The next three poems were written in Germany, 1799'; '1799. Composed in the Hartz Forest' ("Three years she grew"); '1799; Written in Germany'. According to De Quincey (who thought Wordsworth had been 'disappointed at some earlier period, by the death of her he loved, or by some other fatal event'), he 'always preserved a mysterious silence on the subject of that "Lucy", repeatedly alluded to or apostrophised in his poems'.[1] Coleridge's guess was that Dorothy was Lucy. In April 1799, he sent Poole a copy of "A slumber did my spirit seal" and added by way of explanation, 'Whether it had any reality I cannot say. Most probably, in some gloomier moment he had fancied the moment in which his sister might die.' Moreover the Lucy of "Among all lovely things my Love had been"—the poem on the glow-worm quoted on page 129—is certainly Dorothy.[2] And the case for Dorothy is clinched by a recently discovered fragment of "Nutting", which must have been written at Goslar:

> Ah! What a crash was that! with gentle hand
> Touch these fair hazels—My beloved Friend!
> Though 'tis a sight invisible to thee
> From such rude intercourse the woods all shrink
> As at the blowing of Astolpho's horn.
> Thou, Lucy, art a maiden 'inland bred'
> And thou hast known 'some nurture'; but in truth
> If I had met thee here with that keen look
> Half cruel in its eagerness, those cheeks
> Thus [word illegible] flushed with a tempestuous bloom,
> I might have almost deem'd that I had pass'd
> A houseless being in a human shape,
> An enemy of nature, hither sent
> From regions far beyond the Indian hills. . . .[3]

Other fragments of "Nutting", some of them incorporated later in *The Prelude*, demonstrate conclusively that the 'Beloved Friend' of the poem is Dorothy, though this is the only place in the poem where she is actually given a name. The passage is additionally interesting because of the confusion it seems to indicate in Wordsworth's mind between Dorothy and himself. In the other texts of "Nutting" it is the young Hawkshead

---

[1] *Recollections of the Lake Poets*, ed. E. Sackville-West, p. 166.

[2] Wordsworth's letter to Coleridge, 16 Apr. 1802, proves this. But in an early MS. of the poem that belonged to Sara Hutchinson 'Mary' has been substituted for 'Lucy'. Had Wordsworth tried to allay Mary Hutchinson's jealousy by pretending that this poem at any rate was intended for her?

[3] Printed in de Selincourt's edition of *The Poetical Works*, II, 504–6.

schoolboy who ravishes the hazels, and his ferocity is specifically contrasted with Dorothy's gentle ways. Apparently, then,
William and Dorothy were *interchangeable*. In writing about her
he was writing about himself, and *vice versa*.

Assuming that Lucy is, in some sense, Dorothy, what is the
biographical significance of the Lucy myth? Two points in
particular demand discussion. They are Lucy's early and unexplained death and the curious sexlessness of these love-poems.

The crisis with which Wordsworth found himself confronted
in 1798 was the discovery that he and Dorothy were falling in love
with each other. It was a crisis similar in kind and degree to the
discovery he had made in 1787 that he was not really in love with
Mary of Esthwaite Water and the even more painful discovery
in 1793 that he had failed Annette utterly, both as a lover and as
the father of her child. The only essential difference was that this
latest discovery was so horrible in its implications that it did not
bear contemplation. The idea of incest had to be thrust forcibly
out of the conscious mind. But it remained in Wordsworth's
subconscious mind. The earlier discoveries had been met and
ultimately resolved by running away from them physically. Mary
of Esthwaite Water, her inadequacies once discovered, was
simply eliminated from Wordsworth's personal life. She was
'dead', for him at any rate. The difficulties of 1793 had been
solved in a similar way on Salisbury Plain by ejecting them from
his mind and filling it with other things. It is possible that
the dangerous relationship with Dorothy was now solved,
subconsciously, by killing her off symbolically. Lucy, who
had been loved so dearly, was dead. The guilty possibilities
were evaded by the removal, subconsciously, of the guilty
object.

Lucy's sexlessness also becomes intelligible once the identity
with Dorothy is recognised. The emotional intimacies must not
have a physical basis, even subconsciously. And so we get the
rarefied ethereal being whom Samuel Butler found so irritating.
(She 'was only like a violet when she was half-hidden from the
view, and only fair as a star when there were so few stars out that
it was practically impossible to make an invidious comparison'.

Wordsworth had probably murdered her to avoid a breach of promise action![1])

Wordsworth's prudishness becomes excusable if its biographical basis is understood. It is possible to prefer it, indeed, to Byron's and Shelley's melodramatic preoccupation with incest. Shelley's gibe in *Peter Bell the Third*—

> But from the first 'twas Peter's drift
> To be a kind of moral eunuch,
> He touched the hem of nature's shift,
> Felt faint—and never dared uplift
> The closest, all-concealing tunic.

loses its sting, when it is realised what was in fact hidden, for Wordsworth, under the all-concealing tunic. Dorothy was not a cynical woman of the world like Byron's half-sister. And in any case Shelley's account is inaccurate, as Wordsworth was certainly not a prude 'from the first'. The *Somersetshire Tragedy* was apparently too outspoken by Victorian standards, and there are some curious things among the early MS. fragments that have only recently been printed. The following lines, for example, are the first stanza of a Hardyesque lyric that was written at Alfoxden in or about February 1798:

> Away, away, it is the air
> That stirs among the wither'd leaves;
> Away, away, it is not there,
> Go, hunt among the harvest sheaves.
> There is a bed in shape as plain
> As from a hare or lion's lair
> It is the bed where we have lain
> In anguish and despair.[2]

---

[1] See "Quis desiderio . . .?" in *The Humour of Homer, and Other Essays* (1913), p. 102.

[2] *The Poetical Works*, ed. E. de Selincourt and H. Darbishire, IV, 357. Those who detect sexual morbidity in Wordsworth sometimes quote Haydon's anecdote: 'Once I was walking with Wordsworth in Pall Mall; we ran into Christie's, where there was a very good copy of the "Transfiguration", which he abused through and through. In the corner stood the group of Cupid and Psyche kissing. After looking some time, he turned round to me with an expression I shall never

II

On their return to England from Germany in May 1799, the
Wordsworths went straight to Tom Hutchinson's farm at
Sockburn-on-Tees. In the course of his early rambles Wordsworth
had spent several weeks alone with this Tom Hutchinson,
but it was his sister Mary, William's old schoolfellow at Penrith
and by now an intimate friend of Dorothy's also, who was the
real object of their visit. There had been some sort of a flirtation
with Mary in Wordsworth's undergraduate days, which had
apparently revived in 1794 to judge by a curious poem, an
adaptation of one of Horace's odes, that seems to have been
written at Windy Brow, Keswick. Forgetting all about Annette,
Wordsworth paints in this poem an idyllic picture of the
home he and Mary are to share in 'Grasmere's quiet Vale':

> Yes, Mary, to some lowly door
> In that delicious spot obscure
> Our happy feet shall tend;
> And there for many a golden year
> Fair Hope shall steal thy voice to chear
> Thy poet and thy friend.[1]

Mary's consent, it will be seen, is quietly taken for granted. Mary
also spent some months with the Wordsworths at Racedown.
She was a kindly, sensible, ordinary woman, with a 'delicate
feeling for propriety'.[2] Her one peculiarity was her habit of un-
embarrassed, unembarrassing silence. Clarkson, the Anti-Slave-
Trade man, used to allege that the only words she could say were

---

forget, and said, "The Dev-ils!"' (*Autobiography and Memoirs*, ed. A. P. D.
Penrose, 1927, p. 294). But the discussion of the celibacy of the clergy in the letter
to W. F. Hook of 5 Feb. 1840 (see p. 116 above) is not in the least morbid: 'If we
would truly spiritualise men, we must take care that we do not begin by unhuman-
ising them, which is the process in respect to all those who are now brought up
with a view to the making of that unnatural vow.'

[1] The poem, a free adaptation of one of Horace's odes, will be found in de
Selincourt's edition of *The Poetical Works*, I, 296–8.

[2] The comment is R. P. Graves's, the Vicar of Ambleside. It will be found in
A. B. Grosart's edition of Wordsworth's *Prose Works* (1876), III, 509.

'God bless you'.[1] Long before their marriage she had become Wordsworth's devoted slave.

Wordsworth's object in making straight for Sockburn, where he and Dorothy spent the next seven months, is clear enough. The relationship in which he and Dorothy found themselves was rapidly becoming impossible, and he had conceived the desperate remedy of marrying Mary Hutchinson. For the moment he had not the means or the prospects, or even the house, to enable him to marry anybody. And there was the difficult and delicate matter of an honourable settlement with Annette still awaiting solution. But some sort of an understanding was reached with Mary, of which Dorothy was presumably informed. If the crisis had not been solved, it had at least passed into a new phase by the time the Wordsworths left Sockburn, in December 1799, to set up house for themselves at Dove Cottage, Grasmere.

Dorothy's Grasmere Journal begins on 14 May 1800. With the exception of a long interval in 1801, it provides a continuous and intimate record of the period immediately preceding Wordsworth's marriage. Behind the comings and goings, the daily details of the weather and William's latest poem, a drama was being enacted that often comes near to tragedy. The first entry was made on the day that William and their brother John, who stayed with them between his voyages, set off to pay a short visit to the Hutchinsons without her. 'My heart was so full that I could hardly speak to W. when I gave him a farewell kiss. I sate a long time upon a stone at the margin of the lake, and after a flood of tears my heart was easier. The lake looked to me, I know not why, dull and melancholy, and the weltering on the shores seemed a heavy sound.' William did not return as soon as she had expected, and day after day the entries are 'No letter, no William'. 'I lingered out of doors in the hope of hearing my Brother's tread.' 'I would not go far from home, expecting my Brother.' 'No William!' In 1802, as the marriage approaches, the entries become unbearably pathetic. 'Then we sate by the fire, and were happy, only our tender thoughts became painful.' 'William's head was bad ... I petted him on the carpet.' 'William

---

[1] *Recollections of the Lake Poets*, p. 113.

a bad headache; he made up a bed on the floor, but could not sleep—I went to his bed and slept not.' In William's absence she again sleeps in his bed. On his return after seeing Mary 'his mouth and breath were very cold when he kissed me. We spent a sweet evening.' During another of William's absences with the Hutchinsons she writes 'I *will* be busy. I *will* look well, and be well when he comes back to me. O the Darling! Here is one of his bitten apples. I can hardly find in my heart to throw it into the fire.' When he has returned, with the plans for the marriage all settled, the entries seem to become more rather than less affectionate. 'After dinner, we made a pillow of my shoulder—I read to him and my Beloved slept.' The day of the actual wedding, however, is described in level unemotional tones:

> On Monday, 4th October 1802, my brother William was married to Mary Hutchinson. I slept a good deal of the night, and rose fresh and well in the morning. At a little after 8 o'clock I saw them go down the avenue towards the church. William had parted from me upstairs. When they were absent my dear little Sara [Mary's younger sister] prepared the breakfast. I kept myself as quiet as I could, but when I saw the two men running up the walk, coming to tell us it was over, I could stand it no longer, and threw myself on the bed, where I lay in stillness, neither hearing or seeing anything till Sara came upstairs to me, and said, 'They are coming'. This forced me from the bed where I lay, and I moved, I knew not how, straight forward, faster than my strength could carry me, till I met my beloved William, and fell upon his bosom.

It is against this psychological background of reluctant rejection, a love that is being slowly and gently buried alive, that Wordsworth's poetry of the period following the return from Germany must be read. Measured quantitatively, in terms of the number of lines composed, the three years preceding his marriage were the most productive of his life. It was also the period of his best prose. The great Preface, now generally recognised as perhaps the most original single document in the whole history of English criticism, was written in the autumn of 1800; the letter to Charles James Fox, a sociological masterpiece, followed in January 1801 (it was the covering letter to a presentation copy of the second edition of

Lyrical Ballads); and the long letter to John Wilson, a critical supplement to the Preface, dates from June 1802. Was this literary activity possibly a means of alleviating a psychological strain? The contrast with the astonishingly high level of performance maintained at Alfoxden and in Germany is sometimes painfully evident. Of the German poems only two can be described as failures ("To a Sexton" and "Written in Germany, on one of the Coldest Days of the Century"), and not one of the Alfoxden poems is wholly unsuccessful. But of the poems written after the return to England and printed in the second volume of the second edition of *Lyrical Ballads* only "Michael" is great poetry. "The Idle Shepherd-Boys", "The Pet-Lamb", "The Childless Father" and the *Poems on the Naming of Places* and *Inscriptions* are perhaps slightly less tepid than "Rural Architecture", "The Waterfall and the Eglantine", "The Oak and the Broom" and "Song for the Wandering Jew".

By the time they reached Sockburn Wordsworth was undoubtedly fully aware of the nature of his feelings for Dorothy. In "Written in Germany" he had already contrasted the Goslar fly, without brother or 'mate', with his own happier position:

> No brother, no mate has he near him—while I
> Can draw warmth from the cheek of my Love.

But the most explicit reference to her is at the end of " 'Tis said that some have died for love", a poem written soon after they had settled at Dove Cottage. The first five stanzas of the poem recount the grief of a neighbour of theirs for the death of his sweetheart ('the pretty Barbara'), and in the last stanza Wordsworth expresses the hope that he will not have to suffer in the same way. The following are the crucial lines:

> Ah gentle Love! if ever thought was thine
> To store up kindred hours for me, thy face
> Turn from me, gentle Love! nor let me walk
> Within the sound of Emma's voice, nor know
> Such happiness as I have known to-day.

The implication is clear enough. Emma is to the poet what Barbara had been to the man who lived on the side of Helvellyn.

And in Wordsworth's other poems 'Emma' or 'Emmeline' invariably stands for his sister—'Dorothy' at this time being 'rarely worn', according to John Stuart Mill, 'by any person above the degree of cookmaid'.[1]

" 'Tis said that some have died for love" is not a good poem by any means. Perhaps Wordsworth wrote it primarily to show it to Dorothy? The knowledge that he would soon be marrying Mary Hutchinson might seem less intolerable if he could convince Dorothy that she was the one he really loved. Some such notion may well have inspired many of the poems written in the spring of 1802, when the date of the wedding had been more or less fixed. This was the most prolific period of all. Every day almost, as Dorothy's Journal bears witness, a new poem was written, and they are almost all connected with her in one way or another. Several of them record actual incidents of their childhood, such as "To a Butterfly" which was written just before breakfast on Sunday, 14 March 1802. 'He ate not a morsel, nor put on his stockings, but sate with his shirt neck unbuttoned, and his waistcoat open while he did it.' Dorothy had happened to mention that as a child she had chased butterflies but had been afraid of brushing the dust off their wings, and the remark was promptly turned into a poem of two stanzas.

Another and larger group of the poems of 1802—they were not actually published until 1807, in *Poems in Two Volumes*—consists of invocations to or descriptions of birds and flowers, "To the Daisy", "The Green Linnet", "To a Sky-Lark", "To the Small Celandine", "The Redbreast chasing the Butterfly", and similar pieces. Until his association with Dorothy, Wordsworth had never shown much interest in flowers or the smaller birds, and it seems clear that these poems were written, to some extent at any rate, because he knew they would please her. A similar motive may underlie his brief return in the spring of 1802 to the manner of the Alfoxden ballads. Dorothy's Journal makes it clear that she herself preferred her brother's more realistic poems. "The

---

[1] See Anna J. Mill, "John Stuart Mill's Visit to Wordsworth, 1831", *Modern Language Review*, July 1949.

Idiot Boy" was a special favourite of hers, and she quotes from
such poems as *Peter Bell*, "Simon Lee" and "Lines written in
early Spring" in a natural unselfconscious way that suggests that
they meant more to her than the later poems. And when alone
and depressed, her habit was to re-read *Lyrical Ballads*, by which
she probably meant the first rather than the second edition. These
preferences may explain the emergence in 1802 of three extremely
realistic poems—"Alice Fell", "The Sailor's Mother", and
"Beggars", all three of which incidentally derive from episodes
recorded in Dorothy's Journal.

Many of these poems are charming, but they cannot be called
great poetry. The whole of Wordsworth's intellectual and emotional nature is not engaged in them. Dorothy, it is clear, was
no longer the centre of his life. But her place had not been taken
by Mary Hutchinson, but by Wordsworth himself. This is the
period of the 'egotistical sublime'. The one topic that really
interested Wordsworth at this time, and that could still wring the
greatest poetry from him, was his own inner life. The proof of it
is "Intimations of Immortality" (begun 27 March 1802, added to
in May and June, but apparently not completed until 1803 or
early 1804), "Resolution and Independence" (3 May–4 July 1802),
"Ode to Duty" (about February 1804), and *The Prelude* (1804–5).
It will not be possible to discuss these poems in detail, but an out-
line of their relationship to each other and to the poems of the
German period may perhaps be attempted.

The 'Dorothy-cycle' of poems, as it may be called to distinguish it from the 'Annette-cycle' and the 'Mary of Esthwaite-
cycle', begins with "Tintern Abbey". There is the same failure
to integrate disparate material in that poem as in *Salisbury Plain*.
In particular conscious and subconscious elements get in each
other's way in a confusing manner. The distinction on which so
much emphasis is laid between the period when nature was all in
all to Wordsworth and the period when human interests pre-
dominated remains impenetrably obscure. It is not clear that the
passage of five years has added anything at all; the 'still sad music
of humanity' remains a phrase without any content. And if the
picture of himself in 1793 cannot be taken at its face-value—it is

clear, as we have seen, that it cannot—what precise significance
has it? Why is the boy's experience being passed off as the young
man's?

Similar questions do not arise with the poems written in
Germany. In these poems the basic content is as egocentric as in
"Tintern Abbey", but Wordsworth's subconscious mind has
found objective correlatives which disguise the egotism. It is not
clear, however, how far Wordsworth was conscious himself of
the relevance of the Lucy poems and the blank-verse episodes
of his own childhood to the personal problems with which he
was now confronted as an adult. "Intimations of Immortality"
and "Resolution and Independence" mark an increase of self-
awareness. The psychological problem, as he sees it in these
poems, is the melancholia with which he is now afflicted. How
is it that moments of ecstatic happiness are followed, apparently
without any reason, by moods of the deepest depression? In
"Resolution and Independence" he seems almost to correlate
the adult's happiness with his success in forgetting his social
responsibilities:

> My old remembrances went from me wholly;
> And all the ways of men, so vain and melancholy.

The melancholia returns with the realisation that reality cannot be
kept indefinitely at arm's length:

> Far from the world I walk, and from all care;
> But there may come another day to me—
> Solitude, pain of heart, distress, and poverty.

It will be remembered that the poet is saved from self-pity by
contemplating the Leech-gatherer, who is so much grosser a
victim of 'the ways of men' and who yet retains a measure of
cheerfulness.

"Intimations of Immortality" proposes another cure for
melancholia—the attainment of a trance-like condition by re-
creating within oneself the experiences of childhood. The
process, which is similar to that recollection of emotion in
tranquillity he had already described as the source of all poetry, is
described allegorically in the poem:

> Hence in a season of calm weather
> Though inland far we be,
> Our Souls have sight of that immortal sea
> Which brought us hither,
> Can in a moment travel thither,
> And see the Children sport upon the shore,
> And hear the mighty waters rolling evermore.

(In suitable circumstances even the elderly can make contact with the mystical experiences of their own childhood through the faculty of memory.) As a cure for the melancholia brought on by the difficulties and complexities of human relationships the prescription to become again as a little child seems hardly adequate. Social irresponsibility cannot heal the guilt-complex brought on by social failure. The poem is moving, however, because of the intensity of Wordsworth's longing for the impossible. If only he could exclude the real world—if only he could forget Annette and Caroline, with whom he and Dorothy had spent an uncomfortable month at Calais just before his marriage; if only he could forget Dorothy who continued to live at Dove Cottage, an un-upbraiding secretary with a broken heart!

The "Ode to Duty" and *The Prelude* were the necessary conclusion. Granted the egotistical premise ('what must Wordsworth do to be happy?') and that the voice of conscience had only contradictory advice to offer (he ought to marry Dorothy, but incest is a deadly sin), it was inevitable that he should turn for guidance to an external authority. It was not long before he began announcing, in the solemnest tones, that he would lay down his life for the Church of England. Political orthodoxy went hand in hand with religious orthodoxy, and although Sir George Beaumont found it necessary to warn Haydon and Wilkie against Wordsworth's 'terrific democratic notions' as late as 1809,[1] an incipient Toryism is already evident in the sonnets written in 1802. Southey's 'conversion' took place in the interval between the Peace of Amiens (27 March 1802) and the renewal of hostilities against Napoleon on 18 March 1803, and this was probably the decisive period for Wordsworth too.

---

[1] See Haydon's *Autobiography and Memoirs*, ed. A. P. D. Penrose, p. 85.

The Prelude, it is true, which was only begun in earnest shortly before the "Ode to Duty" was written, shows little sign of orthodoxy. Its object however, was not to record Wordsworth's opinions at the time of writing, but to trace the "Growth of a Poet's Mind". It is the supreme example of emotion—that is to say, emotional experience—recollected in tranquillity, and in both its subject-nature and its method it rounds off and sums up what I have called the poetry of the 'Dorothy-cycle'.

If Wordsworth's earliest poems are essentially descriptive, and the poems of his second period base themselves upon observation reinforced by sympathetic intuition, the poetry of the third phase, from "Tintern Abbey" onward, is *par excellence* the poetry of memory. The conflict between his past and his present emotional life provided during these years the tension that seems to be the prerequisite of all great poetry. The fact that there is so much of this poetry must be attributed partly to the degree of the tension, and partly to the remarkable nature of Wordsworth's memory. Apparently he could remember anything that he wanted to. And once registered it was there for ever. As a small boy, he had had to learn by heart an enormous number of lines from the English classics, including Pope. Wordsworth grew up to think Pope an over-rated and unnatural writer, but he never forgot the passages he had memorised from him. As late as 1836, nearly sixty years after he had recited them to his father at Cockermouth, or to the usher at Hawkshead, he told Barron Field that, 'with a little rummaging of my memory', he believed he could repeat several thousand lines of Pope.[1] And his extraordinary memory was not only verbal, he had also an exceptionally retentive visual memory. The memoranda on the circumstances under which each of his poems was composed are punctuated by such phrases as 'I have a most vivid remembrance' ("To a Highland Girl"), 'I have, after an interval of forty-five years, the image of the old man as fresh before my eyes as if I had seen him yesterday' ("Simon Lee"),

---

[1] Quoted by William Knight in an article on "Wordsworth and Barron Field", *Academy*, 23 Dec. 1905. The MS. of Field's abortive and unpublished life of Wordsworth is in the British Museum. Some extracts from it will be found in *The Times Literary Supplement*, 28 Apr. 1950.

'I distinctly recollect the evening' ("The Pilgrim's Dream"), 'I distinctly recollect the very moment' ("A Night Piece"), 'I recollect distinctly the very spot' ("An Evening Walk"). And what he *did* recollect distinctly were such *minutiæ* as the way in which a particular oak-tree on the road from Hawkshead to Ambleside had been silhouetted against the sun in the summer of 1784, or the peculiar colour, almost a lily-white, that the leaves of a fallen ash in the grounds of Alfoxden had faded to in the spring of 1798.

But Wordsworth's memory was not merely photographic and omnivorous like Macaulay's; its value when functioning healthily lay as much, in his opinion, in what it rejected as in what it retained. He was justifiably proud of the minute accuracy of his visual impressions. 'I have hardly ever known any one but myself', he told Aubrey de Vere towards the end of his life, 'who had a true eye for Nature.'[1] But, he added immediately, it was essential for the memory to co-operate with the eye. This was where an unnamed poet who seems to be Tennyson had gone wrong:

> He took pains; he went out with his pencil and notebook, and jotted down whatever struck him most—a river rippling over the sands, a ruined tower on a rock above it, a promontary, and a mountain-ash waving its red berries. He went home, and wove the whole together into a poetical description.

After a pause, Wordsworth resumed with a flashing eye and impassioned voice:

> But Nature does not permit an inventory to be made of her charms! He should have left his pencil and notebook at home; fixed his eye, as he walked, with a reverent attention on all that surrounded him, and taken all into a heart that could understand and enjoy. Then, after several days had passed by, he should have interrogated his memory as to the scene. He would have discovered that while much of what he had admired was preserved to him, much was also most wisely obliterated. That which remained—the picture surviving in his mind—would have presented the ideal and essential truth of the scene, and done so, in a large part, by discarding much which, though in itself striking, was not characteristic.

[1] A. de Vere, "Recollections of Wordsworth" (*Essays chiefly on Poetry*, 1887, II, 276-7).

For Wordsworth, then, the memory was not primarily a recording mechanism, passively registering whatever came before the mind's eye. It was active, a 'power' which selected from the stream of consciousness those items, and those items only, that *deserved* to be remembered. To reinforce it by notes, or by referring to old letters or diaries, would have been to falsify it. The sanctity of the unprompted memory was an article of faith which is triumphantly justified in these poems, and notably in *The Prelude*. The mistake is to read them as autobiography in the ordinary sense of the word. *The Prelude* can only be called subjective autobiography. It is written, as it were, from the inside outwards. The frame of reference, that is, round which it is organised, lies deep down in Wordsworth's mind. The names, dates and places, that occur in it, and give an illusion of objective autobiography, are really subordinate to a private calendar and a geography of Wordsworth's own that has only an indirect relationship to the time and space of the world as we know it.

How indirect the relationship can be is demonstrated by the first paragraph of the poem. Wordsworth, it will be remembered, has escaped into the countryside from some town. He describes himself in the earliest MSS. of the passage as—

> from yon City's walls set free
> A prison where he hath been long immured.

(In the text printed in 1850, the first edition of the poem, this became 'escaped From the vast city, where I long had pined'.) But what the town was, and even what country it was in, is withheld from the reader. The town turns up again at the beginning of Book VII:

> Six changeful years have vanished since I first
> Poured out (saluted by that quickening breeze
> Which met me issuing from the City's walls)
> A glad preamble to this Verse . . .

The 1850 edition (from which I have quoted here) adds a note at this point to the effect that the city in question was Goslar in Lower Saxony. The note was apparently added by Wordsworth's nephew, who saw the poem through the press soon after his uncle's death, but it is almost certainly incorrect. We know from several references in Wordsworth's letters that Book VII was begun in October 1804. Six years before that, in October 1798, Wordsworth was not leaving Goslar but arriving there. He and Dorothy did not leave Goslar until February 1799. It is possible, of course, that the reference in Book VII is not to the time when Wordsworth actually left his 'City', wherever it was, but to the time when he wrote about leaving it. A large part of Book I of *The Prelude* was, as a matter of fact, written at Goslar, and it is conceivable that he did make a start on this passage in October 1798. The only real clue that Wordsworth himself provides to the identity of the 'City' is at ll. 106–7 of Book I (1850 text):

> A pleasant loitering journey, through three days
> Continued, brought me to my hermitage.

It is generally agreed that the 'hermitage' referred to here is Racedown, and in that case the 'City' will have to be Bristol. Bristol is only fifty miles from Racedown, and three days ('two days' in the 1805 text) would be about the amount of time required to walk there. But a close examination makes even this solution unlikely. Though much bigger than Goslar, Bristol (with a population of 40,000 or so) could hardly be called 'vast', and the five weeks' holiday that Wordsworth spent there in August and September 1795 as the guest of the Pinneys was not 'long' and was passed, as far as is known, without any pining or discontent whatever. In so far as it has a local habitation, the 'City' must be London, not Bristol. London was the only large town Wordsworth ever spent more than a few weeks in, and the feeling of release from a prison that this passage records, undoubtedly reproduces the mood, though not the exact circumstances, in which he left London in August 1795, after spending the eight preceding months there. Why, then, did he describe himself as setting out for Racedown from London, and why did he talk of it as a mere two or three days' walk? The answer must be that Wordsworth was writing subjective autobiography. The name of the town was subordinate to the emotional fact, the idea of a 'City'—not so much London as the feeling London had come to stand for. At this level there was no real difference between London and Bristol (or even Goslar), and so the 'City' came to stand for both of them in Wordsworth's mind, until what was true of one, viz. a distance of fifty miles from Racedown, could be predicated of the other. The confusion in Book VII between the place where this particular emotional experience occurred and the place where it was recollected and recorded is only another example of the same thought-process.

The point deserves emphasis, not because the mental coalescence of London, Bristol and Goslar is important in itself, but because the method is typical of *The Prelude*. Time and place play almost as many tricks in *The Prelude*, particularly in the last four books, as in "Resolution and Independence" (which was based on a real meeting with a real leech-gatherer) or the poems about Matthew (a real schoolmaster, though at one or two removes) or even "Ruth" (which was suggested by an account of a real 'wanderer in Somersetshire'). *The Prelude* is only accidentally autobiography, and the factual matter it supplies must always be suspect unless confirmed from other sources. Essentially it is simply the longest and best of Wordsworth's 'Poems of Memory' (to coin a category he never used himself).

At one time Wordsworth used the word 'reverie' to define this poetry of subjective recollection. In the second edition of *Lyrical Ballads*, where "The Reverie of Poor Susan" appears for the first time, he even persuaded Coleridge to give "The Ancient Mariner" the sub-title of "A Poet's Reverie" (which, Lamb wrote, was 'as bad as Bottom the Weaver's declaration that he is not a lion, but only the scenical representation of a lion'[1]). The original title of "Strange fits of passion have I known" is also said to have been "A Reverie",[2] and in the account of his

---

[1] Lamb to Wordsworth, Feb. 1801.

[2] Knight records this as the cancelled title in his 1896 or 'Eversley' edition of *The Poetical Works*. It is, however, almost certainly a mistake. (Knight was an exceptionally inaccurate editor, even by Victorian standards.) The only surviving MS. of "Strange fits of passion" is the Longman MS. now in the Yale University Library. David M. Vieth, who has kindly examined it for me, tells me that the MS. has a cancelled title, but the deleted words are quite certainly "The two Thieves" and not "A Reverie". The transcriber (Dorothy Wordsworth) apparently started

experiences on Salisbury Plain, as we have seen, in Book XII of *The Prelude*, the supernatural spectacles are called 'reveries' (in the 1850 text they become 'visions').[1] Wordsworth probably got the word from Erasmus Darwin's *Zoonomia; or, the Laws of Organic Life* (1794–6), the book from which he got the facts for "Goody Blake and Harry Gill", which has a special section 'Of Reverie'. Darwin's definition is worth quoting because of the light it throws on that mystical condition met several times in *The Prelude* in which 'the light of sense goes out':

> When we are employed with great sensations of pleasure, or with great efforts of volition, in the pursuit of some interesting train of ideas, we cease to be conscious of our existence, and inattentive to time and place, and do not distinguish this train of sensitive and voluntary ideas from the imitative ones excited by the presence of external objects, though our organs of sense are surrounded with their accustomed stimuli, till at length this interesting train of ideas becomes exhausted, or the appulses of external objects are applied with unusual violence, and we return with surprise, or with regret, into the common track of life. This is termed reverie or studiousness.

Wordsworth's interest in 'reverie' suggests a defective sense of proportion in egotistical sublimity. An abnormal psychological condition sometimes came to seem important to him simply because he had experienced it and because it was out of 'the common track of life'. The similar experience recorded in "There was a Boy" acquired a similar false value. Wordsworth took these things a good deal too seriously and their over-valuation detracts from the purely poetic merit of "Tintern Abbey", "Intimations of Immortality" and *The Prelude*. The reservation must be made, just as similar reservations have to be made for Yeats's magic, D. H. Lawrence's preoccupation with sex and T. S. Eliot's obscure allusions. One makes the reservation without denying the substantial greatness of the poetry.

---

to copy out "The Two Thieves", a poem also included among the Longman MSS., and then, having written out the title, proceeded through some oversight with the text of "Strange fits of passion", which has never had a separate title.

[1] In a MS. comment of Wordsworth's written about 1800 on "To Joanna" he uses the word 'trance' to describe this 'dream'-like condition (*Poetical Works*, ed. E. de Selincourt, II, 487).

III

The rest should have been silence. *The Prelude* was completed in May 1805, and from this point a gradual deterioration in the quality of Wordsworth's poetry becomes noticeable. There are no longer any great poems, but at first the poems are still quite good, and in *The Waggoner* (1805), an experiment in jovial comedy, and *The White Doe of Rylstone* (1807–8), with its symbolic supernaturalism, there are interesting attempts to extend the poetic range. The 'dotages' seem to begin in 1808, and hardly a single short poem of any distinction is written between that year and 1814, the year of "Laodamia" and perhaps "Yew-Trees". "Yew-Trees" is an imitation of Cowper's "Yardley Oak", a poem incidentally that had been copied into Wordsworth's Commonplace Book some ten years before (it is the only Cowper poem there), but the famous conclusion is nearer Keats than Cowper:

> beneath whose sable roof
> Of boughs, as if for festal purpose decked
> With unrejoicing berries—ghostly Shapes
> May meet at noontide; Fear and trembling Hope,
> Silence and Foresight; Death the Skeleton
> And Time the Shadow;—there to celebrate,
> As in a natural temple scattered o'er
> With altars undisturbed of mossy stone,
> United worship; or in mute repose
> To lie, and listen to the mountain flood
> Murmuring from Glaramara's inmost caves.

Swinburne thought the blank verse of "Yew-Trees" the best Wordsworth ever wrote, with the possible exception of "Tintern Abbey". It is certainly closer to that of Shelley (for whose technical virtuosity Wordsworth had a profound respect), Tennyson and Swinburne himself than that, say, of "Michael". If the ossification had not set in, this is, no doubt, the direction in which Wordsworth would have developed. "Laodamia" is also 'romantic' in something the same way.

The *magnum opus* of this period was, of course, *The Excursion*. Apart from Book I (which is simply a revised version of *The*

Ruined Cottage and Book II (written in the summer of 1806), most of the poem was written between 1809 and 1813. It was published in 1814. Although not much longer than *The Prelude*— 8,927 lines as against 8,584 lines of the 1805 text of *The Prelude* —it is infinitely more difficult to read because of its invertebrate character and the pomposity of the style. In *The Prelude* the reader's interest is sustained even in the flattest passages by a natural curiosity to know what Wordsworth's next emotional experience is going to be and how he will relate it to the 'Growth of a Poet's Mind'. The mere process of growing up provided a kind of plot. But *The Excursion* is without any recognisable plot at all—it consists essentially of a series of long speeches, partly narrative and partly didactic, by the Wanderer, the Solitary and the Pastor—and when the poem does at last end, it is not at all clear why it need have done. The actual writing, in spite of some good passages, is also deplorably grandiloquent and verbose. The result is that, taken as a whole, *The Excursion* is one of the dullest books of its kind in the English language. Landor made the same complaint, but more politely, in his lines "To the Author of *Festus* on the classick and romantick":

> Wordsworth, in sonnet, is a classick too,
> And on that grass-plot sits at Milton's side;
> In the long walk he soon is out of breath
> And wheezes heavier than his friends could wish.
> Follow his pedlar up the devious rill,
> And, if you faint not, you are well repaid.

I am afraid the modern reader generally faints.

In the dedication to *Peter Bell the Third*, Shelley distinguished four stages in Wordsworth's poetic deterioration. 'He was at first sublime, pathetic, impressive, profound; then dull; then prosy and dull; and now dull—O, so very dull! it is an ultra-legitimate dulness.' Shelley's first stage, before the descent begins, is to be equated presumably with the two editions of *Lyrical Ballads* (1798 and 1800). The second stage, that of mere dullness, presumably refers to the poorer poems in *Poems in Two Volumes* (1807). The third stage ('prosy and dull') must be that of *The Excursion*—a poem described in a note to *Peter Bell the Third* as containing 'curious evidence of the gradual hardening of a strong, but circumscribed sensibility, of the perversion of a penetrating, but panic-stricken understanding'. And the fourth stage, that of 'ultra-legitimate dulness', is no doubt that represented by *Thanksgiving Ode, January 18, 1816, With Other Short Pieces, Chiefly Referring to Recent Public Events* (1816). This volume which contains "Ode 1815", with the notorious passage (later suppressed) in which Carnage is described as the daughter of God, is perhaps Wordsworth's nadir. Some of the later collections represent a partial poetical recovery, notably *The River Duddon* (1820), but the poems written after 1815 are at their best unexciting. The masterpiece is, I suppose, "Extempore Effusion upon the Death of James Hogg" (1835).

The descent into bathos remains unexplained. It is possible that the series of moral crises punctuating Wordsworth's early life finally exhausted the power of response. De Quincey tells a story of a fellow-passenger on the stage-coach appealing to the other passengers for a verdict on Wordsworth's age. 'You'll never see three-score, I'm of opinion.' And everybody agreed, De Quincey assures us, that Wordsworth was rather over than under sixty. This was in 1809, when he was really only thirty-eight or thirty-nine![1] Dorothy also got old before her time in the same way. De Quincey attributed this premature ageing of the Wordsworths to 'the secret fire of a temperament too fervid; the self-consuming energies of the brain, that gnaw at the heart and life-strings for ever'.[2] Whatever the precise explanation, the fact that he looked an old man before he was forty is extremely suggestive. Wordsworth's poetry was emotional rather than intellectual, and the physical basis was perhaps more important in his case than most writers find it. One curious illustration of the interconnection of the body and the mind in the composition of his poetry is that a sore on one of his feet would not heal while he was writing *The White Doe of Rylstone*, but got better at once when he took a holiday from the poem. Two other facts are perhaps also relevant. In or about 1805 Wordsworth no longer wrote great poetry, and

---

[1] *Recollections of the Lake Poets*, pp. 124–5.
[2] *Ibid.*

February 1805 was the date of John Wordsworth's death. John's drowning has been described by de Selincourt as 'the most terrible blow that either William or Dorothy had ever suffered'.[1] For weeks their grief was uncontrollable. William cried like a baby. The ultimate effect, he claimed, was to 'humanise his soul' ("Elegiac Stanzas suggested by a Picture of Peele Castle"):

> I have submitted to a new control;
> The power is gone, which nothing can restore;
> A deep distress hath humanised my soul.

But there is little evidence either in his poems or his letters that John's loss did make him more human. It seems on the contrary to have desiccated his soul. 1805 was also the year when Wordsworth's eye-trouble began. He had carried their Johnny, a two-and-a-half-year's old child, all the way up Kirkstone Pass, and this brought on an inflammation of the eyes which gave him endless trouble all the rest of his life.

In Coleridge, the corruption of the poet had proved the generation of the critic and the metaphysician. Wordsworth's metamorphosis after 1805 was into a talker. As a young man he had been rather silent and tongue-tied, but in his later thirties he became a fluent and eloquent table-talker. Like Coleridge's his talk was essentially monologue. To the young disciple who arrived at Rydal Mount with an introduction and a handful of fundamental problems Wordsworth was always delighted to hold forth by the hour, and the advice was usually sensible as well as being lucidly and vigorously expressed. It was the same in London at Sir Henry Taylor's and Samuel Rogers's breakfast parties. Even Carlyle, a rival talker, ended by conceding a surly approval. Carlyle had been told that Wordsworth 'talked better than any man in England', and though disconcerted by Wordsworth's egotism (Pope's 'partial failure', 'the narrowish limits visible in Milton', 'Shakespeare himself had his blind sides, his limitations'—until it gradually became apparent to Carlyle that 'of transcendent unlimited there was, to this critic, probably but

---

[1] *Dorothy Wordsworth* (1934), p. 187.

one specimen known, Wordsworth himself !'[1]) and the topics on which he sometimes chose to discourse (on the occasion of their first meeting it was 'how far you could get carried out of London on this side and on that for sixpence'), the final conclusion he came to was that 'you could get more meaning out of what Wordsworth had to say to you than from anybody else'.[2] In Scott's opinion Wordsworth was 'too much of the poet' in his conversation at social functions.[3] But this was not the general impression. Jeffrey, when he at last met Wordsworth in the flesh instead of in print, found him 'not in the very least Lakish now, or even in any degree poetical, but rather a hard and a sensible worldly sort of a man'.[4] The presence of a certain hardness in Wordsworth in later life is confirmed by the lively account a Welsh poet, John Jones, gives of a visit to Rydal Mount. Jones was greatly impressed by Wordsworth's shrewdness—'it struck me forcibly at the time, that he would be a capital hand to drive a hard bargain with a Welsh pig-driver at a fair'.[5] His conversation, the witnesses agree, had a vigour and raciness that the later poems are deplorably deficient in. One admirable phrase has been preserved by J. P. Muirhead, the biographer of James Watt, who paid a call on the Wordsworths in August 1841. On this occasion Mrs. Wordsworth reported that there was soon to be a veritable feast of culture at Keswick, with lectures by Lord Monteagle, Whewell and Carlyle on astronomy and 'universal philanthropy'. Would Mr. Wordsworth go to hear them? 'Go!' said the poet, 'I would as soon go to see so many carrion crows!'[6] The manner, however, was not impressive. 'There was an inflexible matter-of-fact manner and spirit in all he said', according to another witness, 'which came out in a rather hoarse and harsh *burr* that made it disagreeable as well as unimpressive.'[7] The diction seems to have

---

[1] *Reminiscences*, ed. J. A. Froude (1881), II, 334.

[2] Sir Charles Gavan Duffy, *Conversations with Carlyle* (1892), pp. 53–4.

[3] Thomas Moore, *Diary*, entry for 10 May 1828.

[4] Lord Cockburn, *Life of Lord Jeffrey* (1852), I, 322.

[5] Letter to *Carnarvon Herald*, 6 Nov. 1852, reprinted in *Academy*, 7 Nov. 1896. The visit took place in 1844.

[6] *Blackwood's Magazine*, June 1927, p. 740.

[7] T. C. Grattan, *Beaten Paths* (1862), II, 123.

been elaborate and polysyllabic—a characteristic nicely hit off by one of the Wordsworth grandchildren: 'Grandpapa', he exclaimed, looking up in amazement, 'is reading without a book!'[1]

But the *bonhomie* was reserved for his social equals. As he grew older, Wordsworth had less and less to say to his humbler neighbours. Their opinions of him were collected after his death by H. D. Rawnsley and form the basis of a paper read to the Wordsworth Society, with Robert Browning in the chair, that is now a minor classic. According to *Reminiscences of Wordsworth among the Peasantry of Westmorland*, the poet became a morose eccentric in his later years who never laughed and had little to say to anybody. 'He was not a man as fwoaks could crack wi', nor not a man as could crack wi' fwoaks.'[2] In both these respects the disreputable Hartley Coleridge was greatly his superior. According to one old man, whose sister had been a servant at Rydal Mount for years, Hartley was 'twice the man that Mr. Wordsworth was'. 'But you see, sir,' he told a correspondent of *The Athenæum*, 'Mr. Wordsworth had character, and dear Mr. Hartley, sir—well, he had not character. It is a great thing in this world, sir, is character. But for all that, sir, dear Mr. Hartley was the better man of the two.'[3] The verdict is a salutary reminder of a certain narrowness in Wordsworth, both as a man and a poet. When he was buried Eliza Fletcher reported to her daughter that 'Every Grasmere face you know of the upper grade was at the funeral, but I was sorry not to see any of the peasantry, he was so peculiarly the poor man's friend.'[4] Once upon a time, in the 1790s, he had been the poor man's friend, but for the last fifty years of his life he had been too much preoccupied with himself to spare much time for the poor—or indeed the not-so-poor. The egotistical sublime, in its later phases at any rate, had perhaps been purchased at rather too high a price.

---

[1] Edward Whately, *Leisure Hour*, 1 Oct. 1870, p. 652.

[2] H. D. Rawnsley, *Lake Country Sketches* (1903), p. 38.

[3] George Birdwood, "Wordsworth", *Athenæum*, 2 Mar. 1889.

[4] *Autobiography* (1875), p. 283.

Chapter Six

THE CRITICAL VERDICT

I

Why did he write? In the complex of conscious and semi-conscious motives, was there one that can be distinguished as the efficient cause of Wordsworth's poetry?

Wordsworth's stock answer, repeated with greater and greater emphasis as his youth receded, was that he was a teacher, and that he wrote his poetry primarily in order to provide his readers with moral instruction. This is certainly the gist of the long letter that he wrote to John Wilson, who is perhaps better known as 'Christopher North' of Blackwood's, in 1802. Wilson had praised *Lyrical Ballads* for the accuracy with which human emotions were delineated there. But this account did not satisfy Wordsworth:

> You have given me praise for having reflected faithfully in my Poems the feelings of human nature. I would fain hope that I have done so. But a great Poet ought to do more than this: he ought, to a certain degree, to rectify men's feelings, to give them new composi-tions of feeling, to render their feelings more sane, pure, and per-manent, in short, more consonant to nature, that is, to eternal nature, and the great moving spirit of things. He ought to travel before men occasionally as well as at their sides.[1]

And as examples of the emotional education that the great poet must take his reader through, Wordsworth went on to mention the excessive admiration paid in the past to 'personal prowess and military success'. 'So with regard to birth, and innumerable other modes of sentiment, civil and religious.' His own "Idiot Boy", he added, was intended to show that 'the loathing and disgust which many people have at the sight of an idiot' is really only 'false delicacy'.

---

[1] Wordsworth to John Wilson, June 1802.

If we can trust the letter to Wilson the central doctrine preached
in the earlier poems is egalitarianism. They were written, apparently, to convince the rich—'Gentlemen, persons of fortune,
professional men, ladies, persons who can afford to buy, or can
easily procure, books of half-a-guinea price, hot-pressed, and
printed upon superfine paper'[1]—that they could learn a great deal
from the private lives of the poor. Wordsworth was no doubt
exaggerating the didactic elements in his poetry, but if not
entirely convinced we can see today that egalitarian propaganda
was certainly one of the motives that contributed to the writing
of *Salisbury Plain*, *The Ruined Cottage* and "The Old Cumberland
Beggar." It may also have operated in *Lyrical Ballads*, though
most of the ballads in the first edition were apparently intended
for the middle and lower classes rather than the rich. But what
about "Tintern Abbey"? Or the Lucy poems? Or *The Prelude*?
In so far as there is doctrine in these poems it is not, except
incidentally in *The Prelude*, the lesson of the Universal Heart but
a form of Pantheism that is being inculcated. And in preaching
the Religion of Nature Wordsworth did not address himself
specifically to either the rich or the poor. The people he was most
concerned about were those who live in towns, 'the obstreperous
city', as he calls it in *The Excursion*.[2] Love, he maintained in *The
Prelude*, does not

> easily thrive
> In cities, where the human heart is sick,
> And the eye feeds it not, and cannot feed.[3]

It had been his special fortune, as he was at pains to point out,
that he had grown up

> Not with the mean and vulgar works of Man,
> But with high objects, with enduring things.[4]

With these convictions Wordsworth's poetic mission-field as the
prophet of nature was necessarily in the towns. It was the townsman and not the countryman who in fact read his poems, and to

---

[1] Wordsworth to John Wilson, June 1802.   [2] IV, 369.
[3] *Prelude*, XII, ll, 201–3.   [4] *Ibid.*, I, ll. 435–6.

whom they are obviously primarily addressed. Unfortunately, however, as an early critic pointed out,[1] the prolonged access which they prescribe to nature in its grandest and wildest forms was only possible in the nineteenth century to the townsman with a large income. The urban rich could save their souls, the urban poor couldn't—a conclusion that is hardly compatible with the enthusiastic egalitarianism of the letter to Wilson.

Wordsworth never succeeded in resolving this logical contra-diction between his belief in equality and his belief in the spiritual benefits to be obtained from an intimate communion with wild nature. When it was proposed to extend the railway line from Kendal to Windermere he resisted the proposal with all the eloquence he could then command (1844) in both verse and prose. But to the advocates of the extension who pointed out that the new railway would now enable the poor to enjoy the scenery of the Lake District he could only reply (in a letter to the *Morning Post*): 'Rocks and mountains, torrents and wide-spread waters, and all those features of nature which go to the composition of such scenes as this part of England is distinguished for, cannot, in their finer relations to the human mind, be comprehended, or even very imperfectly conceived, without processes of culture or opportunities of observation in some degree habitual.'[2] The admission, however, is fatal to a central thesis of *The Prelude*—that the basis of the good life is *unconscious* intercourse with natural beauty. Moreover the townsman who has to undergo preliminary 'processes of culture' and be provided with appro-priate 'opportunities of observation' will at best only turn into another connoisseur of Picturesque Beauty, like the Reverend William Gilpin.

The honest answer to the projectors of the Kendal and Winder-mere Railway—that the privacy of the Lake District was a necessity for his own mental health—was one that Wordsworth

---

[1] George Brimley, *Essays*, pp. 113-14.

[2] Wordsworth reprinted his two letters on this matter in the *Morning Post* in a pamphlet—*Kendal and Windermere Railway* (1844). My quotation is from de Selincourt's edition of *Wordsworth's Guide to the Lakes* (1906), p. 151, which reprints the pamphlet as Appendix II.

himself could not give. It is not that he was a hypocrite, but he was a man exceptionally unaware of his own motives. At this very time, when by opposing the railway he was strenuously denying the poor opportunities already available to the rich, he used to hold forth 'with great animation' at Ambleside tea-parties, we are told, 'of the unfortunate separation between the rich and the poor in this country'.[1] Nor was this an isolated sentimentality; the long 'Postscript' that he added to the Prefaces of his poems in 1835 contains a thoroughly sensible and humane attack upon the New Poor Law. But Wordsworth's right hand did not know, and so could not understand, what his left hand was doing.

It will be apparent that this contradiction between the 'messages' Wordsworth meant his poetry to convey is one more example of the incompatibility of the Two Voices. The egalitarianism can be equated, roughly, with his 'Augustan' voice and the nature-mysticism with the 'Romantic' voice. Put into prose, in terms of conscious intentions, the dilemma could not be resolved. Each 'message' was valid up to a point, but the two half-truths, instead of adding up to a whole truth, a consistent and coherent philosophy of life, only cancel each other out. To overcome the contradiction it is necessary to go behind Wordsworth's various pronouncements about the function of his poetry to the personal motives, of which he himself was often only partly conscious, out of which all that is most genuine and original in it really emerges. In other words, if we are to look for an efficient cause of his poetry, the ultimate explanation for its being written at all, the place where we may hope to find it is not in his Prefaces, or in semi-public letters like those to Wilson or Fox, but in the recesses of his personality, the dark corners that were only partly explored even in *The Prelude*.

The boy's abysses of idealism present the problem in its simplest form. These 'Fallings from us, vanishings' are recorded with some equanimity in "Intimations of Immortality", but it must not be forgotten that they very much alarmed Wordsworth in

---

[1] "Reminiscences of Lady Richardson (1843)" are printed in *Memoirs of William Wordsworth* (1851), II, 440.

his early school-days. The only way in which he found that he could rescue himself when drowning in the deep sea of subjectivity was to grasp a wall or a tree or a gate. The sense of touch, consciously and almost desperately appealed to, provided the one effective means of return to the objective world. The touch is the most primitive of the senses, and in less acute crises the more sophisticated senses, particularly those of sight and hearing, were able to perform a similar function. Wordsworth's excitement when he discovered, at the age of fourteen, how different the oak on the Hawkshead-Ambleside road looked at sunset was clearly a connected psychological phenomenon. The resolution that he made to record 'the infinite variety of natural appearances' may perhaps be regarded, from this point of view, as a more disciplined defensive strategy against the terrors of the subjective world, such as the 'huge and mighty Forms' who haunted him after he had stolen the Ullswater boat. (It will be remembered that, in addition to troubling his dreams for many days, those formidable ghosts also 'mov'd slowly through the mind By day'.) It is possible that the ultimate source of Wordsworth's passionate devotion to wild nature was the gratitude he felt to 'rocks and stones and trees' for saving him from this nightmare world. The hypothesis will help to explain the striking difference in poetic quality between the descriptions of Esthwaite Water and its surroundings and those of inherently more beautiful or more impressive scenery elsewhere. The sights and sounds of the country round Hawkshead included objects that he had in fact 'grasped', with one or other of the senses, when the nightmarish moods described in *The Vale of Esthwaite* had descended upon him. The later enthusiasm for the Picturesque was perhaps only a rationalisation of the adolescent gratitudes. It is certainly significant that a scene exceptionally picturesque by ordinary standards—I am thinking of the magnificent sunset in the Alps so conscientiously described in *Descriptive Sketches*[1]—was insufficient in itself to induce poetry in Wordsworth. Such scenery was too impersonal, too objective. The brilliant catalogues in *An Evening Walk* of the sounds to be heard on Esthwaite Water before and after sunset

---

[1] ll. 336–47.

are in a wholly different category. Here personal memories and
associations have unconsciously given the impressionism another
dimension. Although it is not always visible on the surface the
poetry in these passages almost certainly derives its quality from
the momentary union in Wordsworth of intense objective and
subjective pressures—the eye that recorded and the emotion that
was recollected.

In Wordsworth's second phase the background of subjective
terror reappears in a different form. When he paid his first visit to
Tintern in 1793 he was once again, in his relations with natural
scenery,

> more like a man
> Flying from something that he dreads, than one
> Who sought the thing he loved.

But the 'something' had lost its vulgar supernatural quality. It is
true there are Druids in the first version of *Salisbury Plain*, but
they are much less alarming than the Druids of *The Vale of
Esthwaite*. There is also an unpublished ballad fragment written
at Racedown that is all about a ghost.[1] But the nightmare quality
has gone. The subjectivity of this phase is not an absyss of idealism.
Wordsworth did not need to grasp things now to assure himself
of the reality of the outer world. It was rather what might be
called a social subjectivity—the mood in which he 'Yielded up
moral questions in despair'. The failure of his own plans and
ambitions, his unintended desertion of Annette and Caroline, the
war with France, and the degeneration of revolutionary idealism
into Robespierre's Reign of Terror had combined to deprive him
not only of a social function for himself but of a content to the
very concept of society. And the return to sanity was by a process
of sympathetic self-identification with other social outcasts. In
the anti-social nightmare he was still able from time to time to
'grasp' the basic human traits exhibited by such companions in
his misfortune as Peter Bell's original or the heroine of "We are
Seven". It cannot be an accident that, with only one or two
important exceptions, all the poems Wordsworth wrote during

---

[1] The MS. is in the so-called Racedown Notebook, now in the Wordsworth
Museum, Grasmere.

the five years between the summer of 1793 and the summer of 1798 are concerned with social outcasts and misfits, whose natural goodness and purity are contrasted with the treatment they receive from an indifferent and inhuman social order. By identifying himself subjectively with *dramatis personæ* as objectively different from himself as the hero and heroine of *Salisbury Plain*, the Margaret of *The Ruined Cottage*, the Cumberland Beggar, Poor Susan, Goody Blake, Simon Lee and the others he was able to overcome in himself the temptations to moral nihilism represented by Oswald in *The Borderers* and the wicked mother in "The Three Graves". In the process of understanding them he was learning to understand and accept his own position in an ideal society.

The third phase is more complex and more difficult to define. A more minute analysis will be necessary not only because the egocentric period includes what are generally considered Wordsworth's greatest poems but also because of the remarkable extension of poetic range that it exhibits. In addition to the autobiographical poems like "Tintern Abbey" and *The Prelude* and such quasi-autobiographical poems as "Resolution and Independence", "Intimations of Immortality" and the "Ode to Duty", there are poems like "Michael" and "The Sailor's Mother" that seem at first sight to be reversions to the second phase, as well as more fanciful pieces like the Lucy series and "Ruth" that are different from either group. It is true that a biographical unity in this diversity is provided by Dorothy. Some of the poems are about her, others are devoted to topics that were especially congenial to her, and a great many are about that childhood period that Wordsworth felt he shared with his sister in a special sense. But, though Dorothy's presence or influence serves as a connecting link between these poems, it does not altogether account for the fusion of subjective and objective attitudes in them.

A clue is perhaps provided by the appearance of a new feature in Wordsworth's poetry during this phase. The new feature is the recurring metaphors. In the earlier poems the metaphors are generally conventional and commonplace, but in 1798 they

suddenly attain an almost Shakespearian vigour. A characteristic
example of the metaphors of this third phase is the image describing
the impression Windermere made upon the young Wordsworth,
as he and his friends returned from Bowness, in the second book
of *The Prelude*:

> Oh! then the calm
> And dead still water lay upon my mind
> Even with a weight of pleasure, and the sky
> Never before so beautiful, sank down
> Into my heart, and held me like a dream.[1]

The impact of nature on the passive consciousness was described,
it will be remembered, in similar gravitational imagery in
"There was a Boy". But it is the active appreciation of natural
beauty that is the real theme of *The Prelude*, and this intimate co-
operation between the human subject and the natural object is
expressed in Wordsworth's poems of this period in images of
eating and drinking. The images recur so frequently that they
must be considered symbolic rather than merely metaphorical.
There are three examples in "Tintern Abbey" alone,[2] and similar
images are to be found in some of the finest passages in *The
Prelude*. As a child, it will be remembered, he

> held unconscious intercourse
> With the eternal Beauty, drinking in
> A pure organic pleasure from the lines
> Of curling mist . . .[3]

There were also those mysterious sounds that he heard at night:

> Thence did I drink the visionary power . . .[4]

And the gap in the mist on Snowdon that seemed to him

> The perfect image of a mighty Mind
> Of one that feeds upon infinity. . . .[5]

Other examples of eating and drinking images have already been
quoted earlier in this book.

---

[1] *Prelude*, II, ll. 176–80.   [2] ll. 64, 80, 127.
[3] *Prelude*, I, ll. 589–92.   [4] *Ibid.*, II, l. 330.
[5] *Ibid.*, XIII, ll. 69–70.

The Wordsworthian religion of nature seems to be implicit in these recurrent metaphors. Their primitive, infantile character, for one thing, shows how personal and subjective it was. In order to define his feelings in the presence of wild nature Wordsworth had to use some of the earliest and simplest sensations known to man. In "Expostulation and Reply"—which was written in June 1798, only a month or so before "Tintern Abbey"—both weight and food images are associated, not altogether surprisingly, with a kind of animism:

> Nor less I deem that there are powers,
> Which of themselves our minds impress,
> That we can feed this mind of ours,
> In a wise passiveness.

These natural 'powers' reappear in several early drafts of *The Prelude* and its offshoots, such as "Nutting", as 'Gentle powers' 'powers of earth', 'genii', 'beings of the hills', 'spirits of the springs', etc. They are certainly not entirely conventional, though Wordsworth would no doubt have denied them phenomenal existence. In some of the shorter poems the moon and the stars have also been animated in the same way. It seems difficult to deny to this phase what R. D. Havens has called 'a reversion to primitive ways of thinking' in Wordsworth.[1]

What was the psychological condition which this insistent primitivism reflects? It is possible that the instinctive regression to childhood should be seen as an unconscious attempt to return to the childish pre-sexual relationship with Dorothy; Wordsworth's conception of wild nature is certainly curiously sexless. Or perhaps it was simply a profound reaction against the fragmentary, disconnected mode of life into which he had drifted since he left Cambridge, whose dangers had now been dramatically illustrated when he and Dorothy found themselves in love? I go on using the word, because it is the right word to use, but I am not suggesting, of course, that there was a physical consummation. All that was 'Augustan' in Wordsworth wanted there not to be—and was terrified at its mere possibility. There is a

---

[1] *The Mind of a Poet* (1941), p. 84.

curious tribute to Coleridge's beneficial influence at this period at
the end of *The Prelude* (1850 text):

> Thy kindred influence to my heart of hearts
> Did also find its way. Thus fear relaxed
> Her overweening grasp; thus thoughts and things
> In the self-haunting spirit learned to take
> More rational proportions. . . .[1]

The revival of the subjective terrors recalls the boy's abysses of
idealism, and there is perhaps a parallel between Wordsworth's
'grasping' natural objects and 'eating' an animated nature to
escape fear's 'overweening grasp'. The animism assumed 'More
rational proportions' as Wordsworth began to re-establish the
sense of personal continuity by a conscious technique of emotion
recollected in tranquillity. The process consisted, essentially, in
restoring to consciousness and order the periods and events of his
personal life that were lurking haphazardly in the depths of his
memory. Its masterpiece, of course, is *The Prelude*, but the theme
of personal continuity is to be traced in most of the great poems
of this phase. It is certainly present, as we have seen, in "There was
a Boy". Wordsworth's psychological objective is summed up in
a fragment of Coleridge's that was written at this very time
(*c.* 1803): '. . . There does not exist a more important rule nor one
more fruitful in its consequences, moral as well as logical, than
the rule of connecting our present mind with our past—from the
breach of it result almost all the pernicious errors in our education
of children and indeed of our general treatment of our fellow
creatures.'[2] The mental continuity aimed at by both Wordsworth
and Coleridge was organic rather than rational. The metaphor in
The Prelude's sub-title ("Growth of a Poet's Mind")—unlike the
poem's title the sub-title is Wordsworth's own—was not by any
means a dead one. Indeed, as the deliberate anti-rationalism of
"She dwelt among the untrodden ways" has demonstrated, the
secondary power that multiplies distinctions represented for
Wordsworth one of the principal agents of discontinuity. There

---

[1] XIV (1850), ll. 281–5.
[2] Alice D. Snyder, *Coleridge on Logic and Learning* (1929), p. 60.

is among the MSS. at Grasmere a most interesting unpublished essay by Wordsworth, apparently written at Goslar, which contrasts the weakness of merely rational decisions with the powers of habit on the mind. Its general trend can be gauged from the opening sentences:

> I think publications in which we formally & systematically lay down rules for the actions of man (?) cannot be too long delayed. I shall scarcely express myself too strongly when I say that I consider such books as Mr Godwyns Mr Paley's & those of the whole tribe of authors of that class as impotent to all their intended good purposes, to which I wish I could add that they were equally impotent to all bad ones. . . . I know no book or system of moral philosophy written with sufficient power to melt into our affections, to incorporate itself with the blood & vital juices of our minds, & thence to have any influence worth our notice in forming those habits of which I am speaking.[1]

As against Paley, the Christian rationalist, and Godwin, the rational anarchist, Wordsworth was feeling his way in this third phase, the last genuinely creative phase, to a religion and a political philosophy based upon man's primal instincts. It was literally a matter of 'feeling' his way, and feeling did not always prove a reliable guide. But, whatever the failures in practice, his programme of psychic integration—of the unification of the sensibility, as Mr. Eliot would call it—must surely be commended. Instead of relying solely on the senses, as when he was struggling in the abysses of idealism, or solely on the emotions, as in his second phase, he was now trying to rebuild his personality on the basis of an emotional life rooted in the senses. The 'affections' were not enough. The disembodied affections had led into the ecstatic, explosive intimacy with Dorothy. In future, as in childhood, he would integrate the affections with 'the blood & vital juices'.

II

Why did he write? The question has now received a partial answer. The efficient cause, so far as the poetry had a single

---

[1] MS. JJ of *The Prelude*, Wordsworth Museum, Grasmere.

originating source, was the impelling need Wordsworth felt to integrate the more subjective or inward-looking and the more objective or outward-looking aspects of his personality. The poetry, it turns out, was not so much autobiography as a technique of self-preservation and self-recreation.

As a part of the process of re-establishing his own mental health Wordsworth found himself dramatising in verse a series of situations that paralleled or symbolised the regimen on which he was embarking in his own person. This homœopathic procedure was primarily an unconscious one. The character of the Female Vagrant, for example, cannot have been created in order that Wordsworth might have an opportunity to try out on paper, as it were, a possible attitude to his own personal disasters. But, if he was not wholly aware of the relationship between his life and his poetry, he must soon have discovered that there were interconnections between them. The dilemma of his personal life was that solitude, even when mitigated by the company of one or two intimates, carried with it the potential threat of melancholia, the condition that Coleridge called Wordsworth's 'hypochondriacism', while its opposite, the social life of a city, tended to smother and frustrate all that was most original and creative in him. And the conflicting 'pulls', either to a solitary communion with wild nature or to all-night arguments with fellow-intellectuals in Cambridge, London or Bristol, are reflected in the bases of his poetry. One might say that the periods of solitude or near-solitude provided the subject-matter out of which the poems were finally composed, whereas the form they took and the language in which they were written reflect the urban 'pull' in Wordsworth. But even such a differentiation of the Two Voices would be an over-simplification. It is true that the diction and the syntax of Wordsworth's poetry conform, with a few exceptions, to the literary language of late eighteenth-century London, but the total stylistic impression that his poems leave, again with some exceptions, is very different from that of the poetry of contemporary Londoners. The fact is something of a commonplace, though it is not always realised that Wordsworth's use of language is as different from that of his younger London contemporaries as it obviously is from those of the older poets; as different, for example, from Keats's as from Cowper's. The difference seems to derive from Wordsworth's attitude to his audience—a problem that has not received the critical attention it deserves.

As a preliminary to a definition of Wordsworth's poetic audience, it will be worth while looking rather closely into two voices that are to be heard in his poetry in quite a different sense from J. K. Stephen's. In so far as poetry is read aloud or recited, it is dominated by the spoken voice. But poetry that is written primarily to be read appeals to an *unspoken* voice. The two voices are not mutually exclusive and in some of Wordsworth's poems it makes little or no difference whether they are read to one or one reads them to oneself. But this is not generally true. One of the most important differences between Wordsworth and the other major poets of the eighteenth and nineteenth centuries is that whereas they wrote for the silent reader, *i.e.* for the eye, he wrote most of his poems to be declaimed, *i.e.* for the ear. It was only in revising his poems later that he took into account the claims of the eye. This characteristic is the real explanation of the heaviness of style, the occasional clumsiness and general lack of verbal polish, that Tennyson hit off in the epithet *thick-ankled* ('Wordsworth seemed to him *thick-ankled*').[1] Tennyson *saw* his own poems as well as hearing them. The critical standards that he applied to Wordsworth's verse—he objected, for example, to the want of literary instinct shown in the repetition of the word 'again' four times in the first fourteen lines of "Tintern Abbey"—were those of a poet for whom a poem exists primarily on a piece of paper. It is something he can return to whenever he likes, touching up a rhythm here and a metaphor there, as the mood takes him. For Wordsworth, except in the process of revising his poems for a new edition (when the basis was generally either pasted-up sheets of an earlier edition or transcripts made by his women-folk), the poem existed primarily *in his head*—as a rhetorical whole, that is, of which the part could only be reached after all that had preceded it had been declaimed.

---

[1] *Tennyson. A Memoir. By his Son* (1897), II, 505.

It is significant that, instead of lending his friends MSS. or printed copies of his poems, Wordsworth preferred to read them aloud or recite them. Emerson, who paid his first call on the Wordsworths in 1833, found the Rydal Mount ritual of recitation a little disconcerting:

> He had just returned from a visit to Staffa, and within three days had made three sonnets on Fingal's Cave, and was composing a fourth when he was called in to see me. He said, 'If you are interested in my verses, perhaps you will like to hear these lines.' I gladly assented; and he recollected himself for a few moments, and then stood forth and repeated, one after the other, the three entire sonnets, with great animation. . . . This recitation was so unlooked for and surprising,—he, the old Wordsworth, standing apart, and reciting to me in a garden walk, like a schoolboy declaiming—that I at first was near to laugh; but recollecting myself, that I had come thus far to see a poet, and he was chanting poems to me, I saw that he was right and I was wrong, and gladly gave myself up to hear.[1]

Some of Wordsworth's other American visitors seem to have found it even more difficult to adjust themselves. The poet Bryant, for example, used to give amusing, if irreverent, imitations of the performance.

Wordsworth also read his poems aloud as effectively as he recited them. Hazlitt's "My First Acquaintance with Poets" contains a vivid account of the way he did it: 'We went over to All-Foxden again the day following, and Wordsworth read us the story of "*Peter Bell*" in the open air; and the comment made upon it by his face and voice was very different from that of some later critics! Whatever might be thought of the poem, "his face was as a book where men might read strange matters", and he announced the fate of his hero in prophetic tones.' Wordsworth makes it clear in his 1815 Preface that he expected his poems to be read aloud. 'Some of these pieces', he writes, 'are essentially lyrical; and, therefore, cannot have their due force without a supposed musical accompaniment; but, in much the greatest part, as a substitute for the classic lyre or romantic harp, I require

---

[1] *English Traits* (1856), chap. i.

nothing more than an animated or impassioned recitation, adapted to the subject.' The poems, he adds, will not 'read themselves'. The reader is to be encouraged to contribute his own modulation of the music of the poem. It is clear that Wordsworth regarded the facial expressions and dramatic intonations with which he read or recited his poems as an essential part of their meaning. Without this or a similar accompaniment—that is, if it was read silently by the reader to himself—the poetry would fail to achieve its proper effect. It is probably true that the technical slovenliness to which Tennyson objected in "Tintern Abbey" would not be noticed, if the poem was declaimed with sufficient animation. And in poetry a slovenliness that is not noticed does not exist. It is our modern reading habits that are at fault here, not Wordsworth.

Wordsworth's habit of either reading his poems aloud or reciting them was a corollary of his habit of composing aloud. This was a practice that fascinated his humbler neighbours, and Rawnsley's *Reminiscences of Wordsworth among the Peasantry of Westmorland* is full of stories of the poet's 'bummings' and 'booings'. One of Rawnsley's witnesses, a half-farmer, half-hotelkeeper, remembered how alarming Wordsworth's powerful voice could make the process of composition:

> . . . thear was anudder thing as kep' fwoaks off, he had a terr'ble girt deep voice, and ye med see his faace agaan for lang eneuf. I've knoan fwoaks, village lads and lasses, coming ower by t'auld road aboon what runs fra Gersmer to Rydal, flayt a'most to death there by t'Wishing Gate to hear t'girt voice a groanin' and mutterin' and thunderin' of a still evening. And he hed a way of standin' quite still by t'rock there in t'path under Rydal, and fwoaks could hear sounds like a wild beast coming fra t'rocks, and childer were scared fit to be dëad a'most.[1]

If this anecdote is to be taken at its face value, it looks as if Wordsworth enacted his poems as he composed them. No doubt on such occasions he would have thought he was alone and could not be overheard. The performance on the grass terrace at Rydal

---

[1] *Lake Country Sketches* (1903), pp. 38–9.

Mount, as the Wordsworths' garden-boy remembered it, was a more staid affair altogether:

> . . . he would set his heäd a bit forrad, and put his hands behint his back. And then he would start a bumming, and it was bum, bum, bum, stop; then bum, bum, bum reet down till t'other end, and then he'd set down and git a bit o' paper out and write a bit; and then he git up, and bum, bum, bum, and goa on bumming for long enough right down and back agean. I suppose, ya kna, the bumming helped him out a bit. However, his lips was always goan' whoale time he was upon the gres walk.[1]

The bits of paper are interesting. They do not come into the account given to Rawnsley by a one-time maid of the Words-worths of the procedure indoors:

> . . . Mr. Wordsworth went bumming and booing about, and she, Miss Dorothy, kept close behint him, and she picked up the bits as he let 'em fall, and tak 'em down, and put 'em together on paper for him. And you med . . . be very well sure as how she didn't under-stand nor make sense out of 'em, and I doubt that he didn't kna much aboot them either himself. . . .[2]

Rawnsley's witnesses must be taken with a grain or two of salt. They had none of them read any of Wordsworth's poems, and they regarded him as an eccentric, whose actions rarely had any rational basis. Moreover their evidence, which was only collected in the 1870s, refers for the most part to the last twenty years or so of Wordsworth's life.

But the earlier evidence is on the same lines. Coleridge told Hazlitt that 'Wordsworth always wrote (if he could) walking up and down a straight gravel-walk, or in some spot where the continuity of his verse met with no collateral interruption'.[3] This

---

[1] *Lake Country Sketches* (1903), pp. 15–16. An earlier gardener to interest himself in Wordsworth's methods of composition was one of the Beaumonts' employees at Coleorton who, unknown to Wordsworth, used to follow him round to 'catch the words I uttered'. (I.F. note to "Though narrow be that old Man's cares", *Poetical Works*, ed. E. de Selincourt, III, 430.)

[2] *Ibid.*, p. 7.

[3] "My First Acquaintance with Poets."

seems to confirm the garden-boy's account, though it omits the bits of paper (perhaps they were proofs or fair copies that Wordsworth was only revising?). One early poem that we know was composed orally was "Tintern Abbey", which was not written down until the Wordsworths had returned to Bristol after their short tour of South Wales. Although there are 160 lines in it, and no rhymes to act as mnemonic aids, 'Not a line of it was altered, and not any part of it written down till I reached Bristol'. According to G. M. Harper, the most exhaustive of Wordsworth's biographers, it was his regular habit to retain hundreds of lines in his mind, often for many weeks, before they were completed. When a poem had been completed orally it was often dictated to Dorothy, as Wordsworth disliked intensely the physical exertion involved in writing. There is a tradition that Wordsworth dictated Books I and II of *The Prelude* to her, while he paced up and down a still-existing path at Lancrigg near Grasmere. An Irish yew has been planted to mark the spot where Dorothy sat.[1] Although the account may not be literally true— much of Book I was written down in Germany, many months before the Wordsworths settled at Grasmere—it probably gives a reliable idea of the way many of the poems got on to paper. One of the reasons why the Wordsworths aroused the suspicions of their neighbours in the Quantocks in 1797 was their habit of sallying forth with folding stools and notebooks. 'The man has Camp Stools', the busybody at Bath reported to the Home Secretary, 'which he and his visitors take with them when they go about the country upon their nocturnal or diurnal excursions, and has also a Portfolio in which they enter their observations, which they have been heard to say were almost finished.'[2] It would be nice to know what it was in reality that was 'almost finished'. Was it *The Ruined Cottage*? Had the 'Portfolio' been acquired so that Wordsworth could dictate the final version to Dorothy while they sat on the 'Camp Stools' at some picturesque spot discovered on their walks?

---

[1] *William Wordsworth* (1916), I, 401, II, 6.
[2] A. J. Eagleston, "Wordsworth, Coleridge and the Spy", *Nineteenth Century and After*, Aug. 1908.

Ambulatory composition was Wordsworth's most usual method, but it was not his only method. Charles Greville, the diarist, who met Wordsworth at one of Henry Taylor's breakfast parties in 1831, was told that 'he never wrote down as he composed, but composed walking, riding, or in bed, and wrote down after'.[1] The number of poems composed on horseback is probably small. Wordsworth was a poor horseman and only borrowed or hired a mount on exceptional occasions. The one poem that is known to have been composed when riding is "Among all lovely things my Love had been", which was not only composed on horseback (between 'the beginning of Lord Darlington's park at Raby and two or three miles beyond Staindrop') but is also a record of an earlier ride. The poems composed in bed provide a more interesting category. The time of composition was apparently the morning. In 1830 Wordsworth told some undergraduates at Trinity College, Cambridge, that some of his best thoughts came to him 'between sleeping and waking, or as he expressed it, in a morning sleep'. The observation was recorded in his diary by Henry Alford, one of the undergraduates, and arose out of a discussion of "Kubla Khan", which Wordsworth thought Coleridge might have composed in the same half-awake state in which some of his own poems came to him.[2] Wordsworth certainly attached a special importance to 'the first involuntary thoughts upon waking in the morning'. He once told R. P. Graves, the Vicar of Ambleside, that they ought to be watched closely 'as indications of the real current of moral being'.[3]

Wordsworth always composed orally. Normally he composed aloud. There is some evidence that his voice rose and fell in the process of composition, as though he was reciting the poem before an imaginary audience. Only when the poem had been completed, unless it was an exceptionally long one, was it put into writing. Often it was not Wordsworth himself but his sister who actually wrote down the poem.

---

[1] See Edith C. Batho, *The Later Wordsworth* (1933), pp. 11–12.

[2] *Life, Journals and Letters of Henry Alford* (3rd edition, 1874), p. 62.

[3] Christopher Wordsworth, *Memoirs of William Wordsworth*, II, 481.

These are the principal conclusions that it seems reasonable to draw from the existing evidence as to Wordsworth's methods of composition. His nervous objection to putting pen to paper may explain some of the peculiarities, but it does not explain his preference for reading his own poetry aloud or reciting it. It certainly seems as though oral communication was, for him, the natural medium of poetry. When he defined the poet as 'a man speaking to men' it is possible, I think, that he was using the word 'speaking' in a literal sense, and that the audience he envisaged when composing was a real audience—composed of *auditors*. The relationship, however, was not that of an actor to a theatrical audience so much as that of a priest to a congregation of devotees. Hazlitt, who is confirmed in this matter by Emerson, noted the prevalence of *chant* in the way Wordsworth recited his poems, which 'acts as a spell upon the hearer, and disarms the judgment'. The choice of metaphor is significant. A chant that acts as a spell is an *incantation*. The complement of a spell-bound hearer is a spell-binding poet, an *enchanter*. The metaphor brings out once more the essentially primitive nature of Wordsworth's conception of poetry. He is the bard, the *sacer vates*, whose relationship with his little audience is infinitely more intimate and more profound than the casual liaison between the modern poet and his readers that is provided by printers, publishers and booksellers.

The highly charged, almost hysterical atmosphere within the original inner circle of the Wordsworths, the Coleridges and the Hutchinsons is apparent in a curious letter that Wordsworth wrote to Sara Hutchinson on 14 June 1802, just a few months before he married Mary. Sara had complained that the leech-gatherer in an early version of "Resolution and Independence" was *tedious*, a criticism that provoked the following outburst: 'You speak of his speech as tedious: everything is tedious when one does not read with the feelings of the Author—"*The Thorn*" is tedious to hundreds; and so is the *Idiot Boy* to hundreds. It is in the character of the old man to tell his story in a manner which an *impatient* reader must necessarily feel as tedious. But Good God! Such a figure, in such a place, a pious, self-respecting, miserably infirm and [word illegible] Old Man telling such a tale!' The letter concludes by contrasting Sara's reaction to "Beggars," a much less ambitious poem that Wordsworth had written earlier the same year: 'Your feelings upon the Mother, and the Boys with the Butterfly, were not indifferent: it was an affair of whole continents of moral sympathy.' Wordsworth had not had an opportunity, as far as is known, to read or recite either poem to the Hutchinsons, but the commentary provided by intonation or gesture was presumably not required in their case. Instead he could normally count on 'whole continents of moral sympathy' within this intimate inner audience. The rarity of its failure is proved by the intensity of his disappointment when on this one occasion it did occur.

Like most of the Romantic poets Wordsworth found it hard to say who it was exactly he wrote his poems for. At one time, as he confessed to Wrangham, it was his ambition to write poems which would find their way into the cottages and supplant the superstitious and indelicate chapbooks that were the staple literary fare of country people in his time—'half-penny Ballads, and penny and twopenny histories'.[1] In the 1815 Preface, however, it is the People to whom his poems are addressed—not 'that small though loud portion of the community, ever governed by factitious influence, which, under the name of the PUBLIC, passes itself, upon the unthinking, for the PEOPLE', but the People 'philosophically characterised'. In this sense the People was that select body of cultivated readers who maintain the continuity of literature by familiarising themselves with the best poetry both of their own time and of earlier periods. In the nature of the case, therefore, Wordsworth now admits, an original poet 'must reconcile himself for a season to few and scattered hearers'. The contradiction between the two aspirations—a mass working-class audience on the one hand and on the other a few isolated intellectuals—is perhaps partly bridged in the word 'hearers'. The oral poetry that Wordsworth wrote demanded an audience of listeners who would co-operate with him in the process of communication and transmission. The 1815 Preface is emphatic that the poetic auditor must not be a merely passive participant, 'like an Indian prince or

---

[1] Wordsworth to Francis Wrangham, 5 June 1808.

general stretched on his palanquin, and borne by his slaves'. Now the one place where a tradition of oral poetry persisted in Wordsworth's time was the country, though 'half-penny Ballads' were, it is true, a dying art-form at the end of the eighteenth century. What Wordsworth seems to have been feeling his way towards was a somewhat similar oral relationship among a select body of middle-class intellectuals. It may even be claimed that he did succeed in creating a modern equivalent of the primitive ballad-audience. In the early Wordsworthians— Lamb, Hazlitt, John Wilson, De Quincey, Sir George Beaumont, Haydon, Crabb Robinson, Henry Taylor and Talfourd are probably the best-known of them—he found the sort of intimate and enthusiastic audience, co-operative and yet critical, out of which the great traditional ballads must have originally emerged.

It was a poet-audience relationship different in kind from that of a Spenser, a Milton, a Dryden or a Pope, partly because of its oral basis and partly because of its emotional overtones. To a typical Wordsworthian Wordsworth was so much more than just another good poet. The process of discovering his poetry was more like a religious conversion, an experience from which the convert emerged with the whole of his way of looking at the world permanently and profoundly changed. In a striking passage in *Appreciations* Pater has described those who had undergone Wordsworth's influence as being 'like people who have passed through some initiation, a *disciplina arcani*, by submitting to which they become able constantly to distinguish in art, speech, feeling, manners, that which is only conventional, derivative, inexpressive'.[1] And in the case of the best of the Wordsworthians —De Quincey, for example—the description is scarcely an exaggeration. All that is most original and profound in De Quincey's criticism at any rate undoubtedly derives, as he himself acknowledged on one occasion, from 'many years' conversation with Mr. Wordsworth'.[2]

---

[1] The passage occurs in Pater's well-known essay on Wordsworth, which was written in 1874.

[2] "The Literature of Knowledge and the Literature of Power" (1823).

But if Wordsworth was necessary to the Wordsworthians they were not less necessary to him. It is no accident, for example, that the first and best version of *The Prelude* is addressed directly to Coleridge, or that "Michael" was written for and about Thomas Poole, or even that it was Sir George Beaumont's indifferent painting of Peele Castle which inspired the magnificent "Elegiac Stanzas". And even when the connection is not explicit it is impossible not to be aware, in many of Wordsworth's greatest poems, of that original audience on whom the poem will first be tried out, whose suggestions and criticisms will be considered and very often accepted, and who will copy the MS. out and send it round to their friends.[1] Unfortunately, as he grew older, Wordsworth began to take this intimate inner public too much for granted and to concern himself more and more with the reading public in general. The way to reach this outer public created a difficult technical problem. How could the spoken voice be transposed into the non-spoken voice of the printed page? What substitutes could be found for the facial and vocal accompaniments he normally relied on to tap the moral sympathy latent in his more intimate audience? In the end the solution was provided by the Wordsworthians, who gradually taught the upper middle class how to read Wordsworth. Their eulogies and commentaries bridged a gap that was too wide for Wordsworth to make himself heard across orally. But Wordsworth did not realise this. Instead of relying on the missionary efforts of his disciples he tried, in later life, to meet the reading public half-way. Instead of restricting himself to the oral poetry that came naturally to him, and that he wrote so well, he began to write non-oral poetry, poetry for the eye. Worse still, instead of concentrating on the intimate inner public who formed his natural audience, he started to give the common reader what he thought the common reader needed. He began to *preach*. (The turning-point was perhaps at the end of 1802, when he began to contribute sonnets in aid

---

[1] See the cancelled 'Advertisement' originally intended for the 1807 *Poems*: '... as several of these Poems have been circulated in manuscript ...' (W. Hale White, *A Description of the Wordsworth and Coleridge Manuscripts in the Possession of Mr. T. Norton Longman*, 1897, p. 71).

of the war-effort to the *Morning Post*.) Worst of all, he started revising his earlier poems to make them more palatable to the silent reader. The hours of labour Wordsworth devoted to giving poems composed orally and intended for oral recitation the finish and elegance demanded in poetry written for the eye would be impressive, if they had not been so disastrous. Of the thousands of alterations that he made in one edition after another, only a very few can be considered any improvement at all, and many are ludicrously inferior to the readings they displace. As a general rule it is best to read Wordsworth's poems in the earliest text available. The non-spoken voice that he worked so hard to acquire was a falsetto that should not be allowed to drown the simple sincerity of the spoken voice in which his great poetry was composed.

III

The potential danger in the relationship between Wordsworth and the Wordsworthians was that it might turn into that of a spiritual healer ministering to a congregation of sick souls. It is true that the man—partly because of his acquired hardness and worldliness and partly because of a certain awkward integrity that he never lost—never degenerated into a drawing-room prophet. The disciples were taken for a walk round Grasmere and given tea at Rydal Mount, their letters were answered, their poems were read, but the routine proceeded with a minimum of uplift and unction. Long before the man's death, however, the poet had tended to become dissociated from him, and throughout the nineteenth century the poet Wordsworth was regarded primarily as a healer. John Stuart Mill has testified in his *Autobiography* to the restorative properties of Wordsworth's poetry after an overdose of Utilitarianism, and there is a similar testimony by William Hale White in *The Autobiography of Mark Rutherford*. It will be remembered that Arnold's "Memorial Verses", which were written immediately after Wordsworth's death and were intended as a sort of poetical obituary notice, also select 'Wordsworth's healing power' as the essence of his genius.

Under its influence the desiccated victim of the Iron Time was able to 'feel' once again:

> He found us when the age had bound
> Our souls in its benumbing round;
> He spoke, and loos'd our hearts in tears,
> He laid us as we lay at birth
> On the cool flowery lap of earth;
> Smiles broke from us and we had ease.

The tributes ring a little hollowly today. The old healing power has certainly lost most of its efficacy. And if to be a Wordsworthian it is necessary, as Arnold says in the Preface to his selection from Wordsworth, to read 'with pleasure and edification' everything Wordsworth ever wrote, how many of us are prepared to be Wordsworthians? Will the mid-twentieth century imitate Arnold in reading 'the whole series of *Ecclesiastical Sonnets* [there are 132 of them], and the address to Mr. Wilkinson's spade, and even the *Thanksgiving Ode*'?[1] In America, according to Lionel Trilling, Wordsworth is not read at all now, except in the universities,[2] and in this country too, his popularity has declined almost as catastrophically. Wordsworth is in considerable danger of becoming a classic, like Spenser or Jonson, to whom we pay our respects, but in whom our real interest, if we are to be honest, is decidedly tepid. If his poetry is to be saved from that shelf, it will perhaps be by our returning, as far as that is possible for a twentieth-century reader, to the sort of relationship to it that his original inner audience had to Wordsworth.

The basis of that relationship was a common plight. The middle-class intellectuals who made up Wordsworth's circle of friends lived the same sort of rootless, functionless, fragmentary existence that he had led after his mother's death. The difference between them, however, was not that of doctor and patient but simply of degrees of sickness. And all the evidence now suggests that Wordsworth's soul was not less sick than Coleridge's or

---

[1] Preface (1879), pp. xxv–xxvi.

[2] "Wordsworth and the Iron Time", *Kenyon Review*, summer 1950 (reprinted in *Wordsworth Centenary Studies*, ed. G. T. Dunklin, Princeton, 1951).

Lamb's or Hazlitt's or De Quincey's but more sick. What fascinated and inspired his friends was Wordsworth's continually renewed struggle towards normality and mental health *in spite of his greater sickness*—a struggle which is reflected and worked out in his poems with meticulous if often unconscious honesty and sensitiveness.

The tragic interest of Wordsworth's case is the exceptional degree to which his inner life was predetermined by psychic forces outside his control and of which he was himself only dimly conscious. The recurrent pattern of crisis, psychological disintegration, and gradual convalescence which I have tried to define, is itself evidence of a character in which the area left for the free will and the conscious mind to control was exceptionally small. If I am right in thinking that the pattern repeated itself almost identically at least three times and in each case over a period of almost exactly six years, the special nature of Wordsworth's case included not only a general psychic rhythm, but a pre-determined time-scheme. But if Wordsworth was to a greater degree than most of us the victim of circumstance he was the least acquiescent of victims. At one time I thought of calling this book 'The Heroic Victim'. The phrase sums up for me the final impression that I have carried away from a long and fairly close reading of Wordsworth's poems. So far from surrendering to the neurotic elements in his personality, as so many Romantic poets have done, Wordsworth's early life was one long desperate struggle against them. And whatever one's reservations about this or that poem the general direction of the poetry is undoubtedly towards sanity, sincerity, sympathy, gaiety—in a word, the humane virtues. What makes their successful realisation in Wordsworth's best poems so exhilarating to the modern reader is his continuous consciousness of how hardly the successes have been won, how precarious the achievement is. There were no easy victories for him either as a man or a poet. The failures on the other hand, and there were plenty of them, are refreshingly obvious and blatant.

Wordsworth achieves greatness because his private struggles towards psychic integration have a representative quality. The poems generalise themselves, as they are read, into the reactions of the human individual fighting for its spiritual survival in a society that seems to have no place for it. And this makes him, with Blake, the first specifically modern English poet. The difference between Wordsworth and Blake and poets like Chaucer, Spenser, Milton, Dryden or Pope is, it is not too much to say, almost a difference of kind. Although the exact emphasis naturally varies the earlier poets all shared with their audience (i) a belief in the validity of the literary tradition they inherited, and (ii) an ultimate sense of obligation to the social order (religious-ethical as well as political-economic) in which they had grown up. Wordsworth and Blake did not accept either of these presuppositions. But Wordsworth's example was more important than Blake's for his contemporaries, and perhaps for us too, because Wordsworth, or a part of him, would have *liked* to believe in a literary tradition and an inherited social order. To survive all that was most genuine in him, his *daimon*, the conscience of his conscience, had to fight against the ever-present temptation to conformity and to learn to make its denials and refusals more and more uncompromising. It is, I think, this extremism in Wordsworth, the drastic and even shocking elements in both the man and the poet, that gives his struggle towards integration its heroic quality. Poems like "The Idiot Boy", "We are Seven" and *Peter Bell* are not merely outside the literary tradition— Blake's poems are outside it too—they are written in a deliberate defiance of it. The gross, offensive non-literariness is an important part of their meaning. The revolutionary manner complements the revolutionary matter—which might be described as a series of demonstrations of the superior humanity of men and women who are either outside or at best only on the edge of ordinary organised society.

The progress to the repudiation of literature, as of society, was a gradual one. In the earlier poems, in which Wordsworth was still feeling his way to a non-literary technique, the effect is rather of a misapplication of the literary tradition. The new wine is uncomfortable in the old bottles, though they are still used. In his Hawkshead-Cambridge phase, when he was struggling back to normality primarily through a cleansing and renovation of the

senses, Wordsworth was still using the verse-forms and diction of
Gray and Goldsmith, if the poetry that emerged, when poetry
did emerge, was really completely different from theirs. It is
essentially eye-on-the-object, ear-on-the-noise poetry. In spite
of the conscientiously artificial style the reader is made to see and
hear physical objects as they are in themselves, as mere sights and
mere sounds, wholly divested from the human or conventional
associations they generally had for Gray and Goldsmith. The cattle
in lines 58–60 of *An Evening Walk*,

> When stood the shorten'd herds amid the tide,
> Where, from the barren wall's unshelter'd end,
> Long rails into the shallow lake extend;

may be compared with those in *The Deserted Village*, line 119,

> The sober herd that low'd to meet their young;

or in the second line of *Elegy written in a Country Churchyard*.
Wordsworth's 'shorten'd herds' leaves a vivid impression on the
mind's eye, whereas Goldsmith's 'sober herd' is a metaphor
implying a comparison with some human assembly, and Gray's
'lowing herd' is a mere conventionality (cows do not low as a
herd).

But Wordsworth did not find himself as a poet until after the
crisis year 1792–3. In this phase the personal quest was not so much
for sensuous reality as for emotional reality—a reality that he
found in the healthy instincts and simple affections of the Female
Vagrant, Margaret, Jack Walford, the old Cumberland Beggar,
Poor Susan, Goody Blake and their successors. Except as figures
of fun such humble souls had not found a place hitherto in the
literary tradition, and Wordsworth's extremism is as evident in
Salisbury Plain and *The Ruined Cottage*, in which low life is
described in Spenserian stanzas and Miltonic blank verse, as it is in
Lyrical Ballads, which bases itself on the sub-literary *genre* of the
street-ballad. This literary extremism is much less evident in
"Tintern Abbey" and the poems written at Goslar and Dove
Cottage. Superficially most of the poems of this period are a good
deal less defiant of the literary decencies. But the decorum, as the

analyses of "There was a Boy" and "She dwelt among the untrodden ways" have demonstrated, was a merely superficial one.
Under the surface the poetry is more uncompromising, more
drastically non-literary, even than *Lyrical Ballads*. And the reason
for this is that the repudiation of society, which had been implicit
in *An Evening Walk* and explicit in the poems written between
1793 and 1798, has now been extended and developed into an
implicit repudiation of the whole human race. Wordsworth's
egotism cannot be called misanthropy, it is nearer to solipsism.
The author of the Lucy poems, "Intimations of Immortality"
and *The Prelude* (the list is not intended to be complete) could
only solve his personal crisis—the tragic discovery that he and his
sister were passionately in love with each other—by eliminating
every other human being except himself from his emotional life.
The process was largely, though not, I think, wholly, an unconscious one, and a casual intercourse was, of course, maintained
with friends and acquaintances, including Dorothy. He even got
married and had a family. But nobody seems to have been able
during those terrible years to make any real contact with the
deeper levels of his personality. The intensity with which as a
schoolboy and an undergraduate he had looked out on to the
physical world and the profound emotional hunger which he
had felt for primitive human nature in his second phase were now
diverted into recollection in tranquillity, a process as selective as
it was concentrated. Dorothy, for example, the innocent cause of
the crisis, was excluded from Wordsworth's memories of the
past. It is significant that she plays no part in the account of the
Cockermouth years in *The Prelude*. She was also omitted from
"Resolution and Independence", though the actual historical
meeting with the leech-gatherer had occurred in her company,
and Wordsworth clearly used the record of it in her journal when
writing the poem. It is the same with "Beggars" and "I wandered lonely as a cloud" and a dozen other poems. But after the
Lucy poems, in which her symbolic death was recorded, there was
no place for her in the organs of Wordsworth's poetic imagination, and she was cut out like so much decayed tissue. The
uncompromising ruthlessness of it is awe-inspiring, an act of

necessary cruelty, inevitable but heart-breaking—to himself (there can be no doubt of it) even more than to Dorothy. So Agamemnon sacrificed Iphigenia. In the last analysis it is, I think, the absoluteness of this inner integrity above all that compels my reluctant admiration.

But the Heroic Victim was not granted a tragic end. Arnold's sardonic parable called "The Progress of Poesy" describes Wordsworth's later career accurately enough: the youth who found the spring becomes first of all the mature man who chops 'a channel grand' for a stream that is already exhausted (*The Excursion*), and finally the old man who rakes among the stones. Arnold fails, however, to make clear the moral of his parable. Was it that Wordsworth's genius exhausted itself in the intensity of the early struggles? Or did he perhaps win through in the end to normality, a somewhat hard and selfish normality? In that case the 'dotages' are the evidence not of failure but of success. If the great poetry was the product of a momentary and precarious harmonisation of the Two Voices it could have no *raison d'être* when they were no longer audible separately. The imaginative fusions were the resolutions of pre-existing psychological tensions. In the absence of such tensions there would be no oppositions to balance, no discordancies to reconcile.

Appendix I

TIME-TABLE OF WORDSWORTH'S MOVEMENTS UP TO 1800

For a number of the most interesting details in the following list I am indebted to Mrs. Mary Moorman. It has not been possible to give the documentary evidence on which they are based, and I must refer the reader to her forthcoming biography of Wordsworth. For May and June 1798 I have followed H. M. Margoliouth's persuasive reconstruction in *Notes and Queries*, Aug. 1953, pp. 352–4.

1770

April 7   William Wordsworth born at Cockermouth, Cumberland, the second son of John Wordsworth (1741–83) and his wife Anne, *née* Cookson (1748–78).

1775 (?)   Attends Anne Birkett's infant school at Penrith, Westmorland, while staying with his mother's parents at their mercers' shop there.

1776

April   Dayboy at Cockermouth Grammar School at least until October and may have attended intermittently for two full years. (Much of this time certainly spent with Cookson grandparents at Penrith.)

1778

March   Anne Wordsworth dies at Penrith.

1779

May   Goes to Hawkshead Grammar School, Lancashire. In lodgings there with Hugh (*d.* 1784) and Ann Tyson (*d.* 1796) at Colthouse, a hamlet on the outskirts of Hawkshead. During John Wordsworth's lifetime summer and Christmas holidays usually spent at Cockermouth or Penrith.

1783

December   John Wordsworth dies at Cockermouth. Christopher Cookson (later Crackanthorpe) of Penrith, elder brother of Anne Wordsworth, and Richard Wordsworth of Whitehaven, Cumberland, elder brother of John Wordsworth, now become the children's guardians. Summer holidays (six or seven weeks) regularly spent at Penrith, Christmas holidays (a month) at Whitehaven. Short Easter recess sometimes spent at Penrith, more usually at Hawkshead.

1787

June 20 (?)	Last day of last summer term at Hawkshead School.
June 27(?)–	
August 5	At Penrith with the Cooksons, where Dorothy Wordsworth has been living since May.
August 5–	
October 7	Back at Ann Tyson's, Colthouse, and may have continued at Hawkshead School for these nine weeks.
October 7–28 (?)	With the Cooksons in Penrith.
October 28 (?)–31(?)	At York (staying with Mary Robinson, a newly married cousin?).
November 1 or 2	Takes up residence at St. John's College, Cambridge. Elected a Foundress' Scholar at end of first week.
December 17	Matriculates. Placed in first class in college December examinations. Does not return to Lake District for Christmas.

1788

June	Placed in second class in college examinations.
June 8	Sight-seeing at Dovedale, Derbyshire, en route for Hawkshead. Nine weeks of the Long Vacation spent at Colthouse, lodging with Ann Tyson. Short periods also spent with the Cooksons at Penrith, with the Richard Wordsworths at Whitehaven, and with their married daughter Mary Smith at Broughton-in-Furness.
October	First visit to London? (Presumably staying with his elder brother Richard before returning to Cambridge.)
November	Shows Dorothy round Cambridge on her way to Forncett, Lincolnshire, where their uncle William Cookson is now Rector.
December	College examinations not taken in full but 'considerable merit' in papers attempted.

1789

June	Does well in classics in college examinations.
Mid-June–mid-October	Begins Long Vacation with short visit to Forncett. Apparently proceeded from there to Penrith via Yorkshire, perhaps spending some time with Tom Hutchinson, a Penrith friend, who was now farming at Sockburn-on-Tees. Parts of Vacation also spent at Hawkshead (but not *chez* Ann Tyson, who had now retired), at Whitehaven, and with the Smiths at Broughton.
October 16	Calls on the Cooksons at Penrith en route for Cambridge.
December	College examinations not taken (illness?).

1790

June   'Considerable merit' in subjects taken in college examinations.

July 10–
October 10   Walking tour with Robert Jones in France, Italy, Switzerland and Germany.

October   Short visit to Forncett before returning to Cambridge.

December–
January 1791   Six weeks spent at Forncett before and after Christmas.

1791

January 21   Graduates at Cambridge and then proceeds to London, where he remains in lodgings on his own until end of May.

June–early
September   At Robert Jones's home in Denbighshire. Walking tour with Jones in N. Wales.

September–
October   At Cambridge.

November 22–26   At Brighton en route for France.

November 30–
December 5   Sight-seeing in Paris.

December 6   Arrives at Orleans.

1792

Early Spring   Transfers lodgings to Blois, where he remains until beginning of September.

September–
October   At Orleans.

End of October   Goes to Paris, where he remains in lodgings until early December.

December 15   Anne Caroline, the illegitimate daughter, baptised in Orleans Cathedral.

Mid-December   Back in London.

1793

January–June   In lodgings in London (at first at any rate with his brother Richard at Staple Hall).

July   Four weeks with William Calvert in Isle of Wight.

Early August   Some days spent wandering alone over Salisbury Plain. Proceeds on foot via Wye Valley to Denbighshire, where he stays with Robert Jones.

Autumn   Apparently at Keswick (with the Calverts?). May have stayed with the Hutchinsons about this time at Sockburn-on-Tees.

December   Christmas with the Richard Wordsworths at Whitehaven.

1794

January	Stays with Spedding family at Armathwaite Hall (6 miles east of Cockermouth).
February	Joins Dorothy at the Rawsons' in Halifax. (Dorothy had been brought up by Mrs. Rawson, before her marriage, after Anne Wordsworth's death.)
March	Short visit, with Dorothy, to the Hutchinsons at Sockbridge? Later in month they are at Kendal, whence they walk to Windy Brow near Keswick, a farmhouse belonging to the Calverts. Several weeks spent there together.
May	With Dorothy at Whitehaven, perhaps passing through Cockermouth on the way. They remain at Whitehaven until after their uncle's death (June 14).
July	Apparently spent at Keswick with Raisley Calvert.
August–September	Four weeks' visit to Francis and Mary Barker at Rampside near Barrow-in-Furness. (Mrs. Barker was a first cousin.)
End of September	Returns to Keswick and stays there with Raisley Calvert until early December when both go to Robin Hood Inn, Penrith.

1795

January	With Raisley Calvert until his death and burial (January 12) at Penrith.
Mid-January	Joins Dorothy at Newcastle-on-Tyne, where she is staying with their cousins the Griffiths.
Early February	Arrives in London where he remains (part of time with Basil Montagu in Lincoln's Inn) until August.
Mid-August	At Bristol staying with the Pinneys, who offer him the use of Racedown Lodge, Dorset.
September	Walks over to Racedown to inspect.
September 22 (?)	Joined at the Pinneys' by Dorothy.
September 26	Arrives at Racedown with Dorothy and Basil Montagu's little boy.
Christmas	John Frederick Pinney and his brother Azariah spend a week at Racedown.

1796

January–June	At Racedown (with Dorothy, the Montagu boy, and Peggy Marsh, their one servant).
February–March	John Frederick and Azariah Pinney spend four weeks at Racedown.
June 2	Sets out for London.

1796—*continued*

July 11	Returns to Racedown from London
Mid-July– December	At Racedown the whole time, though there may have been a short unrecorded expedition to Bristol.

1797

January–June	At Racedown, except for a week or two at Bristol in March visiting James Losh. Long visit by Mary Hutchinson (apparently February to beginning of June). Basil Montagu stays four days in March. Short visit by Coleridge in June.
July 2–14	Stays, with Dorothy, at the Coleridges' in Nether Stowey. (Charles Lamb joins them July 9.)
July 14	The Wordsworths enter into occupation of Alfoxden House, Somerset. The Montagu boy and Peggy Marsh join them in August.
October	At Bristol for a few days.
November	Two short walking tours with Dorothy and Coleridge. Basil Montagu arrives on a visit (and stays until January 1798?).
December	With Dorothy in London for first fortnight.
December 15	They return to Bristol, where they stay for two and a half weeks.

1798

January 3	Back at Alfoxden.
May 16–18	Walks over to Cheddar via Bridgwater (with Dorothy and Coleridge).
May 24–25	Another expedition to Cheddar (via Cross near Axbridge). Dorothy and Coleridge return to Alfoxden and Stowey, Wordsworth goes on to Bristol.
May 26	Returns from Bristol with Cottle.
May 27–29	Wordsworth, Coleridge and Cottle walk over to Lynton.
June 4	Goes to Bristol.
June 5–6	Walks back to Alfoxden.
June 23	Lease of Alfoxden expires. The Wordsworths spend a week with the Coleridges at Stowey.
July 2	The Wordsworths leave Stowey and go to Bristol. Lodgings are taken at Shirehampton near Bristol to be near the Loshes.
July 10–13	Tintern Abbey excursion with Dorothy. Rest of July and August in or near Bristol, except for walking tour along the Usk and the Wye with Dorothy and Coleridge.
August 27	Arrives London, with Dorothy, after sight-seeing at Blenheim Palace and Oxford.

14

1798—*continued*

September 16	Arrival at Hamburg from Yarmouth. (With Dorothy, Coleridge and John Chester.)
October 6	The Wordsworths arrive at Goslar, Saxony.

1799

January	Still at Goslar.
February 23	The Wordsworths leave Goslar on foot. A leisurely walking tour through central Germany.
April	They join Coleridge at Göttingen.
April 21	Leave Göttingen for England via Hamburg and Yarmouth.
May 1 (?)	Arrive at the Hutchinsons' farm at Sockburn-on-Tees.
Late October– mid-November	Walking tour in Lake District with John Wordsworth and Coleridge.
December 17	Leaves Sockburn, with Dorothy, for Grasmere.
December 21	Grasmere reached. They spend their first night at Dove Cottage.

Appendix II

Wordsworth's Poems: a Chronological List (to the end of 1815) in the Order of their Composition

Almost every one of Wordsworth's poems can now be dated, though with varying degrees, naturally, of certainty and precision. Wordsworth's own dates, in the I.F. notes and the various collected editions of the poems, are frequently demonstrably wrong, and they generally only specify the year in which a poem was written. More reliable and more precise datings are provided by his sister's Journals and the letters he or she wrote either at the time the poems were being written or soon after. When such information is not available the original MSS. sometimes enable a poem to be dated within fairly narrow limits. In the following list I have generally followed the de Selincourt-Darbishire edition which assembles most of the relevant evidence in the notes on each poem. I have included all the poems printed in that edition—up to the end of 1815—that are indubitably Wordsworth's except some uncompleted or discarded fragments. As there are many similar fragments among the original MSS. at Dove Cottage that have not yet been published, it would be misleading to list the few that have got into print. Within each year the order I have adopted is (i) the poems that can be ascribed to a particular day, month or period within the year, (ii) the poems that certainly belong to that year but which it is impossible to date more precisely, (iii) the poems conjecturally or approximately assigned to it (sometimes several years separate the *termini a quo* and *ad quem*). Except in one or two special cases almost no attempt has been made to include in this list the often drastic revisions that many of the poems underwent. References to *The Prelude* are to the 1805 text. Otherwise the form of the poems and the titles, or in their absence first lines, represent Wordsworth's final readings. The poems' earlier titles, if they had any, follow in square brackets. I have not tried to indicate the inter-relationships of the various poems, or the occasional duplications, *e.g.* the extracts from *The Prelude* and *The Recluse* retained in the collected editions of the poems.

1785	Lines Written as a School Exercise.
1786	
Aug. 7	Anacreon (Imitation).
Autumn	Beauty and Moonlight.
	The Death of a Starling.
1786–7	The Dog.
	Dirge. Sung by a Minstrel [second version Jan. 1788].

1786?	Written in very early Youth [rewritten 1795–7].
1787	
Mar. 2	Sonnet written by Mr. ——.
Spring–Summer	The Vale of Esthwaite.
Mar. 23, 24	A Ballad ("And will you leave me thus alone").
1788–9	An Evening Walk [separate scenes and episodes 1788, epistolary framework 1789, rewritten 1794, largely rewritten again *c.* 1820].
	"When slow from pensive twilight's latest gleams" [unpublished sonnet].
	The Horse [tr. from *Georgics*].
	"Sweet was the walk along the narrow lane."
	Ode to Apollo [tr. from Horace].
1789?	Lines written while sailing in a Boat at Evening.
	Lines written near Richmond.
	Remembrance of Collins.
1790–2	Descriptive Sketches [rewritten *c.* 1836].
1793	
Late Summer and Autumn	Guilt and Sorrow [Salisbury Plain: rewritten and expanded Oct. 1795–Jan. 1796, further changes 1799, final revision *c.* 1842].
1793?	The Convict [rewritten 1797 and 1798].
1794	
Apr.–May	Septimi Gades [from Horace].
	Inscription for a Seat by the Pathway Side ascending to Windy Brow [rewritten early 1797].
1794?	The Birth of Love [tr. from Vicomte de Segur].
	From the Greek [tr. from anon. scolion].
1795	
Summer–Feb. 1797	Imitation of Juvenal (Satire VIII).
Late Aug.–early Sept.	[Preamble to] The Prelude.
1795–7	"If grief dismiss me not to them that rest."
	Lesbia; Septimius and Acme [both tr. from Catullus].
1795?	Lines left upon a Seat in a Yew-Tree [rewritten early 1797 and perhaps 1798].
1796	
Summer–Autumn	Address to the Ocean.
Autumn–Spring 1797	The Borderers [revised for stage performance Nov. 1797].

1796?–	
Spring 1797	The Excursion, book i [The Ruined Cottage: expanded *c.* Jan. 1798].
1797	
Early	The Three Graves. Parts I and II.
Dec.	The Reverie of Poor Susan.
1797–8	"Away, away, it is the air."
	The Old Cumberland Beggar.
	Animal Tranquillity and Decay [Old Man Travelling].
1798	
Jan.?	Goody Blake and Harry Gill.
Jan. 25	A Night-Piece.
Feb.	[The discharged soldier—Prelude, iv, 363–504].
Late Feb.– early Mar.	"On Man, on Nature, and on Human Life."
Early Mar.	To my Sister [Lines written at a small distance from my House].
Early Spring	Lines Written in Early Spring.
	Anecdote for Fathers.
	Simon Lee.
	We are Seven.
Mar. 18	"A whirl-blast from behind the hill."
Spring	The Last of the Flock.
Mar.–Apr.	The Idiot Boy.
Mar. 19–Apr.	The Thorn.
Spring	Her Eyes are Wild [The Mad Mother].
Apr. 12–May	Peter Bell [revised 1799, 1802, 1805 and 1818–19].
Apr.–May	Andrew Jones.
Apr.	"I love upon a stormy night."
Spring	The Complaint of a Forsaken Indian Woman.
June	Expostulation and Reply.
	The Tables Turned.
c. July 13	Lines composed a Few Miles above Tintern Abbey.
Oct.–Dec.	The Prelude [most of i, 271–608, and some episodes and passages finally worked into later books].
Autumn	Nutting.
Nov.–Dec.	There was a Boy.
	Influence of Natural Objects in calling forth and strengthening the Imagination.
Dec.	"She dwelt among the untrodden ways" [Song].
	"Strange fits of passion have I known."
	Address to the Scholars of the Village School of ——.

1798—*continued*
  Late (or early
    1799)   Lucy Gray; or, Solitude.
                Written in Germany on one of the Coldest Days of the
                    Century.
                To a Sexton.
                "A slumber did my spirit seal."
                Alcaeus to Sappho ["How sweet when crimson colours
                    dart"].

1799
  Jan.–Feb.   The Danish Boy.
                Matthew.
                The Two April Mornings.
                The Fountain, A Conversation.
                A Poet's Epitaph.
  Feb.–Mar.   Ruth [revised March 1802].
                "Three years she grew in sun and shower."
  Late Summer
    and Autumn   The Prelude [most of ii].
  Dec. 28   To M.H.
  1799 or 1800   Ellen Irwin; or the Braes of Kirtle.
1800
  Jan.–Feb.   Hart-Leap Well.
  Feb.   The Brothers.
  Feb.–Apr.   The Recluse, Part First, Book First, Home at Grasmere.
  Mar.   Water Fowl.
  First half   The Farmer of Tilsbury Vale.
  Aug.   The Seven Sisters or, the Solitude of Binnorie.
                To Joanna.
  Aug. 29, 30   "When, to the attractions of the busy world" [finished
                1802].
  Sept., Oct.   A Character.
  Oct. 10   "A narrow girdle of rough stones and crags."
  Oct. 11–Dec. 9 Michael.
  1800   The Idle Shepherd-Boys; or, Dungeon Ghyll Force.
                The Pet-Lamb.
                " 'Tis said, that some have died for love."
                The Childless Father.
                "It was an April morning: fresh and clear."
                "There is an Eminence—of these our hills."
                The Waterfall and the Eglantine.
                The Oak and the Broom.
                Song for the Wandering Jew.
                Inscription Written on the Island at Grasmere.

1800—*continued*	Inscription Written upon one of the Islands at Rydal.
	Inscription For the Spot where the Hermitage stood.
	The Two Thieves or, the Last Stage of Avarice.
1800?	Rural Architecture.
1801	
Dec. 4, 5	The Prioress' Tale.
Dec. 7, 9	The Cuckoo and the Nightingale.
Dec.	The Manciple. The Manciple's Tale.
	Troilus and Cressida.
1801	"I travelled among unknown men."
1801?	The Affliction of Margaret.
	The Forsaken.
	Louisa.
	To a Young Lady who had been reproached for taking Long Walks in the Country.
Dec. 1801–	
June 1802	Repentance.
1802	
Mar. 11, 12	The Sailor's Mother.
Mar. 12, 13	Alice Fell; or, Poverty.
Mar. 13, 14	Beggars.
Mar. 14	To a Butterfly ["Stay near me—do not take thy flight!"].
Mar. 16, 17	The Emigrant Mother.
Mar. 23–26	To the Cuckoo.
Mar. 26	"My heart leaps up when I behold."
Mar. 27–	
1803	Ode Intimations of Immortality from Recollections of Early Childhood.
Apr.	"These Chairs they have no words to utter."
	"I have thoughts that are fed by the sun."
Apr. 12	"Among all lovely things my Love had been" [The Glow-worm].
Apr. 16	Written in March while resting on the Bridge at the Foot of Brother's Water.
Apr. 18	The Redbreast chasing the Butterfly.
Apr. 20	To a Butterfly ["I've watched you now a full half-hour"].
Apr. 27–29	The Tinker.
Apr. 28	Foresight.
Apr. 30	To the Small Celandine.
May 1	To the Same Flower.
Spring	To the Daisy ["In youth from rock to rock I went"].
	To the Same Flower ["With little here to do or see"].
	The Green Linnet.

1802—*continued*

Spring	To a Sky-Lark ["Up with me! up with me into the clouds!"].
	The Sparrow's Nest.
May 3–July 4	Resolution and Independence.
May 9–11	Stanzas written in my Pocket-Copy of Thomson's "Castle of Indolence".
May 21	"I grieved for Buonaparté, with a vain."
May 29	A Farewell.
June 8	"The sun has long been set."
July 31 (or Sept. 3)	Composed upon Westminster Bridge.
Aug.	"It is a beauteous evening, calm and free."
	Composed by the Sea-Side, near Calais.
	Calais, August, 1802.
	Composed near Calais, on the Road leading to Ardres.
	Calais, August 15, 1802.
	On the Extinction of the Venetian Republic.
	The King of Sweden.
	To Toussaint L'Ouverture.
	Composed in the Valley near Dover.
Sept.	September 1, 1802.
	September, 1802, near Dover.
	Written in London, September, 1802.
	London, 1802.
Autumn	To H.C. Six Years Old.
Oct. 4	Composed after a Journey across the Hambleton Hills, Yorkshire.
Early Nov.	Translation of Ariosto.
Second half	"Great men have been among us; hands that penned."
	"There is a little unpretending Rill."
Late 1802– Mar. 1803	"It is not to be thought of that the Flood."
Late 1802– Aug. 1803	"When I have borne in memory what has tamed."
1802	To the Daisy ["Bright Flower! whose home is every-where"].
1802?	Translations from Metastasio [5 short pieces].
1803	
Aug. 31	Address to Kilchurn Castle.
Sept. 18	Sonnet composed at —— Castle.
Oct.	Anticipation. October, 1803.
	To the Men of Kent.
	October, 1803 [3 separate sonnets].

1803—*continued*

Oct.	Sonnet in the Pass of Killicranky.
Autumn	Lines on the Expected Invasion.
1803	"Who fancied what a pretty sight."
	To a Highland Girl.
	Glen Almain; or, the Narrow Glen.
	"What if our numbers barely could defy."
	"England! the time is come when thou should'st wean."
	Yarrow Unvisited.
	"I find it written of Simonides."
1803–5	The Matron of Jedborough and her Husband.
1803?	At the Grave of Burns, 1803.
	"There is a bondage worse, far worse, to bear."
June 1802–	
Jan. 1804	"Nuns fret not at their convent's narrow room."
	"'Beloved Vale!' I said, 'when shall I con.'"
June 1802–	
Jan. 1804	"A plain Youth, Lady, and a simple Lover" [tr. from Milton].
	"Return, Content! for fondly I pursued."
	"Methought I saw the footsteps of a throne."
	To Sleep ["A flock of sheep that leisurely pass by"].
	To Sleep ["Fond words have oft been spoken to thee, Sleep"].
June 1802–	
Feb. 1804	"Pelion and Ossa flourish side by side."
	Admonition.
	Personal Talk [4 sonnets].
	"How sweet it is, when mother Fancy rocks."
	To the Memory of Raisley Calvert.
	"The world is too much with us; late and soon."
	"With Ships the sea was sprinkled far and nigh."
	"Where lies the land to which yon ship must go?"
	"These words were uttered as in pensive mood."
	"'With how sad steps, O Moon, thou climb'st the sky.'"
	"Brook! whose society the Poet seeks."
	To Sleep ["O gentle Sleep! do they belong to thee"].
1803	"It is no Spirit who from heaven hath flown."
1804	
Jan., Feb., Apr.	The Prelude [most of iii, iv, v, vi and ix].
Feb.	Ode to Duty.
Early	At Applethwaite, near Keswick.
Apr.	The Simplon Pass.
Late Spring	Vaudracour and Julia.

1804—*continued*

Sept. 16	Address to my Infant Daughter Dora.
Oct.–Dec.	The Prelude [most of vii, viii, x].
Dec.	Inscription for the Moss-Hut at Dove Cottage.
	French Revolution as it appeared to Enthusiasts at its Commencement.

1804

"I wandered lonely as a cloud."
"She was a Phantom of delight."
The Kitten and Falling Leaves.
The Small Celandine.

1805

Spring	Distressful Gift.
Mar.–July	Elegiac Verses in Memory of my Brother, John Wordsworth.
	To the Daisy ["Sweet Flower! belike one day to have"].
Late Apr.– mid-May	The Prelude [most of xi, xii, xiii].
June 3	Stepping Westward.
June 1805– Feb. 1806	Rob Roy's Grave. To the Sons of Burns.
Nov. 5	The Solitary Reaper.
Dec. 1805– Jan. 1806	Character of the Happy Warrior.
Late 1805 (or early 1806)	Fidelity.

1805

Incident Characteristic of a Favourite Dog.
Tribute to the Memory of the Same Dog.

1805–6

From the Italian of Michelangelo [4 sonnets and some lyric fragments].

1806

Jan.	The Waggoner.
May?	Power of Music.
May?	Stray Pleasures.
May?	Star-Gazers.
July	Elegiac Stanzas suggested by a Picture of Peele Castle, in a Storm, painted by Sir George Beaumont.
Summer– Autumn	The Excursion [ii and parts of iii, iv, v].
Autumn	The Orchard Pathway.
Sept.	Lines [on Fox's imminent death].
Nov.	November, 1806.
Dec.	The Blind Highland Boy.

1806—*continued*
Dec. (or Jan.
    1807)   A Complaint.
Late (or early
    1807)   Thought of a Briton on the Subjugation of Switzerland.
Late   "O Nightingale! thou surely art."
1806   To the Spade of a Friend (an Agriculturist).
                  "Yes, it was the mountain Echo."
                  The Horn of Egremont Castle.
1806–7   On Milton.
1806?   On Seeing some Tourists of the Lakes Pass by Reading.
1806? (before
    Apr. 1807)   "O mountain Stream! the Shepherd and his Cot."
1806? (or much
    later)   "Come, gentle Sleep, Death's image tho' thou art" [tr.
                  from Thomas Warton].
c. 1806?   Translation of the Sestet of a Sonnet by Tasso.
1807
Early   Gipsies.
                  Song at the Feast of Brougham Castle.
                  "Though narrow be that old Man's cares, and near."
Feb.   A Prophecy, February, 1807.
                  To Lady Beaumont.
Mar.   To Thomas Clarkson.
Sept.   The Force of Prayer or, the Founding of Bolton Abbey.
Oct.–Jan. 1808   The White Doe of Rylstone; or, the Fate of the Nortons.
1807   Composed by the Side of Grasmere Lake.
1808
Mar.–Apr.   St. Paul's [The Vision of St. Paul's].
Spring   To the Clouds.
                  The Tuft of Primroses.
Mid-Apr.   George and Sarah Green.
Nov.–Dec.   Composed while the Author was engaged in writing a
                  Tract occasioned by the Convention of Cintra.
                  Composed at the same Time and on the same Occasion.
1808–10   Pelayo.
1809
Spring   "Is there a power that can sustain and cheer."
Spring-Summer   "Hail, Zaragoza! If with unwet eye."
                  "And is it among rude untutored Dales."
Summer–
    Autumn   "Advance—come forth from thy Tyrolean ground."
                  Hofer.
Oct.   "Alas! what boots the long laborious quest."

1809—*continued*

Oct.–Nov.	On the Final Submission of the Tyrolese.
	Feelings of the Tyrolese.
Late 1809–1813	The Excursion [vi–ix and parts of earlier books].
Second half	"Brave Schill! by death delivered, take thy flight."
1809	"O'er the wide earth, on mountain and on plain."
	"Call not the royal Swede unfortunate."
	"Look now on that Adventurer who hath paid."
1809–12	Epitaphs translated from Chiabrera [7 certainly 1809 or 1810, one possibly 1812].
1809?	"Say, what is Honour? 'Tis the finest sense."
1810	
Early	"The martial courage of a day is vain."
1810	1810.
	"Avaunt all specious pliancy of mind."
	Indignation of a High-minded Spaniard 1810.
	The Oak of Guernica.
	"In due observance of an ancient rite."
	Feelings of a Noble Biscayan at one of those Funerals, 1810.
	"Ah! where is Palafox? Nor tongue nor pen."
1810–11	The French and the Spanish Guerillas.
1811	
First half	Characteristics of a Child Three Years Old.
Aug.	Upon the Sight of a Beautiful Picture.
	Departure from the Vale of Grasmere.
	Epistle to Sir George Howland Beaumont, Bart.
1811	Inscriptions. I: in the Grounds of Coleorton. II: in a Garden of the Same. III: written at the Request of Sir George Beaumont. IV: for a Seat in the Groves of Coleorton [III, IV, Nov. 1811].
	1811 ["They seek, are sought; to daily battle led"].
	1811 ["The power of Armies is a visible thing"].
	Spanish Guerillas.
1812	
July	"The fairest, brightest, hues of ether fade."
Oct.	Composed on the Eve of the Marriage of a Friend in the Vale of Grasmere, 1812.
Dec.	"Six months to six years added he remained."
Dec.(or Jan.1813)	Maternal Grief.
1812	Song for the Spinning Wheel.
1813	
Nov.	November, 1813.
1813–14	Yew-Trees.

1813?	Inscription Written on Black Comb.
	View from the Top of Black Comb.
1814	
July	"From the dark chambers of dejection freed."
Autumn	Yarrow Visited.
Autumn?	Effusion in the Pleasure-Ground on the Banks of the Bran, near Dunkeld.
Autumn?	Composed at Cora Linn.
Autumn?	The Brownie's Cell.
Nov. 13	Lines Written on the Death of late Vicar of Kendal.
1814	Laodamia.
1814?	"Surprised by joy—impatient as the Wind."
1814? (or earlier)	"Mark the concentred hazels that enclose."
	"The Shepherd, looking eastward, softly said."
	"Even as a dragon's eye that feels the stress."
	"Hail, Twilight, sovereign of one peaceful hour!"
	On a Celebrated Event in Ancient History.
	Upon the Same Event.
1815	
Early	"'Weak is the will of Man, his judgment blind.'"
Dec.	November 1.
	September, 1815.
	To B. R. Haydon.
1815	Artegal and Elidura.
1815? (or earlier)	Composed in one of the Valleys of Westmorland, on Easter Sunday.
	Through Cumbrian Wilds.

INDEX

Appendixes I and II, which are virtually indexes in themselves, are not included here.